THE GARDEN OF COSMIC SPECULATION IS A
LANDSCAPE OF WAVES, TWISTS, AND FOLDS,
A LANDSCAPE PATTERN DESIGNED TO RELATE
US TO NATURE THROUGH NEW METAPHORS
PRESENTED TO THE SENSES.

Landscape of Waves—Linearism, mixed media, 30

IT IS PARTLY BASED ON THE NEW SCIENCES OF COMPLEXITY DEVELOPED WITH THE AID OF THE COMPUTER OVER THE LAST TWENTY YEARS— STRANGE ATTRACTORS THAT ORGANIZE SUCH THINGS AS THE FLOW OF WATER, THE MOVEMENT OF SOIL, THE PATTERNS OF WEATHER.

The Snake Mound with the Henan Attractor inscribed.

DNA UNDERLIES ALL LIFE AND COMES IN SEVERAL STATES, SUPERCOILED OR CONGESTED AND UNFOLDED BEAUTIFULLY IN THE DOUBLE HELIX. WE HAVE SHOWN THESE OPPOSITE QUALITIES BECAUSE THEY EXIST IN NATURE AND ARE NOT MERE HUMAN PROJECTIONS.

The Senses of Taste and of Anticipation, and ribosomes.

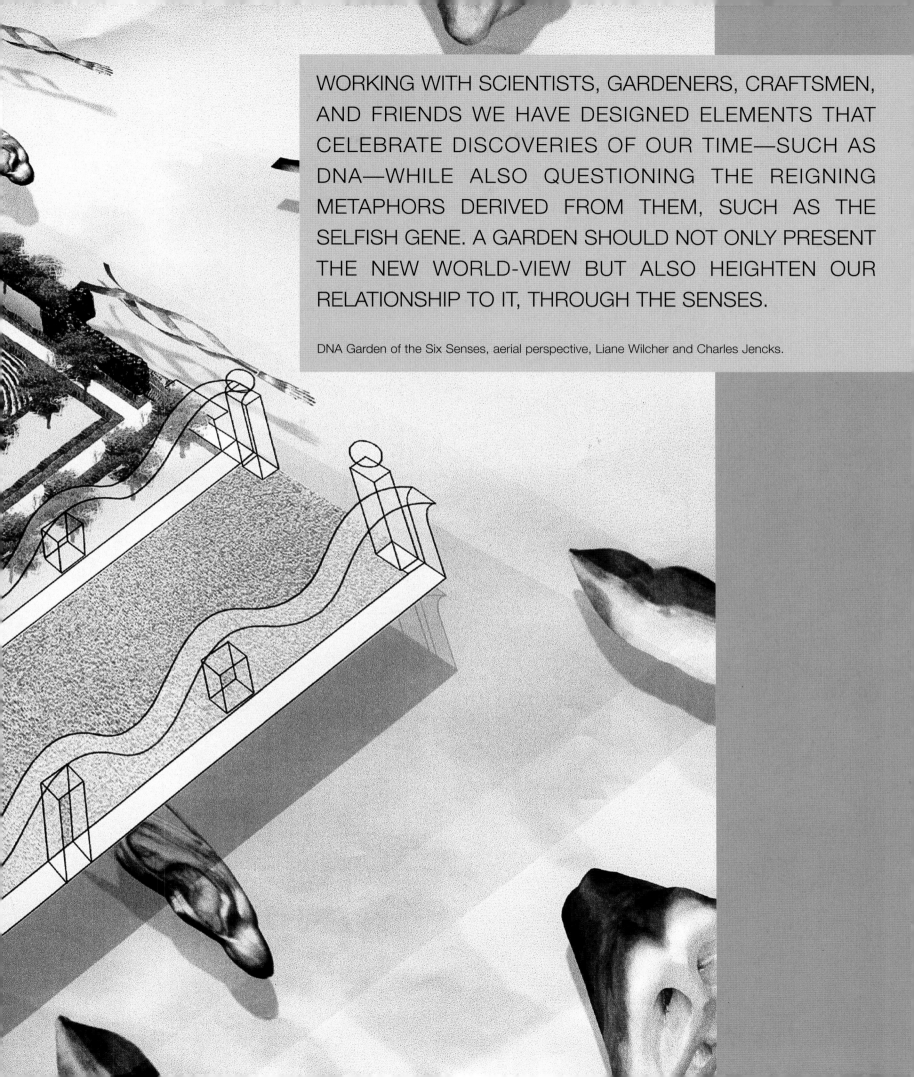

WORKING WITH SCIENTISTS, GARDENERS, CRAFTSMEN, AND FRIENDS WE HAVE DESIGNED ELEMENTS THAT CELEBRATE DISCOVERIES OF OUR TIME—SUCH AS DNA—WHILE ALSO QUESTIONING THE REIGNING METAPHORS DERIVED FROM THEM, SUCH AS THE SELFISH GENE. A GARDEN SHOULD NOT ONLY PRESENT THE NEW WORLD-VIEW BUT ALSO HEIGHTEN OUR RELATIONSHIP TO IT, THROUGH THE SENSES.

DNA Garden of the Six Senses, aerial perspective, Liane Wilcher and Charles Jencks.

LABYRINTHINE, FRACTAL, SURPRISING, AND QUESTIONING, THE FORMS RELATE TO THE SURROUNDING HILLS, THE FUNCTIONS THEY PERFORM, AND THE RECENT DISCOVERIES OF COSMOLOGY—HERE, A BLACK HOLE. UNDERSTANDING DEMANDS A CERTAIN SLOWING OF TIME—WHY ELSE ENTER A GARDEN?

Black Hole Terrace (right) and Octagonia (above). Photograph by Chris Webster.

FRANCES LINCOLN

THE GARDEN OF
COSMIC SPECULATION

CHARLES JENCKS

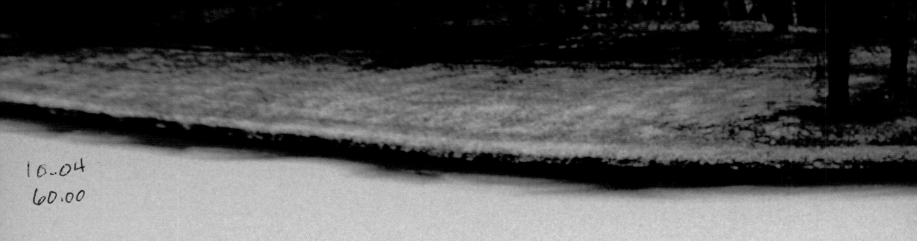

10.04
60.00

Maggie, mère des souvenirs

Portrack Garden is opened through the Scotland's Gardens Scheme.
The garden is also open to groups who apply in writing to:

Charles A. Jencks
PO Box 31627
London W11 3XB

All donations to Maggie's Centres:
Scottish Charity Number SCO 24414

Frances Lincoln Ltd
4 Torriano Mews
Torriano Avenue
London NW5 2RZ
www.franceslincoln.com

A catalogue record for this book is available from the British Library.

ISBN 0 7112 2216 9

Set in Joanna MT and Helvetica Neue

Printed and bound in China by Kwong Fat Offset Printing Co. Ltd

First Frances Lincoln edition 2003
9 8 7 6 5 4 3 2 1

CONTENTS

ACKNOWLEDGMENTS

It is too obvious to say and impossible to say adequately that my greatest debt of gratitude in building the garden and writing this book goes to my late wife, Maggie Keswick, who initiated some landscape work at her family house in 1988. The book and garden are dedicated to her memory, a constant inspiration for me to continue work in completing what started as our joint vision. As partly explained in the text, she invited me to help design a kitchen garden, something I resisted but then finally accepted with the proviso that I not take it over as had happened in the past with our joint design. This stipulation was not to be realized, partly because she became ill and partly because, untrained as a designer, she lacked the confidence to settle on a final idea and see it through. There were important exceptions, such as her design of the lakes, the very things that make the mounds come alive but, for the most part, Maggie provided the impetus for design and the functional brief rather than the drawings and models. Nevertheless, her love, grace, critical wit, and calm wisdom were both inspiration and buttress for the continuing project.

Many other people helped build the garden and helped with ideas on how it might be shaped and planted, but above all one stands out: Alistair Clark, the head gardener. He not only runs the garden and snags the endless problems of plants that will not grow according to symbolic instruction, but he has constructed much of it, particularly the most difficult part, the Universe Cascade. It is rare to find someone who will both make the effort to understand contemporary science and turn it into growing sculpture. I am deeply indebted to him for such commitment and skill, as were Maggie, Clare, and John Keswick: he has helped shape Portrack for more than forty years.

As will also be apparent in the text, I have been most fortunate to find skilled craftsmen in the Borders area of southwest Scotland, two of whom I have worked very closely with for fifteen years and who have become friends: the gifted carpenter and craftsman Bobby Dixon and the expert metalworker John Gibson. Their translation of drawings, words, gesticulations, and models into artifacts is to be seen throughout this book.

Some artists I have worked with in a collaborative way on small projects, such as the nose sculpture by Chris Barrowman and the fused glass by Anthea Summers, while the large-scale mounds were built with the aid of Hugh Hastings and the long, undulating dry-stone walling was constructed by Hugh Drysdale. Again I am grateful for their skill and patience, something quite visible in the illustrations.

Madelon Vriesendorp has often visited Portrack and spent hours with me helping to draw up, and model, various parts of the DNA Garden. I look back on our enjoyably bizarre moments together as much as I look forward to more in the future. Her surreal wit and skill with translating it into l'*image juste* is deeply appreciated by me as much as her audience and her husband, Rem Koolhaas.

To keep the gardens of Portrack in a high state of order and the design intentions clear is no mean feat, especially because of the grass that needs cutting, the weeds pulling, and my mistakes fixing. Doug McCormick, Neal Brown and, more recently, Andy Cook have continued over the years to fine-tune the elements that they have partly constructed with such good humor. There is no question a garden needs delicate, affectionate care over a long period, nothing less, and they have given that to Portrack. The same can be said of Hattie McCormick's work in the house. She has provided the center of gravity, and levity, that makes the place a home, and a welcome refuge to which to return and gather strength from time to time.

This book is concerned with garden art and translating the insights of science and philosophy into workable objects. It is not an autobiography or personal history, though bits of my own past are here. But I must mention that my children have been a constant presence and valued support over the years, Lily and John and Justin and Cosmo. I hope they take delight in the gardens and see that they live and change in the future, according to necessities and design. Gardens, like cities, are whispering games in which the key is to pass on meaning even as it changes. They may reach momentary equilibrium, but should never be pickled. Respect is shown by continuing and transforming the plots.

Louisa Lane Fox and I are now embarked on finishing some and starting others, but happily I'm not sure exactly where they will lead. Design is like conversation; if you knew the outcome it wouldn't be worth having, and I'm grateful that—with respect to the undefined questions of what is to be planted—Louisa has entered into the discussion with creativity and zeal. Her suggestions will complete some of the unfinished ideas.

The Snake Mound in the frost.

Many scientists have visited Portrack in the last fifteen years and a few have contributed to the dialogue I have just mentioned. Paul Davies and I discussed many times the birth, laws, and development of the universe and he collaborated particularly on the basic equations that now crown the greenhouse. Joanna Migdal and Brookbrae turned these designs, and the globes to either side, into expressive metalwork. Steven and Hilary Rose and Nancy Lane helped work through ideas for the DNA Garden, as did Mae-Wan Ho and Peter Saunders. Lee Smolin, Martin Rees, and Roger Penrose were intermittent companions in discussion on cosmological points, especially around the Black Hole Terrace, into which they were, from time to time, drawn by gravity. James Watson and Matt Ridley were kind enough to clarify many issues connected with DNA, and also commissioned sculptures that extended some ideas developed in the garden. Laura Lee and Marcia Blakenham also asked me to design another version of DNA for a Maggie's Centre in Glasgow and I am beholden to them, as to the others, for being good clients—demanding but not interfering.

The cosmic engineer Cecil Balmond, though not directly involved with calculations and working drawings, has given me advice for and poetic insights on work at Portrack—we share a commitment to celebrating patterns of the universe. And the group who helped organize the Portrack Seminars over many years, David Ray Griffin, Charlene Spretnak, and Richard Falk, also debated cheerfully and thereby helped clarify many of the philosophical and ecological ideas expressed here.

Trevor Hearing of Studio Arts filmed the garden for Border Television and kindly granted permission to use material from his thoughtful production. Once again I am very indebted to my P. A. Bunny Firth for the initial, skilful layout of the book. To communicate all at once a design idea, a scientific concept, and an aesthetic message is a complex affair of effort and luck, and she has put in a great deal of work and creativity in leading toward the final design. I have also benefited greatly from the sharp eye of my editor, Michael Brunström, who has not only weeded the prose, but also nurtured ideas and pruned some metaphors (except this one).

The content of the book has, from its initial conception, been skilfully steered from a distance by my agent, and oldest friend, Ike Williams at Fish & Richardson. Ike set the challenge to turn a triple plot into a single narrative—the personal, scientific, and design stories. It has not been easy or quick but I hope it has been worth the effort. Finally, it is to John Nicoll and his late wife, Frances Lincoln, who published my first book in 1971, that I owe a different kind of thanks. John, as Frances before him, puts the author's interests right up there with the publishers', something as rare and important today as leadership in politics.

A train passes through the winter garden.

PART ONE: THREE STORIES OF A GARDEN

When you design a garden, it raises basic questions. What is nature, how do we fit into it, and how should we shape it where we can, both physically and visually? Some of these questions are practical, others are philosophical, and the latter may not occur to us while laying out a garden, but they are implied. When, in 1988, I started designing a garden with my wife Maggie Keswick, at her mother's house in Scotland, we were not concerned with the larger issues but, over the years, they came more and more to the fore. The result has become what I have called the "Garden of Cosmic Speculation." The reason for this unusual title is that we—Maggie, I, scientists, and then friends that we consulted—have used it as a spur to think about and celebrate some fundamental aspects of nature. Many of these are quite normal to a garden: planting suitable species which are both a pleasure to eat and easy to grow in a wet, temperate climate. And others are unusual: inventing new waveforms, linear twists, and a new grammar of landscape design to bring out the basic elements of nature that recent science has found to underlie the cosmos.

My goal, in designing the garden and writing this book, is partly a traditional one: to celebrate nature and our delight in it. Today, after a century of extraordinary discoveries in biology, such as evolution and the role of DNA, and cosmology, the birth if not origin of the universe, this means that there are new subjects for garden art and a new view of nature that might be presented.

Moreover, there are new means of making gardens, both new tools and artificial materials for use. Still, however, plants grow mostly as before, people walk on paths and want their gardens to be beautiful. So there is much here that is both new and old, particularly the desire to relate to the benign aspects of the universe while, at the same time, presenting its violent and tragic quality. Serious garden art is a heightening of both aspects of nature, its beauty and terror. Japanese Zen gardens, Persian paradise gardens, the English and French Renaissance gardens were, in some respects, analogies of the cosmos as then understood. They also told stories of physical and cultural evolution.

For instance, the Villa Lante for the Cardinal Gambara tells the story of paradise lost and regained (see following pages). It starts on the side of a large hill and slopes down. From a primitive *boschetto*, representing the distant past when we were in a state of nature, it progresses through three terraces, culminating in the new Golden Age of the Cardinal who built it. The universe is thus conceived in miniature as heading toward the present-day brilliance of Italian arts and sciences, a rather happier direction than later theories of evolution were to propose. Benign, malevolent, or simply neutral, the course of natural history has often been an inspiration for landscape design. Even the early botanic gardens had a cosmic orientation. They were an illustration both of God's plenty and a scientific collection of the world's order. Indeed, one can argue that Egyptian and Chinese gardens were also motivated by cosmic ideas.

Thus the garden as a microcosm of the universe as a whole is quite a familiar idea. The problem is that this cosmic orientation has been obscured by later ideas and a thousand other concerns. I nonetheless feel it is the most compelling motive behind the creation of a garden. What is a garden if not a miniaturization, and celebration, of the place we are in, the universe? Why else build it, if not for the pleasure of heightening our five (and more) senses? After all, like other species, we have senses in order to perceive and understand what is going on. Hence the "Garden of Cosmic Speculation," a set of five areas which have been shaped to celebrate some aspects of what we now know about the underlying forces and forms of nature. This book and the garden are also, in part, a speculation about the underlying truths. We have never seen a black hole nor the birth of a universe; these things are still mysterious and may remain forever so. But in the last thirty years they have become standard scientific terms and essential ideas for looking into nature.

In that sense the garden and this book are experimental and intended to challenge accepted notions, both of what a garden looks like and of the mechanistic metaphors that underlie modern science. The intentions are polemical, but not reactionary. I do accept most standard models of contemporary science, and will provide minimum summaries and descriptive drawings for the interested reader who wants to follow the ideas and the way they lead to design. But I am often critical of the words, images, and metaphors with which they are depicted, the interpretive framework that is reductive and based on the view that the universe

Clare's gate. The entrance to the DNA Garden.

is a giant machine. So a double type of design and critique are at work, where the meanings of both science and gardening are questioned at the same time. On one level, the garden is a design to be enjoyed; on another, it is an attempt to reinterpret the way we relate to the universe through models and new ideas. But I hope the second motive does not obscure the first, because if it did the point of the garden would be lost.

Gardens, like works of art, are not made to be illustrative but to be artifacts to be experienced in their individual ways, and the reality of creating a garden is that it becomes, inevitably, part of a family story, with the kind of personal ups and downs that implies. You cannot create it, or recount it, without revealing some basic truths of your life, and these happy and tragic moments will be as much a part of my account as the rest. Garden art is a genre close to autobiography because it takes years to achieve, and the events of one's life get wrapped into its meaning. "We did this and thought of that and then this happened to us which meant that we had to reconsider the whole enterprise from a new angle." The landscape becomes a record of what individuals do to nature, and of what nature does to them: a circular, or, if time is put into the equation, a spiral enterprise.

This can lead to amusing reversals, such as the time I tried to replant moss where it had always grown before. Nature, on this second attempt, did not want moss and grass grew instead. But this led me to a third option: designing a structure for willow trees to provide more shade for the moss so that it would not dry out; yet, when this structure was complete I liked it so much that the willows were never planted. As if to confirm my change of mind, the moss followed suit and decided to grow. This is a form of non-linear design, based on a personal response to nature's response.

Not only was nature changing my mind, and its tactics, but also the study of nature was shifting. As the garden developed since 1988, so too did such sciences as cosmology, and this allowed a dynamic interaction between the unfolding universe, a progressing science and a questioning design. In effect, it allowed a dialogue between those scientists meditating on nature and our garden forms that could present some new truths. When I started the design the universe was thought to be made up of fundamental entities called superstrings and to be about 15 billion years old (plus or minus 5 billion). By the time I completed the major layout the prime candidate for the basic structure was a vibrating membrane, and the universe had become a multiverse with a 13-billion-year history (plus or minus 2 billion). That is progress of a kind even if it is not certainty.

But such change presents a problem. What, for instance, would cathedral builders have done with such a fast-moving cosmology, out of date by the time they had excavated the site and laid the foundation stones? How can one keep pace? Should a false

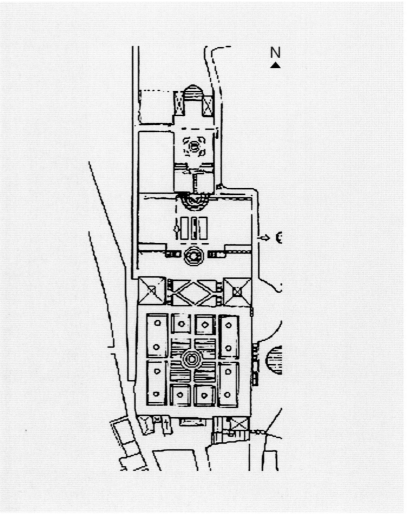

(or falsifiable) theory be built in concrete? One of the great investigators of the cosmic mystery, Roger Penrose, asked me this several times as I showed him various scientific speculations in the garden. Yes, our theories will become superannuated, but there are at least three rewards for building them into a semi-permanent form. The mistakes positively date the design in time, as all falsified theories do. They shout out: "This was what was thought before Einstein's theory." Secondly, they relate us directly to the unfolding cosmic process of understanding, tying us into evolutionary history. Lastly, they contain part of the truth that will persist into the future. That is, while science does change, it also shows some cumulative progress, a development that includes fragments of truths that have led to the present ones. If one doubts this manner of progress, think of the periodic table, a fairly good illustration of cumulative development, not to be totally smashed or overthrown, but modified and added to in the future. Similarly, a garden of cosmic speculation provides these partial hints of truth, as well as other pleasures.

In this, and in much more personal ways, constructing a garden contains an inevitable element of autobiographical story. It is a kind of existential calisthenics and, over the years, it brought me closer to my family, and mother-in-law Clare, and led to many enjoyable moments of mutual creativity with my wife, who initiated the whole thing, Maggie:

Thus there are three stories to tell: the personal one of a family as it changes and faces crises; the public one of how a garden might relate us to the universe and its laws; and the practical one of design theory and building—how friends, craftsmen, and the head gardener of Portrack, Alistair Clark, helped construct and maintain it. These three stories will be told separately and, where they overlap, simultaneously, because that is the way they happened and were mixed up. So it is with gardens, life, and love.

The ideas also had a life of their own and were developed further in other places. Several more landforms and several more versions of the DNA structure discussed in Part Five were constructed. Another "black hole" may be built in Pune, India, and a public park has been commissioned for Milan. All these projects continue themes explored first in this garden.

But I start with a constant inspiration, the universe as guide and measure, because that was the idea that initiated the design.

The Villa Lante, Bagnaia, begun in 1566 by Vignola. The flow of water from the top of the site, over cascades and rippling fountains, is used to narrate the development of civilization from its primitive beginnings in the Golden Age of Nature to its culmination here in Italy, a supposed New Golden Age of a reformed church. Planting, sculpture, and iconography support this story of culture evolving out of nature.

Cosmic Passion

Contemporary science is, I believe, potentially the greatest impetus for creativity of our time because it tells us the truth about the way the universe is. Today, more than ever before, it is uncovering basic events and laws that ask to be put in a wider framework. To put it paradoxically: science is clearly providing a new iconography for art, but one without clear icons. The new concepts are flowing out of the laboratories with such speed and fecundity that this period will probably be seen as the greatest age of discovery—especially in cosmology, biology, and the sciences of life. For those who follow developments, even in the daily newspaper, it is almost too stimulating and provocative. And yet many of us remain blind to these discoveries because they are not reinterpreted on the cultural level and given artistic expression. The icons, or expressive conventions, have not found their Michelangelo, or even their Henry Moore, perhaps because contemporary science itself is so complex and inchoate, or perhaps because things are moving so fast, or perhaps because of the way science is framed—with inadequate or alienating metaphors.

Whatever the reasons, contemporary science has not yet transformed the cultural landscape nor led to a renaissance in thought. This is something of a surprise since, as I will discuss, the new sciences of complexity, cosmology, and genetics have revolutionary implications. In any case, I believe that the ideas of contemporary science do provide the basis for a cultural reawakening and that a new iconography must be made more tangible through art if it is to be assimilated. This is what I have sketched here in words, drawings, and photographs. Throughout the book you will find conversations I have had with scientists and designers while creating the garden. As Ilya Prigogine, the Nobel laureate has framed it, there is now the possibility of a new dialogue with nature, and that conversation is what this book and garden are attempting. I, like he, think we are living through one of the most exciting shifts in conceiving the universe.

Cosmic passion, the desire both to know and to relate to the universe, is one of the strongest drives in sentient creatures, on a par with those which exercise novelists: sex, money, and power. Every creature in the universe tries to increase its knowledge, to figure out what is going on, what will happen next, how things are evolving and—the point of this passion—how we can relate to this process, fit in with its patterns, celebrate and, on occasion, criticize it. An art fitting to the cosmos, what I would call "cosmogenic art," does not always take nature as beneficent or beyond improvement. The laws of nature may be omnipotent, but they can also be challenged. A garden is a perfect place to try out these speculations and celebrations because it is, of course, a bit of man-made nature, a fabricated and ideal cosmic landscape, and a critique of the way the universe is.

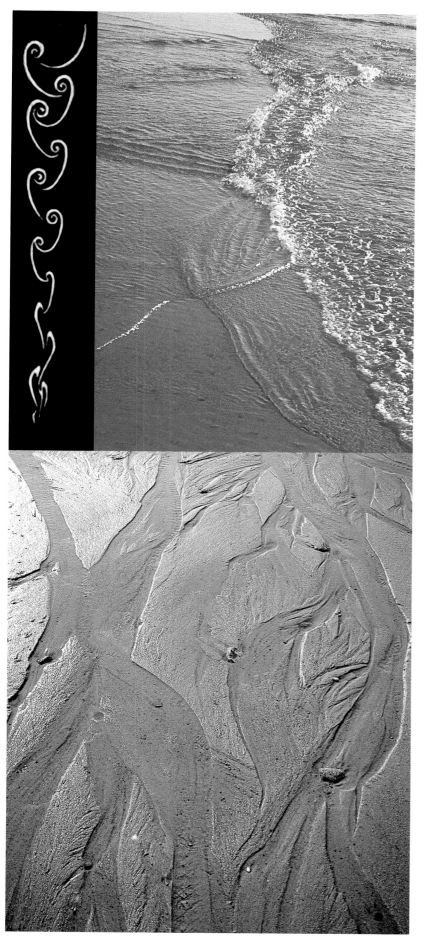

Even if one does not feel such commitment, a series of sticks and carrots are driving cultures irreversibly toward a cosmic view. The negative pressures are such things as global warming and an accompanying mass extinction; or the fact that an asteroid big enough to destroy New York City or Greater London missed the earth in June 2002 by a mere 75,000 miles. Another one—known as 2002NT7—will come within 32,000 miles of the earth on February 1, 2019, and will possibly hit us. Global catastrophes with a cosmic dimension are now part of the daily news, and global consciousness. Inescapable. The positive pressures, the enticements, include the way everything is gaining a cosmic name, understanding, and dimension. For instance, instead of measuring days and minutes by wobbly turns of the earth, time has been put on a cosmic footing and one second is now measured at 9,192,631,770 cycles of a Cesium atom. Feet, inches, meters—all weights will soon go this way, as the universe, not man (as Protagoras claimed), becomes "the measure of all things."

Yet however strong the cosmic impulse, because of a mechanistic view of nature, it may be undeveloped, or repressed. The modern world-view that emphasizes a universe based on warfare, selfish genes, and an arms race between species, can be as alienating as the Christian orientation that has us exiled from nature on account of original sin. These two views even concur in giving us dominion over nature, as if we actually controlled it. What misguided hubris; we cannot even control global warming.

Clouds and their fractal patterns have been solidified in rock design by the Chinese who see the Tao, or the Way of nature, as a ceaseless flow of energy. This is etched in rocks, or more delicately in the beach sand when the tide goes out—ripple marks within curves and meanders. Veins, bifurcations, and branchings, like those in the body or a tree, emerge as a consequence of flowing liquid. Patterns common to living and non-living matter are found at all levels throughout the universe. Waveforms, here on the beach, collide, sometimes creating interference patterns, other times a delicate rhythm because of the surface tension of water; the whale's body and play celebrate these basic, universal forces.

Probably everyone feels a natural kinship with the universe, especially when they are young. Even different species, such as dogs and whales, cavort about quite spontaneously, displaying an exuberant love of life, as if they knew they belonged here. You see that when a dog greets its owner, or when a young whale rises out of the water, slides on to its back and whacks its flippers against the sea. They express a knowledge of being at home in a place, the enjoyment of fitting into a part of nature. Empathy with the natural order is hard-wired into animals. The historical species closest to us, the Neanderthals, celebrated their presence, and a love of nature, before they disappeared some 20,000 years ago. They mourned and buried their dead, looked after their sick and infirm, and memorialized nature in grave sites. The archeological evidence is that a cosmic orientation goes back 80,000 years or more, and predates all the organized religions and science, which are more recent arrivals.

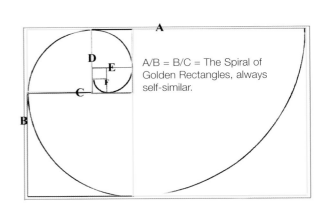

A/B = B/C = The Spiral of Golden Rectangles, always self-similar.

SPIRALS

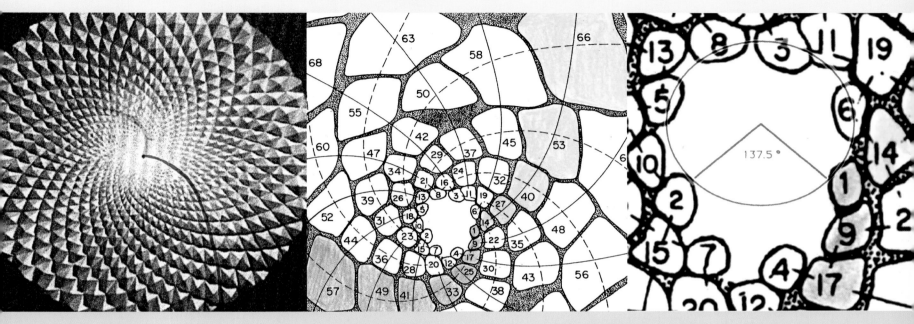

How does a pineapple know how to create beautiful spirals? It turns out that many plants and other forms of life have hit on the secrets of formal organization long before we followed them into this mysterious discovery. The Fibonacci spiral can be found at all scales of nature and cannot be accounted for simply in terms of Darwinian natural selection. Take a sunflower and count the florets running into its center or count the spiral scales of a pine cone running from its bottom to the top and you will find an extraordinary truth: recurring numbers, ratios, and proportions. On these and many other growths there are typically 5 elements spiraling to the left and 8 spiraling to the right, or 13 and 21, or 34 and 55 etc. These numbers follow the Fibonacci series (named after Leonardo Fibonacci, the 13th-century Florentine who discovered it). Each term is the sum of the previous two. When laid out in grids the harmonic patterns also form what are known as Golden Section rectangles: self-similar rectangles that can be inscribed into each other endlessly with no space left over. How does nature know to be so elegant and efficient? Why do 80 percent of 250,000 species of higher plant have comparable orders? Natural selection? Not only.

The recurrent pattern is a form of robust self-organization, the most probable way the leaves or pine scales can occupy space given the rate at which they grow. The explanation, which eluded botanists for many years, has recently been discovered to lie in the close packing of space. I mention it here because it is typical of many other recent discoveries that are celebrated in the garden. It turns out that one floret of the sunflower grows after another at the key angle of 137.5 degrees because this is the angle best suited for occupying space over the growing time of the plant. The structural elements of a pine cone, daisy, pineapple and so many other spiraling plants can support each other most efficiently this way. They can fill in the available space most simply—huddle together for mutual support most economically—without either wasting space or getting in each other's way. How did they know how to do this, and how did they know it would produce the beautiful Fibonacci series?

The Fibonacci spirals and Golden Sections created by a daisy are analyzed in the beautiful drawings of Gyorgy Doczi, while an analysis of a monkey puzzle tree (*Araucaria excelsa*) shows the order in which the leaves grow and migrate—at an angle of 137.5 degrees—generating spirals and Golden Section rectangles. Follow the spiral numbers from the youngest leaves at the center: 1, 9, 17, 25, 33, 41, 49, 57. . . . All have a difference of 8. The opposite spiral is 1, 14, 27, 40, 53, 66. . . . Difference: 13. The pattern is called an 8/13 phyllotaxy, a typical Fibonacci sequence. (After G. Doczi, *The Power of Limits*, Shambhala, Boston and London, 1994, and A. H. Church.)

One Clue in the Garden—Self-Organizing Harmonies

Beyond the mechanistic and theistic traditions is a third understanding that is barely twenty years old, although it has many precedents. Partly it comes from what are called the new sciences of complexity, and it finds that most everything in the universe is self-organizing—following one harmonic pattern or another. This quality of self-organization gives things identity, beauty, and coherence. It makes them semi-autonomous and valuable and, to a degree, it extends even to inanimate matter. Chemical reactions pulsate, storms self-organize, and they both form rhythmical structures such as the spiral, a form I have used repeatedly throughout the garden.

The spiral shape is found in the tiny DNA molecules that we share with all life forms. The shape is also found in ammonites, prehistoric ammonites that became extinct 250 million years ago, and since fossils of these are plentiful in Scotland I have used them as latches on garden gates, and parts of a waterfall. The spiral shape occurs in the pine cone and the pineapple, in the hurricane, and in the second largest structure of the universe, the galaxy. Why should such patterns be so important, why should I enlist their support in aid of a new world-view? Because instead of emphasizing mechanical determinism or the laws of an external deity, they bring to the fore creativity, freedom, and self-organization along harmonic lines.

Over many years of evolution, of trial and error, nature discovered deeper cosmic patterns such as the spiral and then exploited them. Natural selection may have fine-tuned the process, but the perfect angle of the Fibonacci spiral comes from the pre-existing geometry of space occupation. In effect, the universe has pre-ordering possibilities before natural selection ever gets to work. Cosmogenesis produces pattern, harmony, and organized complexity before there is life.

This is what one of the leading complexity scientists, Stuart Kauffman, calls "order for free" but because it is so important and because it contradicts the principle of increasing disorder or decline (entropy) and other truths the Modernists brought to the fore, it should perhaps have a single term. Another investigator, Gyorgy Doczi, calls it "dinergy," a new word made up from the Greek *dia*, meaning "across, through, opposite," and energy for the creative energy of organic growth. Actually, self-organizing patterns emerge out of the universe and its laws: they are present, curiously, before nature or behind nature. They give it and us identity, dignity, semi-autonomy. They may predispose the universe to evolve along one path rather than another—almost, if not quite, in a purposeful direction. For me they are a source of great wonder and awe, a fitting icon for a garden.

As luck would have it I have even found good examples of such pattern-formation in inorganic structures right underfoot, in the

River Nith. This fast-running salmon and trout waterway flows very close to the garden. From this ever-changing current some strange Liesegang rocks can be fished, and they can be turned into icons of self-organization. Such icons afford one clue to the meaning of the garden that "symmetry breaking" is as important as "symmetry making."

Other icons remain veiled, to be discovered by the viewer or reader. There is much in the following story, and photographs, that will be left unsaid. After all, if the universe is, like mankind, a mystery in its birth and final destination, then a garden, its microcosm, is a place where not everything should be spelled out. Einstein said: "God is subtle but not malicious." The laws of the universe do not change capriciously, but need teasing out. A garden should present a corresponding puzzle to be fathomed, some things very clear and others veiled.

The implications of the new sciences of complexity are so important that they became explicit, the underlying theme for the garden, and my wife and I used them to speculate on and celebrate the laws of the universe—subtle, complex, beautiful, but not malicious.

Liesegang rocks, discovered in the nearby River Nith, are an example of "symmetry breaking," a basic truth of the universe. These beautiful/ugly rocks were formed of sandstone when iron deposits broke the overall unified symmetry of white sand and pulsated in red concentric circles. The patterns have a similar form and origin to the famous chemical reaction Belousov–Zhabotinskii and the circles and spirals of the self-organizing slime mold. Here, the rocks are mounted on brass plates whose flat identical symmetry has also been broken by simple operations: bending, heating, hitting etc. An iconography emerges to reveal an interesting discovery of our time. It is not just to beautiful symmetrical shapes like a circle that we owe the interest of our universe, but to symmetry breaking. No breaking, no history of the universe—nothing but dull identity.

PART TWO: THE CREATION OF A GARDEN

Maggie

Many people noted Maggie's lightness of bearing, her delicate charm. As one friend said, when she walked she did not touch the ground. Ideas came to her from everywhere she traveled. Pigeonholes were traps to be jumped over. She was brought up by her mother as a Catholic, but had no trouble combining that faith with Buddhism, Taoism and other beliefs she found sympathetic. She liked to say she came from a family of traders, or merchants, in the Borders of Scotland as if living in an area that had been fought over allowed her to see two sides of a question. She was the only daughter of John and Clare Keswick of London and Holywood in Scotland (mispronounced it sounds like its more famous counterpart).

The Keswicks spent the early part of Maggie's life, in the 1940s, shuttling back and forth between China and Britain. John, later Sir John, had been taipan of a leading trading company, Jardine Matheson of Hong Kong, and he had been knighted because of his contributions to Sino-British trade, as well as for many other lesser-known deeds in the Second World War and afterwards. Through his contacts he managed to take Maggie, Clare, and other friends on many trips throughout China during the 1960s and 1970s when tourism was non-existent and visas hard to come by. Maoism was still hanging on and although the party line was anti-capitalist John kept the trust of officials there because he had stood by the Chinese during the War and was one of the few capitalists who tried to master the language. Most of his business, and diplomacy, was conducted at banquets or interminable meetings in hotel rooms, so it is probably fair to say that the largest part of his Mandarin and Cantonese vocabulary related to food. In any case, he treated the Chinese with respect, as equals, and in those days, for a powerful capitalist, that was rare.

Constant travel and contact with Chinese also gave Maggie a sense of openness, the ability to relate to strangers whatever their background. This was lucky for me since, as an American teaching in London at the Architectural Association, where we met, we often had very different views of things, and we enjoyed our differences.

Indeed, on our second meeting we literally fell out over questions of taste and ideology. I had shown her two different types of modern architecture: the high-minded Brutalism of the Roehampton Estate in southwest London, which I preferred, and a populist version of more traditional architecture that was also mass-produced, but which had pitched roofs and comforting planning. She could see that, as architecture, the first was superior, but as social housing much less successful. As we left these estates arguing our sides passionately, in exasperation she asked me to leave her car and, when I didn't, she stopped, and did. But then, at my entreaties, she got back in. Before the end of the afternoon we had exchanged our ideological positions two or three more times.

This trial by motorcar was the first of many. We found there was a certain pleasure in trading opinions. I mention all this because it was a pattern that was to last throughout our joint creation of the garden, on her parents' property in Scotland. After all, we used to tell each other, you can learn something from someone with whom you disagree, whereas you already know your own feelings and prejudices. Besides, as sociologists began to discover, couples that don't argue together don't stay together—as long as they know how to turn their disagreements into new bonds. My view is that couples have to be strong as individuals, give each other the space for creative difference, or else their relationship withers—but it does take effort and not a little friction.

By the time we married, in 1978, I was thirty-eight and well into my career as a writer, a visiting professor at UCLA in Los Angeles, and polemicist for a new movement, post-modernism. This I had started in architecture a few years earlier, aided by Maggie's insight and critical quips, and the movement took off around the world. Soon it influenced the fields of art and philosophy, and then other disciplines, becoming in the whirlwind something of a zeitgeist (although it questioned the very notion of a single spirit of the age). My version of post-modernism emphasized the way different codes of architecture should be brought together in order to deal with the richness and plurality of contemporary cultures.

In the late 1970s the issues became international, and the result was that the two of us would fly around the world together, I giving talks on the nascent movement, she on Chinese gardens. As a youth

Maggie outside the Getty Museum, 1977. Clockwise, from top right: Frank Gehry, Allen Jones, Michael Graves, and John Margolies.

growing up partly in Shanghai, Maggie had visited the gardens around Suzhou, Yangzhou, and Hangzhou, and, with many later trips, had continued to study them. Because she had such insight into Chinese culture and landscape, I, as well as others, urged her to write a book on the subject, a task she found painfully difficult. She invented all sorts of reasons for going slow; she cited precedents that mocked her own irresolution, including a 16th-century Chinese text called *Random Thoughts on Disconnected Ideas*. She even managed to lose half of the 140,000-word manuscript somewhere in a Los Angeles suburb and, with typical light-hearted irony, called her procrastination "creative dithering." Whatever one called it the process paid off and, in 1978, she finally produced *The Chinese Garden*. The book became a classic in its field. The disconnected ideas were drawn into a rich and potent mixture, not unlike the Oriental garden itself. Going slow allowed complex meanings to emerge.

When she lectured, particularly in America, students were taken by her English accent and graceful delivery. She would traverse the stage back and forth in front of the slides, coaxing out the meanings of the Oriental garden with a kind of shadow play. She would gesture the flowing force of the Tao as it meandered its way through mountains and lakes—convey it like a sensuous Thai dancer with her fingers and body. I will not say she was very conscious of her performance, although she had acted when at Oxford, but soon after this she was voted (by some unofficial body) as the most accomplished lecturer on the art circuit, after Vincent Scully and Rosamund Bernier. It was her lightness, accent and sensibility that appealed to the Americans, and maybe her legs. What united us particularly were our common interests, our love of travel, and above all our shared sense of humor.

Portrack

Portrack is a Georgian farmhouse built in 1815 and elevated in stature by an addition of 1879, but thankfully it has always kept a modest scale. The Victorian architect, James Barbour, understood the importance of using bay windows and gables to break up a mass and the result is a picturesque compilation in black and white with a slight spooky air about the pointed tower. Used as the dower house of the adjoining estate, it was further opened up, with a few large windows, when John and Clare settled in during the late 1950s. It was named after a ruined castle whose remains still exist not far from the banks of the River Nith, and this structure may have dated back to Roman times when there was a natural ford over this ever-changing current (see the site plan, pages 36–7). Previous owners had formed a large lawn by the main entrance to the south. Earth-movers had flattened the land in front, possibly for games such as croquet, and pushed the spoil toward the approach road creating a buffer and, in effect, a linear garden between two banks of

planting. Here "the long walk," as Clare conceived it, was planted with all sorts of colorful and scented species, an eclectic paradise garden in the English sense. At one end was a curved vault of yellow flowering laburnum, at the other a mixture of shrubs, lilies, hostas, bulbs, herbaceous plants, and roses, while the middle was also calculatedly informal. Various tufted mosses held the banks while above them rhododendrons and small trees kept the eye moving. The sense of a crafted wilderness of juxtaposed species, of nature's plenty, is why I associated it with the paradise garden, in which there is supposed to be one of everything. But it was only later, when Maggie and I started designing linear snaking forms, that I could see what a deft invention it really was. Not only did it block out the noise of the road and allow a lawn in front of the house, but it also resulted in a surprising contrast to the utilitarian landscape. There, amidst the rolling Scottish hilltops grazed low by sheep and cattle, one suddenly comes upon a very thin, secret garden. Perhaps all gardens aspire to this condition—one of the oldest conceits is the *giardino segreto*—but it really is a surprise to find it tucked between a road and open lawn.

Other interventions around Portrack were more piecemeal, made spontaneously on the foot, or from the window. John planted an old bit of remaining forest, called Crow Wood, with a variety of specimen trees—beeches, blue cedars, red acers, and big-leafed rhododendrons that give clumps of different color. By an existing burn, he laid out a row of cherry trees and, to hide the railroad from London to Glasgow that passed over the River Nith, he planted a row of tall poplars. Throughout the landscape he dotted clumps of bamboo, white-bark birch and masses of differently colored rhododendrons and azaleas. These last, on first sight, seem uncontrollably dissonant but, on second view, provide some welcome visual energy, especially in May and June when they explode into reds and oranges. In any case, Clare and Maggie shared John's taste for strong bright colors, again something that was influenced by the Chinese. Characteristically, he put together a large collection of odd grotesques with which he would delight visitors: small charmed figures often made of jade and known as Three-Legged Toads. Magical icons, they signified good luck, avariciousness and prosperity; but their outstanding property was a compulsively beautiful ugliness. Absolute contrast. Like Chinese rocks, which I came to love and use in a cascade at Portrack, they challenged categories of thought, particularly the notion that only living things constitute the natural world.

Portrack House. The Victorian Picturesque, with a slight hint of Charles Adams, with opposite forms juxtaposed for functional and aesthetic reasons: a small white country house stands out against the dark green landscape.

Clare's Long Walk, an eclectic Paradise Garden laid out as an undulating path hidden from the house, bordered by rhododendrons, hostas, lily of the valley and flowering shrubs. At the end of the lawn is a bank with many different types of thick moss.

Snakes and Dragons

The work that Maggie and I started at Portrack had practical motivations. She wanted to excavate a mosquito-infested swamp and create a place for our children to swim. In the back of her mind was the nearby Cluden Falls, a small stream in which she had played when young and, as a drawing titled it, "one of my favorite places in Dumfries." We hired a local contractor who had earth-moving equipment, Hugh Hastings, to dig ten feet into the swampland to increase the flow of water in an existing burn, or stream. We were both amazed at how quickly a few diggers and ploughs could excavate a pond and form the earth into different viscous shapes that came naturally out of the process. Was this another example of Stuart Kauffman's "order for free"? In any case, as the diggers piled up the mud in a long line, we discussed the shape this earth might take and, as usual, could not reach a quick conclusion.

As we debated the shapes of the earth and water, I said that whatever they might be I knew one thing for certain: they should become part of an overall program, a strategy for the gardens, fields, and farms that surrounded us. Perhaps a new grammar of landscape. Maggie granted this and then we looked at aerial photos and old plans and saw, indeed, there was an underlying structure to the hills and valleys that could be brought out. We both drew curves connecting up the local hills. These had been left by a glacier and, by joining some large features, we could create five or six undulating landforms that had a huge scale. So far so good: we both agreed on a formal grammar of snaking curves.

Then, having seen some latent snake images emerge, we argued over our friend Frank Gehry's play on words and animism. In the mid-1980s he built a conference room in the shape of a fish, and designed several snake and fish lights that had caught the public's imagination. "I'm giving a new scale to architecture," he would say to humanists and those modernists still concerned with an abstract system of proportion, "the fish scale." The ludicrous pun usually touched a nerve, just as did his abstract images, because they were deftly balanced between functional necessity and explicit representation. But the debate raised a deeper question: how vulgar and explicit should our projections on to nature become? Is the cosmos really like an animal? Does it have some animating spirit or "world soul," as many cultures have thought? Or, as the Chinese used to think, is there some Tao—the Way—underlying nature? After some disagreement, we decided to combine two images and substances: a "water dragon eating a land dragon."

Maggie and I both admired the way the Chinese used the image of a dragon in their undulating white walls, and the way this metaphor could be both implicit and explicit. There is one wall in the Yu Yuan in Shanghai, going up and down and in and out, that ends in a ferocious dragon's head; the mixture was positively post-modern (if ancient). Maggie's researches into Chinese geomancy

sparked off a further apt metaphor for seeing the local landscape in animistic terms. This part of Scotland consists of deep, smooth valleys, and low, long curving hills. Chinese landscape painters, following Taoist monks and philosophers, saw similar hills and mountains as "bones of the earth" energized with the "chi," the "vital breath" of subterranean dragons. The challenge was to make the image grow out of the contours so that when it became an explicit dragon it felt both inevitable and surprising.

With this in mind we set out to form the swampland as an earth dragon zigzagging back and forth with generous curves that diminished toward the tail. On the head, which projected twenty feet into the water, we placed two giant rocks, dotting the eyes as it were, and then surrounded the head with large liquid jaws, those of a much bigger water dragon. The earth eaten by the water. It sounds arbitrary, but the forms have subsequently been absorbed by a riotous nature.

Because bulldozers so easily produced linear and drop-like shapes, we conceived the area as having a hidden order waiting to be revealed. Or that, at least, when I drew sketches of the whole site, is what I thought: there emerged eight or nine blobs, or serpents, or worms, or slugs or, better than any image, a new language of abstract form which had an underlying logic. Partly it came out of the site and earth-moving and partly, as I shall explain, it came from a metaphor that was beginning to form in my mind, "a landscape of waves."

During those long summer nights, when it stayed light till 11:30, we would argue over which way the program should go. In the back of Maggie's mind was a radical plan for turning the layout of Portrack around and approaching it with a long, meandering, tree-framed avenue that would pass on one side of the Dragon Lake. She had heard Anthony Archer-Wills give a talk on water gardens and artificial lakes and got the idea of having him construct a waterfall at Portrack. This she did, overseeing the work carefully along with Hugh Hastings and his team of earth-movers. They gingerly put in place about ten large Dumfrieshire boulders and composed them as if they had always been there, and then created a little island that also looked eternal. "The Land of the Immortals" was the Chinese reference, but one would hardly recognize the allusion unless it was pointed out. Maggie always favored

OPPOSITE, TOP: Maggie's sketch of Cluden Mills and Falls, 1987, a nearby river in which we swam, that became a model for her excavations and waterfall. OPPOSITE, CENTER: The Dragon Wall in the Yu Yuan, Shanghai, with a figurative head at the end of an undulation. In spite of the fact that Chinese connoisseurs considered such explicitness vulgar, images and sculptural rocks give welcome punctuation to a garden. ABOVE AND LEFT: In the undulating dry-stone wall at Portrack, and elsewhere, this image is coded with other metaphors. As if to confirm the idea, birds, ancestors of dinosaurs, have subsequently made nests in our dragon heads.

understatement and, where appropriate, sensitivity to Scottish conventions. This led to our first major disagreements. I, more than she, was bored with traditional design, however convincing its last exemplars had been, and saw no reason to repeat anything done well for three hundred years. "Don't reinvent the Georgian spoon, buy one," was my approach. She, by contrast, wanted one of the great radical traditionalists, Leon Krier, to do an extension to the main house. He, a good friend, was not only drawing seductive city plans to reconstruct a fragmenting Europe, but also leading a vast army of followers, including Prince Charles, in his charge back to the past. In fact, Leon is something of a visionary and like all prophets who sacrifice themselves to an idea he is also part Don Quixote, part the stern lawgiver. When we have our periodic, heated discussions I call him "Ayatollah," a designation he accepts because he knows I value his criticism and inventiveness. Krier also influenced Maggie's drawing style and, as we will see, she was not to go very far from the traditional view until after she started painting with Cecil Collins and worked on a scheme with Frank Gehry.

In any case, from my background, I knew that architectural invention has at least two opposite sources: the formal and the programmatic—either can drive design forward when the other gets tired. So now that we had a tentative agreement over the new wormlike grammar of the Dragon Lakes, I went to work on five or six main areas which might be brought into a narrative. Should a novel have one plot, or many?

The First Plot—The Senses of Sensual Knowledge

Because they are made over time, gardens create the stories by which they are made, and what is a garden, if not the celebration of the senses, a heightening of the way we perceive the universe? Imagine a garden on the moon or on a dead planet, such as Venus or Mars, with only a few colors. There is nothing much to touch except hard, dusty surfaces, and no scents except the occasional stench of a volcano. Minimalism, sensory deprivation, nothing to perceive, little growth of the mind. By contrast, the earth seems to be designed to stimulate every nerve ending and external organ that can pick up a signal. Flowers clearly amplified the senses of smell and sight when, some 140 million years ago, they came on the scene. Their strong polychromy, contrasting with the predominantly green background, would have startled all the sentient creatures had they been keeping records and, to further the fantasy, it might have stimulated them to look harder and longer, as if hypnotized by the new brilliance. The same shock of the new would have been created by the new power of perfume; it would have dominated the usual smells of rotting flesh and inert matter. Since flowers came to perform a sexual function, they must also have heightened other senses, for instance, hearing—the sound of insects buzzing and performing their frenzied dances.

Looking for further proof that a garden is a built sensorium, I thought of its primary function, the cultivation of food. This obvious conclusion led me from the nose to the mouth, and something that Maggie had always planned: a kitchen garden. There is no question that the sense of taste is celebrated in a kitchen garden along with the sense of smell since, routinely, it is made with herbs that release their perfumes on a footstep or a gust of wind. Thus, the five senses could be the initial program for an instrument whose major function, inherently, is to tie us sensually into the cosmos. I imagined this as giant organs—nose, eyes, mouth, hand, ears etc.—reaching out, perhaps lightly waving in the breeze like insect feelers. Later I understood the extraordinary way our senses transform impulses of energy into feelings, and my friend Madelon Vriesendorp drew a surrealist image of the magnified senses.

The question became how to extend the senses on to a larger plane, to the level of thought, logic, and understanding. One night, with a thesaurus in hand, Maggie and I hit on a program for the whole site. We found it was possible to relabel all the existing functions, and parts of the garden, with a normal and abnormal sense, and also a different use of the word "sense." Thus the kitchen garden became, quite logically, the Garden of Common Sense, the place where you grow what you eat. The tennis court, surrounded by its high walls of a fast-growing cypress that Maggie hated, became the Sense of Fair Play. The existing Crow Wood, because of its dark, tall tree cover and the behavior of its mad crows, became the Garden of Taking Leave of Your Senses, a place of illusions, tricks and confusions. All these puns "made sense" in terms of their use and thus we had two different codes, two related programs.

There was the narrative of the five senses, later augmented to six and more, and the faculty of the mind analogous to a physical sense. The latter uses had a lot of applications in a garden: the vague impression of giving "a sense of security." In Italian gardens the surprising jet of water which the gardener releases when you are standing over it (*gia d'aqua*) heightens the "sense of humor." Then one could imagine the discernment of quality, the "sense of value," and the meaning of a word—its "sense." The logic was compelling, leading quickly from one area and subject to another. As the site plan on the next page reveals, these different "senses" divided up the landscape into overlapping gardens.

TOP: Flowers and birds emerged 140 million years ago, bringing to a green world an escalation in sensuality: polychromy, scent, and sound. This collage is a step on the Universe Cascade (see page 218), painted by Lily Jencks. FAR LEFT: A General Sense of Anticipation. Senses transform energy waves into neuronal events of the brain that have to be interpreted by the mind. LEFT: Drawing of the senses by Madelon Vriesendorp.

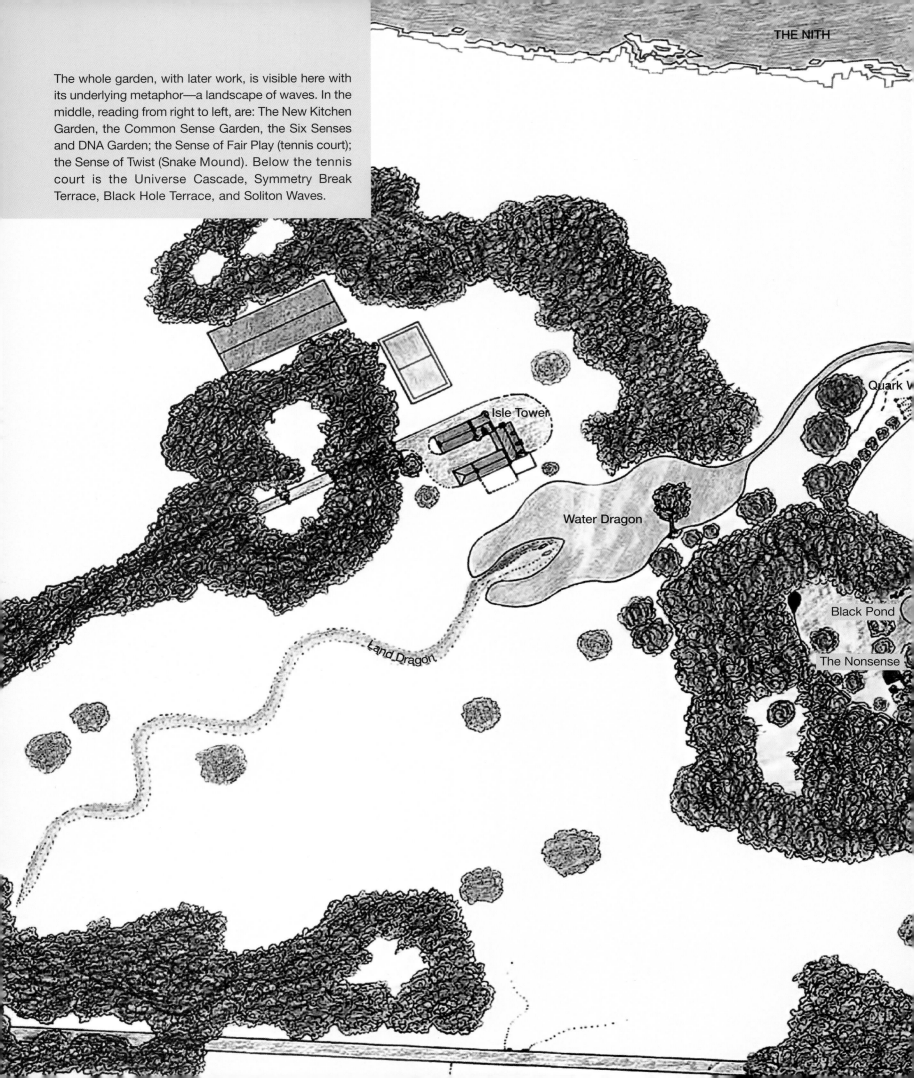

The whole garden, with later work, is visible here with its underlying metaphor—a landscape of waves. In the middle, reading from right to left, are: The New Kitchen Garden, the Common Sense Garden, the Six Senses and DNA Garden; the Sense of Fair Play (tennis court); the Sense of Twist (Snake Mound). Below the tennis court is the Universe Cascade, Symmetry Break Terrace, Black Hole Terrace, and Soliton Waves.

Isle Tower

Water Dragon

Land Dragon

Quark W

Black Pond

The Nonsense

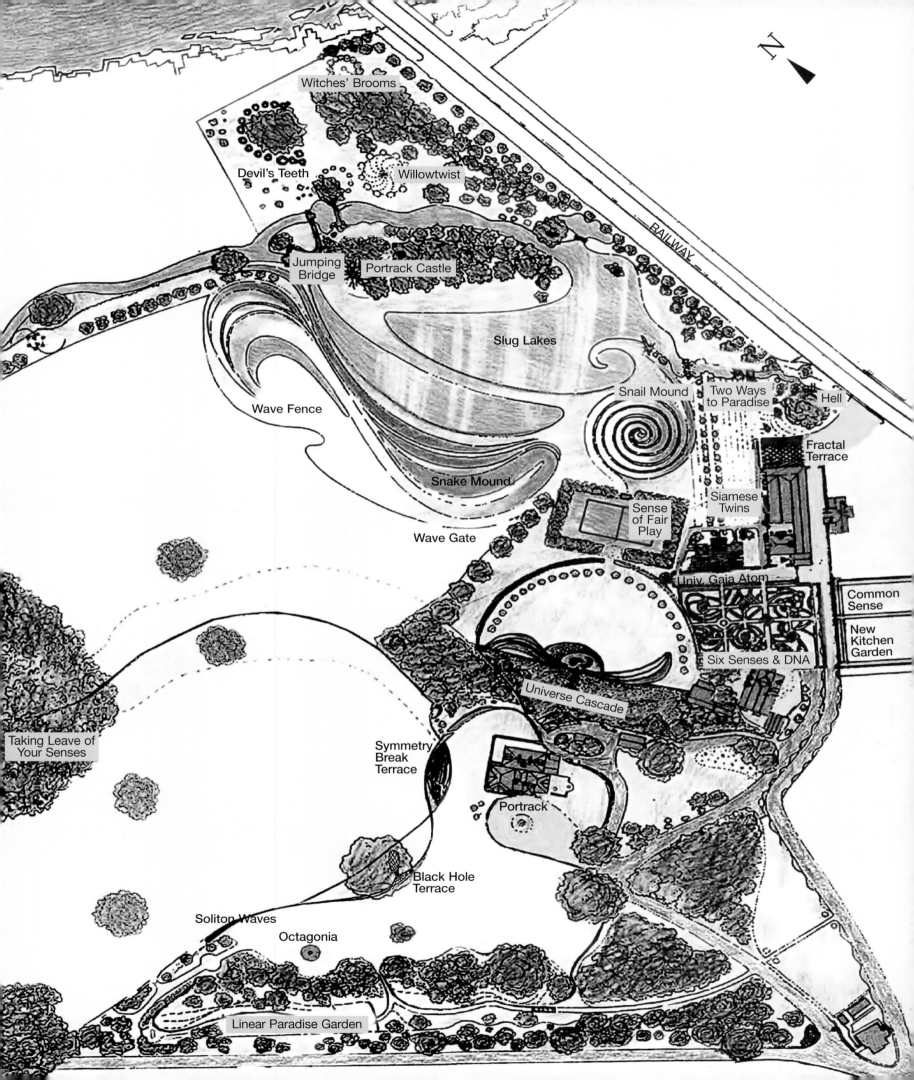

Sense and sensibility, sense and nonsense. In Crow Wood, where a thousand crows make their nest in large sycamores and elms, there was a bizarre, eerie atmosphere that reminded us of Bomarzo, a 16th-century Italian garden. This strange landscape has sculpted, in huge stones on the site, a battle of the Titans, the open jaws of Hades, an elephant with a castle on its back, and a tipped house leaning at such an acute angle that you lose balance. Maggie and I had gone there in the 1970s before it had been cleaned up and sanitized for tourists. As we pushed through the undergrowth and came upon stone giants engaged in some sort of love tussle it evoked the wilderness as wildness. Thus the program for our strange woodland of crows became a garden called "Taking Leave of Your Senses." This was to create a new form of disorientation.

At its heart we re-erected part of a model building that was being thrown out. James Stirling's mock-up of his Neue Staatsgalerie in Stuttgart, that exemplar of post-modernism, had been on show at the Royal Academy in London in 1986. Since they did not have a use for this fragment of a building, we put it on a plinth in Crow Wood. To continue the theme of disorientation, I designed an abstract columnar screen in alternating silver and black, and a bizarre stair for climbing up to its deck. Because this platform was unusable in a conventional sense, we christened the whole folly "The Nonsense." Words covering one lintel, from a poem by Baudelaire, both underline and displace the meaning of the pavilion. The symbolism of different media—words, building, and nature—interact in surprising ways, an idea carried throughout the rest of the landscape. Thus the structure was an important first step in creating a hybrid medium somewhere between sculpture, literature, architecture, and landscape—a first example of cross-coding I was to christen "cosmogenic art."

As if to prove its title, The Nonsense suffered, over the years, a few indignities. One day Leon Krier and his wife Rita Wolf came to visit Maggie and me, so we took them to Crow Wood to see the building, a structure Krier might have had a very oblique role in creating. Krier had been a key draftsman in James Stirling's office in the late 1970s but, as I was well aware, they had fallen out over several issues including design credits and the influence of Krier on Prince Charles. The Prince had attacked Stirling for not caring enough about what the public thought of his housing and had tried to stop Stirling's project for the center of London, saying the scheme looked like "a 1930s wireless" (that is, an old-fashioned radio set). And, as far as Stirling thought, the Prince had kept him from getting any more British commissions. The architect

Bomarzo Garden, c.1560, created by Count Orsini near Viterbo, Italy. The hell's face with its quote from Dante ("All Hope Flees"), the battle of the Titans, and the leaning house, are some of the many esoteric and popular themes mixed in this sensual garden of mysteries.

countered by comparing Charles to Hitler, an escalation in the Style Wars that was picked up on the front pages of the tabloids. When I showed Krier The Nonsense his response was pretty much what I expected. Pulling a long face, saying "How ugly," he gave it a thumbs down. A week later, as I was walking over to Crow Wood, I heard an explosive noise that sounded like a motor accident. There was The Nonsense, with a long tree branch smashed through its roof, a tangle of broken wood, leaves, metal, and glass. The Ayatollah's Thumbs Down had had its way; the deconstruction he disliked was further deconstructed. The catastrophe was, however, quite beautiful, particularly in the way the broken branch fitted like a new angled pediment over the classical base. But what was really nonsensical was that the offending branch had fallen uphill! Maggie and I had always worried about the branch above The Nonsense. Little did we imagine that it would be the one below it that would score a bull's eye. Luckily, insurance paid for its reconstruction, and so it settled back into its original pristine tangle. Subsequently nature has moved in again, this time more kindly, putting up shoots through its falling words. In a garden, co-creation with nature always becomes a major theme in itself.

Judgment, catastrophe, co-creation. Leon Krier gave The Nonsense the thumbs down. A week later the first of several catastrophes at Portrack struck the building. Today nature is slowly taking over.

THE NONSENSE

The front of The Nonsense was designed by James Stirling from fragments of the Neue Staatsgalerie in Stuttgart; the back, designed by Charles Jencks, was based on a triangular geometry. Stirling's pavilion was never intended to be used, so its conversion into a lookout was functionally nonsensical; for instance, on reaching the top, the view is blocked by a beam that also makes sitting difficult. The steep stair is designed for single alternating steps, while the syncopating squares in gray also disorient the sense of balance.

The words are from a poem celebrating the confusion of the senses, Charles Baudelaire's "Correspondences," which describes reality as a forest of symbols that mix up the senses:

La Nature est une temple où de vivants piliers
Laissent parfois sortir de confuses paroles;
L'homme y passe à travers des forêts de symboles
Qui l'observent avec des regards familiers . . .
Les parfums, les couleurs et les sons se répondent.

Confusion, synaesthesia, or the correspondences between everything in the world—and yet a crystal order.

TOP: James Stirling, CJ, Maggie, and Eduardo Paolozzi.

Common Sense through the Six Senses—Skottish

The Nonsense and this wilderness garden, Taking Leave of Your Senses, are a planned form of disorientation, to be set off by its opposite, common sense, the great virtue of British philosophy at the time of Hume and the Scottish Enlightenment. Practicality, functionality, hard-headedness, even the Yankee virtues of straightforwardness and no-nonsense are all derivatives. The problem with common sense is that it can become too common, that is, predictable. Yet this also can be positive if you are growing food. Crops are laid in straight lines, logical categories marked "carrots, peas, potatoes"—as if the plot were a laboratory. Such was the first program for the kitchen garden, but hardly the last one. Maggie and I produced six or seven layouts, all of which we ended up rejecting because of their conventional nature.

However, one of these I became particularly fond of, a play on the concept of nationhood: it was the idea of turning the plot into a new "Scottish Garden." Although there is a tradition of Scottish landscape design which recaptures the wild, romantic countryside of the Highlands, it is conceptually not that different from the English Picturesque and, as far as I could determine, there has never been a garden that has been entirely and distinctively Scottish. At the same time, there are paradoxes to our perception of tradition. As the historian Eric Hobsbawm has written, many relatively recent customs, coined at the time of Queen Victoria, have been accepted, mistakenly, as ancient and British. Bearing these contradictions in mind we worked out a grid made up of rocks, concrete, brick and stone slabs which wove through each other, coupled to the weave of plants, like a tartan. This we could claim to be indigenous, even "national." It is known that the Scottish invented most of the tartan, clan patterns—or at least made them fashionable—about the time of Walter Scott. Instant tradition itself has a long tradition, especially if one recalls how an 18th-century hoax turned into a real cultural artifact. This was the confabulation of nationalist pride known as *The Poems of Ossian, The Son of Fingal* concocted by the poet James Macpherson

out of ancient Celtic poetry. These proved fruitful in constructing national identity. Later the designer Charles Rennie Mackintosh produced some original work by deriving a national vernacular based on local materials, flora, and fauna—so there were instructive precedents for pseudo-tradition leading to real breakthroughs.

The Ambiguous Words of Nature

Regression or spur to invention—you could think of instant tradition in two ways. Curiously enough the tartan pattern had played a role in one of our designs many years earlier. When we were reconstructing our London home, according to an iconographic program, Maggie got fed up with symbolism cluttering surfaces, distorting shapes, or simply taking too long to design. Among other appropriate signs, I fashioned an abstracted book for the face of her library door, but she said emphatically, "This time symbolism stops at my door!" Ironically, however, when it came to designing her own desk and filing system, she covered it with a *trompe l'oeil* of the family tartan, so I pointed out rather smugly, "You see, symbolism is quite OK as long as you are doing it." Such was our amicable repartee as we pushed on with our different versions of the kitchen garden, until one day—after half of the tartan pattern was in—she said, "Enough! I don't like the way the bricks go around these corners." On occasion she had non-negotiable opinions. We debated in front of the head gardener, Alistair Clark.

Alistair is an intelligent, attractive, and balanced character, who constructed most of the gardens at Portrack and he tends them with great love and care. Trained in horticulture, he has ruled over the greenhouses for thirty years producing, among other notable features, an unusual array of begonias that look like explosions of little red flares. His wide-ranging skills might have made him the head of a corporation rather than the head of a building team, and he puts his social skills to good use when he leads tours around the gardens. It was his diplomacy and wry sense of humor that were called on, particularly when Maggie and I reached an impasse, as we did here over the merits of brick, or later over the acceptability of concrete. But it was the southern Scottish virtue of patience that he had to exercise with skill for the next few years because Maggie and I had reached stalemate. We could not quite agree on which areas should be stone slab, round rock or brick, and so the idea of the tartan remained half-born, a residual pattern which formed the structure of later plans.

The Garden of Common Sense as a Skottish Tartan. A sensible grid with linear planting framed by paths that weave through each other; it is based partly on Maggie's family tartan. The geometry, word play and pairing of opposite words had three more transformations: first into a Physics Garden relating to the basic laws of the universe, then the DNA and Six Senses Garden, and finally the Ambigrammi Game, still under construction (see pages 48–49).

What we did agree on was an undulating wall, descendant of those dragon walls we both admired, and this became the spur for a new garden game and a set of word plays and word ploys that are called ambigrammi. These are amazingly designed words that can be read two ways, right side up and upside-down. They show that

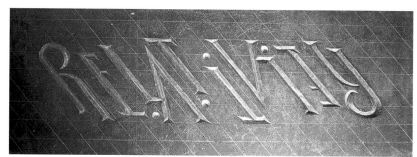

the symmetry underlying the universe also underlies signs and conventional signifiers. This is surprising since words are mostly social constructions that are accidental, fortuitous connexions of sound and sense, usually of arbitrary length. Why should they share geometrical patterns with trees and our body? Symmetry has been the codified route to beauty since the first century BC, when Vitruvius envisaged a man whose well proportioned body would generate circles, squares, and, by extension, temples.

Symmetry means more than the bilateral similarity of our body or of Renaissance gardens. It means an invariant pattern that remains after transformation. If you rotate, shift or mirror-reflect certain well-designed letters that remain the same when thus transformed, they can become symmetrical ambigrammi. It all depends on whether they form a word. Ambiguous from a semantic perspective, whether they should be read right side up, upside-down, or back to front, they are at the same time very clear from a formal perspective. An example would be the capitalized AH . . . HA. The H can be flipped and rotated through 180 degrees and remain the same, while the A can only be flipped on a vertical axis and remain meaningful—unless it is ambiguously redesigned as a V with, say, half a crossbar. In this case the 180-degree rotation

Ambigrammi to be read upside-down, based on some designs by John Langdon. The symmetry of these letters mirrors symmetries in the universe and, as I was to discover, its important principle: symmetry breaking (see pages 178–181).

would become HV . . . AH, which would be formally but not semantically meaningful. Several ingenious mathematicians and designers such as Douglas Hofstader, Scott Kim, and John Langdon have recently developed a few ambigrammi, and one can imagine the corpus being slowly extended. One area that has not been exploited is that of epigrams that read differently when ambigrammi are combined into phrases. For a garden art where symmetry and asymmetry are always basic themes, many opportunities open up. For instance, as one walks a path one way it says "turn on," the other way "no turn"; at a gate where one constantly reverses direction it says "reversal" going both ways, and what is more in positive and negative reversal, thus becoming a double ambigrammo (see pages 48–9 and 179).

Words, letters, signs, symbols should reverberate throughout a landscape, an idea common to Chinese gardens and poet-gardeners such as Ian Hamilton Finlay. In a garden not far from Portrack he has used single words and short phrases to intensify the feeling of a place or view, or to form a contrast with it. As Baudelaire insists in "Correspondences," (see page 40) "Nature is a temple . . . of confused words . . . a forest of symbols." This idea is also biblical except, for the enlightened, it was possible to overcome the symbolic confusion. Words, things, and symbols are all perceived united in a garden as they were in the Bible: "In the beginning was the Word, and the Word was with God, and the Word was God." That is quite a symbolic unity.

There are obvious parallels between gardening and creating a cosmos. God created the universe as He did the garden of Eden, by cutting up undifferentiated nature into parts and naming them rightly: "And God called the light Day." He brought into being and exactly named the other major aspects—that is "the night," "the firmament," "the seas," and "the beast of the earth after his kind, and the cattle after their kind" (i.e. the categories were logically and empirically cogent). Then "God formed every beast of the field, and every fowl of the air and brought them unto Adam to see what he would call them." In effect, He gave Adam the job of nomothete-in-chief, who could also create and order by getting the names correct: "And Adam called his wife's name Eve; because she was the mother of all living." This is interesting because it implies that names and things pre-exist together in a kind of scientific heaven and that one can either get Eve's name right or wrong. The nomothete, like the creator of a garden, is thus in the ambiguous position that the Bible indicates. On the one hand, naming authenticates things as it brings them into being, just the way seminal modern artists such as Duchamp and Picasso would invent an object and category of correctness in one act (the Readymade, the Cubist portrait). A gardener lays out areas, grows and names them, and by this act confers an ontological status on the parts they would not have if they had just occurred by chance.

On the other hand, like a scientist or Adam getting the name of Eve right, the gardener has to discover an order already existing, somehow hidden in the nature of things.

This creation by correct naming, as Umberto Eco has shown in *The Search for the Perfect Language*, has led accidentally to a whole series of sciences, such as modern linguistics. And how does my digression relate to gardening? While God and Adam may not have named all the world's elements, the existing landscape comes already divided into parts given conventional terms—"tree," "river," "cloud"—as if a divine creator were speaking sentences through discrete things. Each has its power to be countered or enhanced by words placed against it (see page 48). At Portrack words and signs are beginning to accrue to each design, each area, some that are evocative as in a Chinese garden, some that are confusing as in a synaesthetic poem, some that are ambiguous as

in an ambigrammo, and some that are descriptive as in a science museum. Written signs can give other layers of meaning not readily available, can cross-code the landscape and make it richer, deeper, perceived more slowly like an endless text of Proust. As Maggie pointed out to me, a Chinese garden is finished after the "naming ceremony," during which friends, poets, botanists, and children perambulate the site and compete for the most appropriate *bon mot* or literary allusion. Like Adam, they have to get Eve's name right—producing both an invention and correct discovery—after which some calligraphic artist comes along to immortalize the insight in beautifully cut stone. At Portrack the naming ceremony remains to be done, but there are a few signs in the ground. Moreover, as I was to discover later, the DNA and RNA that underlie all of life create a kind of language with letters, words, paragraphs, and whole plots.

With these various plans, the kitchen garden, or Garden of Common Sense, began to grow different meanings like barnacles accreting over generations. Although Maggie and I stopped work on it because of the tartan incident, we had agreed a basic narrative and I had come to an important realization: that our senses are protagonists for gardening—indeed life. The proof is language.

Think of how we express understanding. When we say, "I *see* what you mean" we use the sense of sight as a metaphor for comprehension—seeing is a synonym for knowing, or insight. "I *hear* what you are saying" is another phrase that shows that the second sense is also a metaphor for understanding. And then there is the saying contrasting the two: "You appeal to a man through his sight, a woman through her ears."

One does not regularly say, "I *feel* what you mean," but you can say, "You *touch* me"; so the sense of touch is a natural metaphor of the emotions ("You *touch* my heart"). You would never say, "I *smell* what you mean," unless you were a dog. But you can say, under certain conditions: "I want to *eat* you up" (possess you), or the more acceptable "You're delicious." That is proof enough—the five senses permeate our knowledge, affection, action and understanding. Aristotle, refuting Plato's emphasis on an abstract, disembodied set of forms, opens his *Metaphysics* with a daring claim, which I think is true: "All men [and women] by nature desire to know. An example of that is the delight we take in our senses. For even apart from their usefulness, they are loved for themselves, and of all of them none so much as vision." Aristotle claims we prefer sight because it reveals knowledge more clearly and the differences among things. It is said, "a picture is worth a thousand words" because it codes more information than words, in less space and time. From this central importance of the senses comes the plan of the kitchen garden, the Garden of the Six Senses, as I shall explain in Part Five.

It is sufficient at this point to mention that driving forward our senses is the overpowering desire to know about reality, to understand our place in the universe and how things have evolved to their present position. Our senses are active, not passive, because they are motivated by this curiosity. It is one of the strongest urges and on a par with the desire for eating, immortality, and power. Ultimately, we want to know about everything, the universe. If, contrary to Hollywood, knowledge, rather than sex, is the Basic Instinct, it is because the big question, of where we come from, drives the others. Everyone has some sort of answer to this question, whether it is personal, mythic, or based on shared scientific or religious explanations. We cannot escape metaphysics; it follows us from a cosmic landscape right into the house, and this brings me to my mother-in-law who lived at Portrack.

Inscribed windows and doors punctuate the Snake Wall at cross axes.

UNDULATING WALLS

Within an undulating wall, I designed three windows focused on three major axes. The windows are surmounted by contradictory phrases, part of a garden game that awaits completion. According to plans, four or six players will shake a huge die and chase each other over steps, a form of snakes and ladders with various incentives built into it, both imaginative and, like all competitive games, nasty. The players will start from a central door, above which the words PHYSICAL REASON are written. Above two other windows, on parallel axes, are cut the oxymoronic phrases EDIBLE HARMONY and KITCHEN JUSTICE— since this is a kitchen garden. Reason was inevitably symbolized by a square, justice by a triangle, harmony by a circle—old Renaissance signs that are appropriate for this, the old side of the garden wall. The wall itself was built by Hugh Drysdale, accomplished in the art of dry-stone walling.

AMBIGRAMMI

As the players move away from the starting point, the Renaissance period as it were, toward the future, a pavilion which is growing in the yew, they will cross various words cut in the stones underfoot (ambiguity, symmetry, sometimes, relativity etc.). Players will chase each other, as in croquet, and knock each other backward when they land on, or pass over, the opponent. The winner will be the one who not only reaches the far pavilion first, but the one who invents the shortest sentence from the words that are crossed. Here is the trick. In science you are rewarded for thinking of the shortest, most simple explanation that can explain complex reality. Occam's famous razor cuts away any extraneous meat from over-fat explanations. If one picks up words cut in the stone as one crosses them, there would be perhaps a string of ten. Then, when everyone reaches the far pavilion, the winner is the one who, adding connective verbs and articles, constructs the shortest sentence that makes sense. The Garden of Common Sense.

The ambigrammi can be read upside-down and sometimes backward. If you are overtaken by a competitor and knocked backwards, you pick up the penalty of another word. Someday the game will be tested.

Clare and the Zeroroom

For Maggie's mother, Clare, the answer to the big question was never in doubt. She was brought up a convinced Christian in the very big and very Catholic Elwes family of Northamptonshire. Her family estate, called Billing, was an environment that gave her the faith that was to be the backbone of her life. The youngest of eight children, she, her sister, and six brothers led a charmed life suffused with music and country house pleasures. It centered upon her parents. Her father was the famous tenor Gervase Elwes, and her mother the redoubtable Lady Winefride. Clare became a consummate actress and storyteller at the age of five by sharpening her performances in front of her appreciative brothers. She, like Maggie, and our daughter Lily, had a fierce determination in her eyes, yet it was overlaid by laughter-lines and a vivacious sparkle as if she might suddenly contradict the very high-minded values she upheld.

Her faith was tested by tragedy several times. On the day of her fifteenth birthday, when coming home from school, she saw a headline on a newspaper hoarding: "Famous Tenor Killed." Her father, then on a singing tour in America, had been dragged under a train in Boston. This was the first of the three misfortunes that cut across her life, unpredictable catastrophes that came out of the blue. Her Catholicism and generosity got her through these rough times partly because they tied her to wider communities in which she could share the grief. Clare's public persona might be aristocratic and distant on occasion, but she was also closer to most people than the average egalitarian, and she would break through the ice of awkward social situations by recounting bizarre stories. These were often about her life, which was unusual by today's standards. For instance, she managed to stay away from the local school for most of her youth by being taught at home.

A typical family anecdote concerned her marriage, in 1940, when she was at the slightly advanced age of thirty-five. Proud of being a virgin to that age, she had a very public wedding to John Keswick at the heart of English Catholicism, Westminster Cathedral. Three maiden aunts, hard of hearing and carrying ear trumpets, sat in the front pew. John, marrying into the Roman religion, had decided to try his vows in Latin. So when the moment of commitment arrived, instead of saying, "Yes, I do," he said, "Volo." The three aunts lent forward and whispered loudly, "Did he say no? Did he say no?" A few days later a lawyer arrived at John's office and said the marriage had not been consummated, legally. Why? Because Clare's very long set of first names, Clare Mary Alice Cynthia Catherine Celia, had been said in the wrong order. After they had made a second, and now successful attempt, at a registry office, John said: "Clare, if we have any children they will have one name—if we have a daughter she's called Margaret Keswick, and that's that."

While Clare was firm in the faith of the established church, Maggie was less certain. I remember lying in bed one evening watching the author David Lodge, whom we both admired, on television. When he said of his own beliefs, "I was brought up a Catholic, but I'm now an Agnostic Catholic," Maggie shot bolt upright and replied, "Yes, so am I." Because of her double upbringing, in Shanghai as well as Scotland and in Chinese as well as Western culture, she could have equally said, "I'm a Buddhist Catholic," and we often discussed hybrid belief systems such as those of the émigré priest Father Bede Griffiths, who settled in India.

One day Clare asked me to redesign a small passage that led out on to the garden. It held a jumbled mess of too many coats, gumboots, tennis rackets, garden pots, books, and the bric-a-brac one needs in a country house. A new cloakroom? I decided to use

ABOVE: A portrait of Clare Elwes by her brother Simon Elwes on the Island of Capri when she was eighteen, 1923. RIGHT: The Zeroroom: the cloakroom with repeated doorhandles and tennis rackets.

this redesign as a pretext for something entirely other, for preparing one for the garden and testing our uncertain place in the universe. Since the 16th century, and the Copernican Revolution, which displaced earth from the center of the cosmos, there has been much anxious speculation about our location, which it has been customary to equate with our significance. According to a simple equation the center means importance, and the periphery equals insignificance and, even though the idea of cosmic location has an absurd logic to it, philosophers, poets, and scientists continue to invoke it. The anxiety it engenders is expressed in John Donne's poetry. He lamented the loss of Christian wholeness implied by the new theories of atomism and mechanism. "An Anatomy of the World," written in 1611, includes the lines: "And new philosophy calls all in doubt/And element of fire is quite put out," and nears the end with, "They see that this/Is crumbled out again to his Atomies./'Tis all in Pieces, all coherence gone." The new mechanistic philosophy revealed a world, as Alfred North

Whitehead later wrote, that was "a dull affair, soundless, scentless, colorless, merely the hurrying of matter, endless, meaningless." The "loss of self in Modern literature," the identity crisis, which is an omnipresent theme of modernism, has its roots in existential dislocation, the loss of co-ordinates, a dizzying affair.

"In the vast heavens, where are we?", an innocent question, can lead to extreme psychological distress. Pascal, the Catholic thinker who made his wager with God, also expressed his angst at confronting a universe which expanded on and on, out of scale with any conceivable thought: "Le silence éternel de ces espaces infinis m'effraie." ("The eternal silence of these infinite spaces terrifies me.") Infinite spaces are frightening, even nauseating to some. When the telescope and calculus reached a certain sophistication in the 17th century there was no avoiding the crisis of infinity. It could be seen, operated on mentally and even represented in some architecture, for instance in the Baroque churches of Guarino Guarini. By the 19th century the painter Paul Gauguin made it a subject of one of his paintings: *D'où venons-nous? Que sommes-nous? Où allons-nous?*

"Where do we come from, what are we, where are we going?" These are the big questions, and what better place to face them if not in the smallest room in the house? Some people meditate, when they do, on the loo and there is a pleasing irony in confronting grand questions among hats and coats. The cloakroom thus became a strange mixture of the everyday and the unlikely: tennis rackets, in white jackets, march between doorknobs that hold them in place. Moldings, which look ordinary, dissolve from positive to negative. And aerial photos and drawings, showing our place in the universe, tilt out slightly from the wall to confront you, as they progressively lead from the big picture, our galaxy, to the smaller scale of the garden plan, and then, through the door, into the real garden.

Science and religion give us some grounding in the universe, even if a contradictory one, but so too do aerial and satellite photographs. The ultimate grounding is our new eyes. They reveal new patterns and ways of reconceiving our place in the universe as a zoom of scales. According to a Pascalian reading this new vision shows that the cosmos is out of scale with us, and that we are not at the center. How can we conceive of the thirteen-billion-year-old spacetime that we occupy? How can we imagine this scale? Nothing in daily experience is like it. Paradoxically, according to another reading, every place is at the center of an expanding spacetime balloon.

There were other lessons from this jump into the void that I was not to understand until much later, when I started to construct the "Universe Cascade," but well before this, Maggie and I threw ourselves into another project which was inspired by the first excavations we had made.

THE ZEROROOM

The Zeroroom: a preparation for entering the garden. One approaches through a narrow cloakroom with a rhythmical perspective of tennis rackets and moldings that travel strangely through the wall. To either side, our cosmic place in spacetime is revealed in photos and drawings. These zoom in on our present location in a sequence of eight jumps. First, we are found in a little square to the left of the galactic center. This shows we are located in the "suburbs" of the Milky Way, about two thirds of the way out. Although scientists often used this metaphor to underscore our insignificance, to mock our pride, it turns out, in a twist of fate, that it is the only place where life can emerge. The only habitable zone is Suburban Galaxy.

The second jump in scale, and square in the satellite photo of the earth, shows we are in Great Britain, at the top of the globe. The third shows a further zoom into the region of Scotland. Each aerial photo, map, or drawing has a square that refers to the map below, for easy orientation, so that one can mentally zero in on the present space and time. Unlike Pascal, we know these two coordinates are connected. Finally, the jumps in scale reach the garden plan, in color. Then one looks straight ahead into a mirror, an image of oneself, and also two eyes cut into the door. Below them is printed a continuous band that only makes sense when you read it slowly. IUIUIUIUEYEYEWEYEYEWEYEYEW. You look through the holes of the eye and you see a yew tree, and then the landscape. Lost in space, you are found in spacetime; you open the door into the garden.

Heaven–Hell

When she was young Maggie had discussed with her father the idea of clearing out a swamp and tangle of small bushes that had grown just south of the London to Glasgow line, which ran through their property. They often took the night train along this track in their journeys to and from the capital, and John considered it an eyesore. He planted a diagonal row of tall poplars to screen out the trains and this diagonal line extended almost up to the bridge going over the River Nith, where he loved to fish for salmon. For him and the family the noise and sight of the train was a disturbance—its sparks even caused fires—and ought to be blocked out both visually and psychologically. It was not until much later, when Maggie and I reflected on the extraordinary idea of "the machine in the garden," that we began to see it as a hidden opportunity, but at this stage the idea was to suppress it.

John died suddenly in an accident while fishing on the Nith. It was a freak occurrence reminiscent of the way Gervase Elwes had died. Apparently, while trying to get his small car out of a bog, it suddenly sped backwards and pinned him to the ground. No one could figure out how he had ended up underneath the car unless he had put it in gear and was trying to lift it over a hump in the ground when suddenly the wheels caught the ground. The accident remained a perplexing mystery, without any completely plausible explanation. But no one saw any point in trying to suppose a crime, least of all Maggie or Clare, both of whom remained stunned for many weeks. After John's death we changed the pattern of our lives, spending more time at Portrack to be with Clare who was now without other family, except for her niece, Clare Wagg, who lived nearby. Maggie, an only child, was as devoted to her father as her mother was and the shock of this never really left her. She often drew the little rock that was put up as a memorial with an inscription in Chinese, the initials JK, a cross, and the simple words "5th July 1982, Here on the Bank of the Nith, shortly before his 76th birthday." It was not the last tragedy to strike. While this is not the place to dwell on its impact and implications, like the other ones, it changed life at Portrack completely.

In 1989 Maggie and I started work on clearing the trees south of the railroad, leaving the poplars, and digging out a pond for swimming. Our children, Johnny and Lily, who were then eleven and nine, joined in the clearing, but the main work was again done by Hugh Hastings and his team of earth-movers. As they were reshaping the small burn into a large pond, I noticed that many of the felled trees had been cut up into regular little cylinders. The convention is first to slice the tree into easily movable sausages, and then burn them. When I inspected the results I was astounded.

There they were: perfect, two-foot-high horizontal slices contrasting with the curves and contortions of the growth. Once again I thought of Stuart Kauffman's "order for free" and said to

Maggie, "We can't burn these pieces of sculpture, let's turn them into a stumpery, into a row of teeth." Their interiors had rotted out, so I gave Lily and John a lecture on tooth decay, a pick, a chisel, and a small bribe, and asked them to get to work. The result became the Devil's Teeth, a small moss mound centered below large overhanging branches, which formed, with the sky, a dome. Alistair pickled these stumps with the preservative Cuprinol, so they would not rot any further, and now we have an open-air circular temple of trees. Several more stumperies were built from the offcuts of our excavations: a large hemicycle surrounding a giant sycamore, which culminates a path, and twelve upturned roots, which completely encircle a central tree: Witches' Brooms on one reading, but because I was studying the way a thicket of neural networks is

supposed to work, they became known as the Circular Brain.

Upside-down trees are disturbing, contorted in death, but the tangle of thousands of roots is an arresting sight and an interesting transformation has occurred. Today most of the roots have withered and an extraordinary second growth of moss and mushrooms has replaced the "neurons." And the themes have clarified. Decay, Death, Devil's Teeth, Witches' Brooms: the idea for this area of the garden grew in our mind as a primeval wilderness, the place of death and rebirth. Maggie and I called it by several names: Paradise/Hell, the River Styx (because of the burn flowing through it), the Underground, the Unconscious (because of the murky current), and Destruction. In some cosmologies Heaven and Hell are both underground and shrouded in mist or water. As places of primitive

power they may destroy and regenerate. Such ambiguities of life's double power need expression. "Creative destruction"; death for something new.

With such thoughts in mind Maggie designed a little island in the Chinese image of the Land of the Immortals; then I designed an arched bridge, the Easy Way to Paradise, and she designed a waterfall and stepping stones, the Hard Way. We were working well together, ideas were coming thick and fast and complementing each other. The Wilderness Garden began to take shape and then, as if to confirm our speculation, Dutch Elm disease struck and one tree after another crashed down. In spite of the objections of Clare, and the advice of gardeners, we decided to preserve these fallen giants leaning one against another. They form a spectacular graveyard. Contorted, dead sculptures shoot up their knobbly arms and legs against a riotously growing background of ferns and rhododendrons. Maggie had planted gunnera, which, with their giant floppy leaves, are menacing plants that might eat you. Real death and a symbolic netherworld started to come together. Clare and Alistair, however, were worried about the spread of another disease, honey fungus. By contrast, Maggie and I had visions of a primeval forest, the first landscape at the beginning of time and, to give it a literary theme, the famous painting by Nicolas Poussin, *Et in Arcadia, Ego* ("Even in Arcadia, I"): Death. This area of fallen and regenerating nature became Heaven–Hell and so it has remained.

There was one more trick nature played on us at this time. We had imagined two tiny mounds of earth covered with moss, one positive one negative, both circular temples to nature. They were inspired partly by a *giardino segreto* we had seen outside Verona: a secret garden that had grown up around ruined circular walls. Trees surrounding the walls left a hole focused like the lens of a camera on the sky, creating a virtual dome overhead. It was an old illusion, proved by the Pantheon in Rome and repeated by earth artists such as Michael Heizer and James Turrell. So we decided to make another version, exactly where moss had always grown. But then came the surprise. After we cleared the site of undergrowth and replanted moss in the bowl, it refused to take root. The perversity of this— nature refusing to do what it had always done—meant we left it alone for several years, and only recently have I come back to the idea and created what I have called a Willowtwist, a structure up which willows might grow (see following pages). These will return

TOP: Devil's Teeth—self-similar forms of nature transformed from tree stumps. When trees age and finally fall the farmers cut them into horizontal cylinders to transport and burn them. When cleaned up and preserved they can be turned to other uses (inset). FAR LEFT: *By the Nith*. A stone marks the place where John Keswick died; drawing by Maggie, September 5, 1988. LEFT: A Wedge Bridge—the Easy Way to get across the burn and, in the distance, the waterfall and stepping stones—the Hard Way.

THE WILLOWTWIST

The Willowtwist is a structure made from one single, long sheet of aluminum, cut and split twice so that one arm leans forward, another back and the middle twists to form a central loop. The simplicity of the solution was worked out on a cardboard model that was deflected to give a dramatic rise and fall. One enters at the low end and walks along a circular path that also goes up and down, while views through the curves frame the pines and sky.

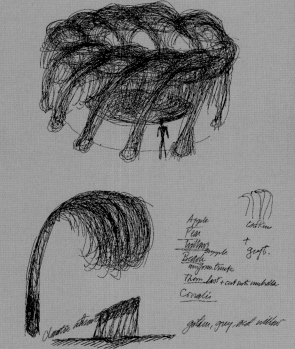

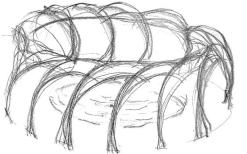

the area to a more sheltered darkness, and dampness. Perhaps the most recent return of the moss will be permanent, but it is not certain. As Alistair points out, moss often grows where it should not, on rocks exposed to the sun, and then dies where it should flourish, in damp, sheltered places. With a subtle shift in context, nature bends its own rules.

The Snail and the Poetics of Going Slow

By November 1990, Hugh Hastings and his bulldozers and diggers had widened the stream and dug out a pond, twelve feet down in parts, deep enough for swimming. Here, like the discarded stumps, was another opportunity. What should we do with the leftover soil, a gift from the hole in the ground? Maggie thought of spreading it over the fields, where cows and sheep might benefit from the nutrients, but I thought if there is going to be a free pile of earth, let it be a sculptural object, experiment with it.

Hastings' earth-movers got to work digging out mud and sculpting the land extremely fast. To keep up, I produced one plasticine model after another and walked out to the building site with an updated drawing every day. Because it is hard to shape sand and gravel precisely, one redesigns in response to what has happened and tries to reshape blobs into desirable figures. Using drawings, models, and, in the field, sawdust and stakes with flags and string, one shapes the earth like an action painter, yelling at men in bulldozers, "More to the left," directing dumpers with soil like a traffic cop, "Over there." They may understand the grand design but they are often too close to the action to see the pattern emerge. I have often found design and its realization to happen this way: you have to continuously remodel an idea, in many media, and then make adjustments as you go along. The rewards are great: something new may emerge, something better than you could have imagined or designed on paper.

Because the digging of the swimming hole was moving so fast and changes would be expensive, Maggie concentrated on shaping the water while I designed the Snail Mound. I had to give it this common name in order to communicate an unambiguous shape to Hastings' men, and to distinguish it from other shapes on which I would soon be working. The "Snail" drawings and models showed a double-curved ascent, two paths that only meet at the top and that lie at an angle.

In my mind were several different ideas (see following pages). I thought of the most important shape behind life, the double helix of DNA. This has two spirals of ascent and they reminded me in turn of a utopian design of 1919 that had a diminishing spiral: Tatlin's tower. A wonderful quality of this is the way it illustrates the dance of history's surprising dialectic; it often proceeds in a counter rhythm, as two steps forward one step back, a progress in fits and starts, an ascent that has descent built into it. Another idea in the

back of my mind was the 16th-century spiral stairway at Chambord which the French king, François I, had designed so that if he saw an unwelcome guest coming up one way, he could escape down the other. I would not understand the beauty of this until much later, when the mound was used in a way I had not foreseen: during a memorial service it separated those going up with flowers from those coming down empty handed.

Another precedent was the oldest pyramidal form in history, the stepped ziggurat of the Egyptians and its later incarnation, the Renaissance mound. And a final motive was the function of the whole thing, a focus toward which one could move, an axis for the various views and a place to survey the entire garden. Too many ideas behind the design? Not at all: never design with one reference or function in mind, never—that would be a waste of money and a one-liner. It would destroy the mystery and surprise of the garden; it would make consumption too quick and easy. Renaissance garden designers, following ideas developed in the seminal Villa Medici at Fiesole, noted the importance of slow perception. A landscape garden should not be a place through which one races on the way to somewhere else, but rather a place of imaginative exploration. "Go slow" is a warning sign with multiple meanings: tease out the hidden signs, discover new ones. "Festina lente" was even advised in the Renaissance garden—"Make haste slowly"—a wonderful oxymoron that I was later to use in a garden design (see page 234). Does it mean "Make haste in order to prepare so that you can later

go slow in the garden," or "Just hurry up and calm down"? A goal of symbolic design is to provoke viewers into discovering latent and even unintended meanings, a provocation that will only work if they assume there is something there to find.

In this way design and discovery amplify each other. As I was thinking about the spiral Snail, for instance, I happened to be reading about the pavement maze at Chartres Cathedral. This has the captivating idea behind it of presenting the pilgrimage route to Jerusalem as a type of counter-intuitive play: in order to get to the Holy City at the center of the labyrinth the pilgrim has to face away from his goal. Once there, in order to leave, he has to face back toward it. How suitably perverse for the pilgrimage of life. I decided to remint the idea. When climbing the DNA/Snail/Ziggurat you have to go down in order to go up; and when going down, by contrast, you are forced to go up. The ascent of life has descent built into it—not easy and counter to expectation. Go slow. The idea is to surprise, perplex, entice, confound, madden, amuse, as you discover these contradictions of life.

To relate the mound to the water we designed the tail of the snail in the shape of a French curve and brought it over the deep part of the pond; then Maggie had it lined with wood edging so that it would keep its shape. The tail allows one to descend almost into the middle

Self-similar curves extend from the snail-hook (right) to the causeway, center, then into the snake mound, (left).

of the pond, to be surrounded by water and to see different shapes from various angles. In fact, one of the virtues of a spiral mound is that it dramatizes discovery: unexpected vistas and shapes suddenly come into view. Another unsuspected bonus is that a mound looks very different in changing seasons: in the snow, for instance, its shapes are simplified and it can glow like a polished cylinder.

The mound building was so quick and satisfying that Maggie said, "Let's excavate another bit and expand the pond and create a causeway." From her researches in the East she knew that a thin causeway cutting across a lake is one of the most dramatic elements found in a Chinese garden. She imagined this as covered with a line of trees, something we never carried through, but she did make a move that had not occurred to me (though apparently Alistair had also thought of it). One day, struggling as usual to get the earth and water into a satisfactory relationship, I found Maggie atop the snail waving and shouting to the men digging a trench: "More to the right, Hugh, more to the right." In effect, she was pushing the emergence of the water a few feet out of sight, behind some trees, to obscure its source. Not seeing where the burn comes from gives it a mystery and leads the eye and imagination further back. The source was so mysterious that some people thought that, in order to make the ponds, we had actually diverted the River Nith—an economic not to say legal impossibility. But Maggie's concern for introducing a hidden source was absolutely right. It has given the ponds and landforms an enigmatic atmosphere that is quite uncanny, hard to figure out.

Another truth emerged on reflection, and when I went on to build other landforms in Edinburgh and elsewhere. The exact shape of the curves and their fine-tuning is key for creating what gives these mounds their strength—the sharp edges and defined shadows. It is the morning or evening sun, a raking light, that makes them come alive with subtle differences in tone. In certain lights bright carpets of green seem to hover above dark looming volumes. One has to sculpt continuous, gentle undulations—"sweet curves" as the Scots say—not wobbly profiles. Such refinements are essential for the success of landforms, and their realization was due largely to the skill of the gardeners working at Portrack. Neil Brown, Doug McCormick, and Alistair created these sharp continuous curves by constantly surveying their work on the turf from different positions. Since large curves create strange perspectival distortions—and can look good from one position and bad from another—one has to review progress as one goes along, and this Alistair would do from many positions, near and far, above and below. While Hugh Hastings did the rough, large-scale earth moving according to constantly revised designs, the next stage of turfing and shaping needed just as much continuous modification. After working on six landforms, Alistair has sharpened his own skills and eye for the well-turned shadow.

THE SNAIL

Two paths—a double helix—rise up the Snail Mound on one side and fall gently on the other so the ascent goes up and down. Various ideas were behind this: DNA, the double staircase at Chambord that allows two people to pass without meeting, a ziggurat, the contrary movement of the giant floor-paving maze at Chartres, Tatlin's Monument to the Third International—multiple meanings that have to be decoded, slowly. Maggie had dug out an old marsh, creating a series of connected, curving ponds, and a leftover pile of earth. We moved the pile with diggers and bulldozers and we could see that this equipment naturally generated blob-curves that were like the shape-grammar of rooms I had been designing. The scale, equipment, and material—sand and gravel—make a broad-brush approach inevitable: it is hard to get earth to within five feet of the place you want it and have it stay there and accept grass. The constant rains of western Scotland smear out all but the largest gesture, making design extremely primitive. Nevertheless, the basic ideas of twists, folds, and waves of energy are in the mounds.

FOLLOWING PAGE: The Snail Mound in snow: a polished cylinder, or a spacecraft.

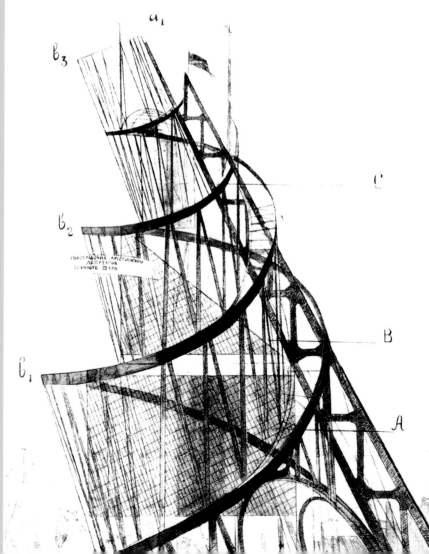

Waveforms, Twists, and Catastrophes

At this point in the garden's creation I was involved in another pursuit altogether, an investigation into post-modern theories that were changing our world-view, some coming from science. Since these explain the direction the landscape was to take, a detour into the house is necessary as well as a look at a room in the house where I first turned theory into form. As usual with her mother's house, Maggie initiated the process of change and identified the necessities. In this case it was the need for a big room, a kitchen and breakfast room where we could all meet informally, work at a big table and, at the Christmas and New Year holidays, dance Scottish reels. It was to be a family room centered on work. Functional problems had to be solved, but uppermost in my mind was the thought that a new grammar of form might emerge from the new sciences of complexity. Developed in the 1960s, these included the study of systems with feedback, such things as embryonic growth and the change in the weather. Chaos Theory, the fractal geometry of nature (see pages 126–7), the new cosmology and a host of what are also called "nonlinear sciences" came to the fore.

The first designs superimposed shallow, curved lines on the pre-existing square geometry, and these echoed the rolling hills of the landscape outside. The Borders area of southern Scotland is gently undulating rather than rugged and precipitous, as it is further north. The landscape resembles folds in a curtain, and flat, layered pleats, inevitable metaphors to be tried out on the new furniture and fabric. There were also conflicting axes of the room—on opposite walls—that generated a new organic shape. In order to accentuate the jump in axis, and using an underlying structural mesh, I designed a twist and a warped curve to hang off the ceiling.

The problem was to get all the curves on the floor and ceiling in synch with each other, to have the undulations of the seats correspond with those that bounce light above the columns. There were maybe a hundred undulations that had to be resolved, a daunting task. I asked Bobby Dixon, the carpenter who has done so much work at Portrack, if he could pull together all these curves while working on his back. Never one to resist a challenge, he responded, "Aye, Mr. Jencks," as he always did when I gave him something hard to do: "I kanna." His Scots accent, as unfamiliar to me as my American to him, was one of a number of bonds between us. We were united by a different language we could approximately understand, and our method of working, through improvisation. I would draw and build a model and then he would comment on it and invent a method of solving the problem. The undulating ceiling was a case of such improvisation: it was conceived first in stucco, but then built in hardboard that was bent over a frame. He or I would constantly take chances and court failure. "If you're going to innovate Bobby, you have to jump off a cliff and, as you're falling,

learn to fly." "Aye, Mr. Jencks"—he never refuses a challenge, but will ponder for several days and think of ways he can transform a design into reality.

After we had worked out the twist grammar at many small scales, I felt confident about trying it out on the landscape where Maggie wanted another mound (see pages 70–71). The result was the most satisfying of our joint endeavors, for the curves of the lake and the landform echoed each other, responded to each other, without being the same. Again, the idea was self-similarity rather than self-sameness. We called it the Snake Mound, to distinguish it from the Snail. It snakes some 350 feet and twists first toward the water and then, in a series of terraces that warp like a racetrack into the curve, it twists toward the pasture and the sheep. There is a certain compressed energy in these lines and the self-similar shapes of the ponds. As one moves around them at dusk they give a peaceful, looming feeling, almost that of a slumbering body, something I never suspected. Only later did I realize that much land art and, for instance, prehistoric landforms such as Silbury Hill near Avebury, and Stonehenge, evoke a bodily presence that must have been perceived and perhaps even intended.

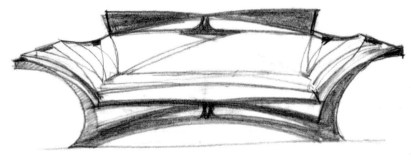

ABOVE, LEFT: Twists and gravity waves warp spacetime. The main shift in the room's axis is underscored by the s-twist on the ceiling while the warps in the furniture set up lines of energy, virtual gravity waves, that radiate from them. Of course, real gravity waves at this scale are too small to measure, but one feels the way objects impress their presence on a space as if sending out rays of energy. TOP LEFT: The s-twist in the ceiling marks the shifts in axis. TOP RIGHT: Bobby Dixon. BELOW LEFT: In light sculpture, two sheets of wood are given one twist, then warped and splayed to create slices of light.

WAVEFORMS
AND TWISTS

The standing light, below, is morphed from a female body holding the image of the Symmetry Break Terrace, a connexion of architecture, body and landscape. The two shifts in axes that became an ordering principle of the room are shown, near right. These and the lighting units then lend to the undulations in the seating and ceiling—a landscape of waves.

Twists and warped curves on the ceiling underline the shifts in axes. These forms, inspired by one of the complexity sciences—Catastrophe Theory—show that a sudden change in a system can be represented by a twist. I will relate how real catastrophes later impinged on our lives, but in this case it was the theory that fascinated me. Twists make possible the mapping of sudden changes within a system—a wave on still water, a prison riot, or the point where a stretched string snaps, or anger turns into rage. Twists also occur in other natural systems I was to investigate such as the Möbius strip and the soliton wave: the twisted energy packets that can travel through each other and keep a memory of their past. Other waves dissipate; solitons remember.

I used this multipurpose room to work out a new grammar of twists and waves, and applied it to the ceiling, walls, floor and details. All the elements are pulled together in off-white folds, fractals whose waves are self-similar but not exactly the same. Modernists, such as Mies van der Rohe, had been obsessed by repeating identical forms in contrast to nature, which, using fractals, varies the form slightly each time it reiterates the program. Post-modernists were beginning to follow nature into the realm of self-similarity.

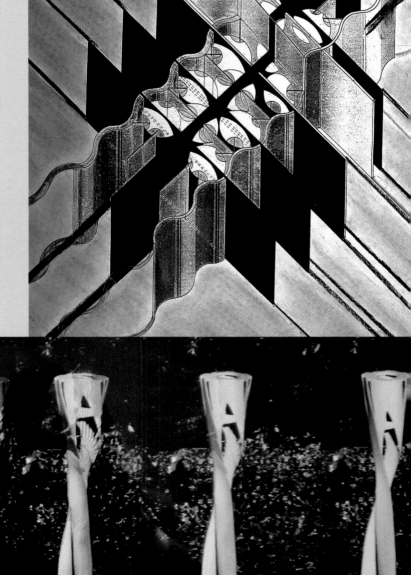

WAVES IN THE GARDEN

Self-similar waves twist almost to a point on the back of the landform before they unfold the other way. The twisting wave recurs at all scales in the garden.

Since constructed mounds are shaped by machines they naturally form linear, viscous shapes which resemble what are known as "strange attractors" or "chaotic attractors." Two of the most interesting are the Lorenz Attractor, "The Butterfly Effect," with its fortuitous butterfly-shaped wings, and the Ueda Attractor (right, above), both of which have inspired the designs.

Curved and counter-curved shapes are structural and often found in nature, for instance, in the meander of a river. Waveforms underlie so many natural activities: sea waves, of course, and sand forms left by the incessant waves on the ocean beach (see page 21); the vortices caused by pulling a solid object through stationary liquid; the swirls of air currents where warm and cold air meet; and the rock curls evident in mountains, a result of a long, slow, geological process of movement.

I wanted to create a new form of landscape design, one based on the waveforms that unite the atom to the galaxy, radio waves to brain waves, ammonites to sunflowers—the pattern that connects, a new poetics.

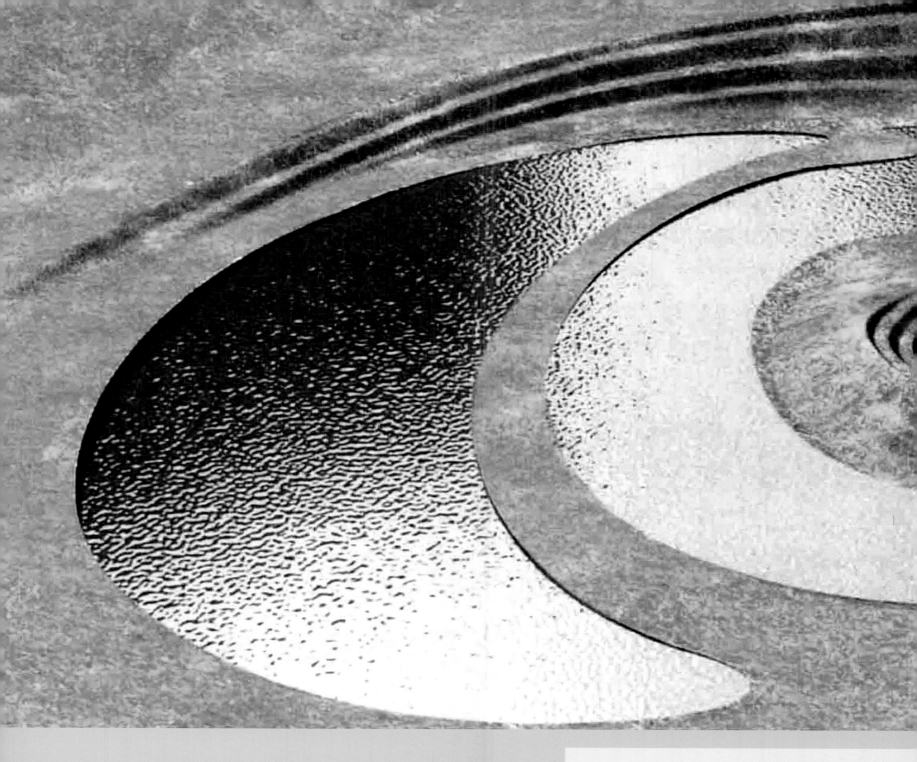

THIS PAGE AND FOLLOWING PAGE: Landform for the Gallery of Modern Art, Edinburgh, proposal 2000, completed August 2002. This design, commissioned to enliven a flat lawn and shield noise from the side road, faces two ways: to the Gallery and across the road to its sister, The Dean Centre. Its connecting "S" form also derives from the Henan Attractor (right), and its self-similar curves that fold inwards. Earth, water, and airflows generate waveforms that self-organize around certain attractor basins so there are natural affinities between this shape and the way the earth is moved and people walk. The landform can be used as an open-air gallery. (With Terry Farrell & Partners and Ian White Associates.)

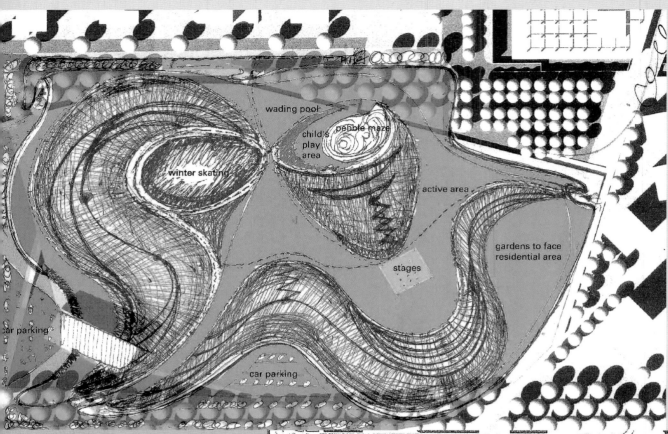

wading pool

child's
play
area

pebble maze

winter skating

active area

gardens to face
residential area

stages

car parking

car parking

The wave and twist grammar has been extended in further work underway at Portello Park in Milan, 2002 and 2003. Landforms and separate gardens appeal to different ages and uses, notably a hospital, nursery, hypermarket, and a set of residences. Further changes in design (with Andreas Kipar) are likely.

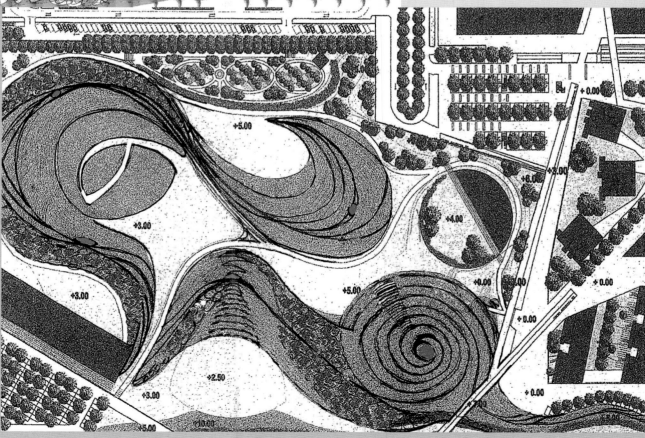

+5.00

+3.00

+3.00

+4.00

+3.00

+5.00

+2.50

+3.00

+5.00

+10.00

+0.00

+3.00

+6.00

+0.00

+0.00

+0.00

+0.00

Soliton Waves

Having been trained in Modern architecture at Harvard, at the end of the Gropius era, I imbibed a kind of Puritan functionalism. According to this doctrine, utility comes first, expression second, and I still follow this priority—or rather, I am always looking for functional excuses and problems to solve, as alibis for formal invention. In the garden this led me to rethink several necessities. After we completed the beginning of the kitchen garden and the landforms, there were two big problems: the mass invasion of rabbits, and the occasional assault by deer, sheep, cows and bulls. These realities led to another application of the twist and waveform: a series of gates and running fences. A sad truth of farming country in Britain today is that these necessities have become ugly and badly kept. Where once there were grand walls of stones cleared from the fields, there is now a tatty mixture of wooden posts and barbed wire, or electric fences sagging dolefully.

Alistair asked me to design four or five swing gates to keep the rabbits out of the kitchen garden. I had been studying the soliton waveform for some time and had the idea that—if I could find a blacksmith accomplished enough to experiment—I could use it in the design of these gates. Hattie McCormick, who is a first class cook and runs Portrack, suggested a craftsman in the vicinity: John Gibson. Thus started a collaboration on metal sculpting that was to last for many years. I showed John my drawings of the soliton wave gates, and he bent some metal strips to follow the twists and Möbius curves. We placed them on a blown-up drawing, and template, and moved them around until the twists gave just the right expression of an energy wave.

Soliton waves are particularly interesting because, as mentioned, they can travel through each other and keep their identity, that is, a memory of the past. By contrast, the typical wave seen on a pond dissipates and, when it encounters another, either adds up or cancels out. The Red Spot of Jupiter is a soliton, a laser beam is a soliton, as are the tidal bores that can reach twenty-five feet in height and travel at a constant speed for five hundred miles. Solitons were first theorized by the Scottish engineer John Scott Russell in 1834, after he had an unusual experience while riding his horse along the Union Canal near Edinburgh:

> I was observing the motion of a boat which was rapidly drawn along a narrow channel by a pair of horses when the boat suddenly stopped—not so the mass of water in the channel which it had put in motion; it accumulated round the prow of the vessel in a state of violent agitation, then suddenly leaving it behind, rolled forward with great velocity, assuming the form of a large solitary elevation, a rounded, smooth and well defined heap of water, which continued its course along the channel apparently without change of form or diminution of speed. I followed it on horseback, and overtook it still rolling on at a rate of some eight or nine miles an hour, preserving its original figure some thirty feet long and a foot to a foot and a half in height. Its height gradually diminished, and after a chase of one or two miles I lost it in the windings of the channel.

Russell's solitary wave, or soliton, keeps its identity because the smaller waves that constitute it bounce back and reinforce the overall shape and frequency. This feedback is the reverse of turbulence. It is obviously balanced on the delicate edge between order and chaos: if the width or depth of the canal were varied greatly, the resonance would not occur.

In the garden, solitons are presented in a layout of terraces, in wave fences, and, particularly, in a group of ten gates. Here waves of energy are shown traveling through the metal elements as a series of twists. When viewed straight on these twists are seen, paradoxically, as an absence of metal—a void—and, from the side, as a traveling hump rather like the curl in a whiplash. Alternating bands of solid and void, black and white, green and gravel are repeated throughout the garden. The visual illusions provoke different readings.

Functionally, however, the void or hump leads the eye one way to the hinges, or the other way to the latch—a hangover from my Modernist commitment to showing how things work. These key points are often picked out with fossils and a surrounding Möbius strip, another twist that has very interesting, paradoxical properties (combining two surfaces into one continuous surface). Both content and function were considerations informing the design. On the one hand, I was looking for formal affinities to the spiral fossil, and strips of metal far enough apart to create optical vibrations, and, on the other hand, strips close enough together to keep out baby rabbits.

A soliton wave traveling through a gate as a twist in metal.

SOLITON WAVES

Soliton sketches from science show trapped solitons, and energy waves going through each other—keeping a memory, not dissipating. Given the coherence of such waves, they can do unusual things, such as pass intact through each other. Or a high, thin, humpbacked soliton can overtake a short, fat one, combine for a while as a single wave, and then remerge, as if the two remembered their separate identities. Solitons have been found in such diverse systems as planetary atmospheres, crystals, plasmas, and nerve fibers, and have been used to create such systems as superconductors and optical fibers.

In general they can be considered as focused energy waves or coherent patterns. They can be represented in two basic ways: either as the traveling hump in a whiplash, or as the twist in a flat strip, such as a leather belt. The latter is "topologically trapped" and can be eliminated only by an anti-twist. "Humps" and "twists" are two signs I have used—especially in a series of metal gates— to represent the traveling of focused energy

through the universe. The twist also appears in other parts of the garden: in the DNA sculpture as the hydrogen bond (page 149), as the Sense of Touch (page 155), as support for Symbiosis (page 213) and in the Willowtwist (page 57). Its recurrence underscores the overall metaphor of the garden as a landscape of waves.

Light and dark bands throughout the garden set up vibrating patterns and visual illusions. Waveforms of energy, alternating waves, waves of light—photons—that interfere with each other creating overlapping waves. Thus light waves are turned into electrical waves and then brain waves. The waveform and the twist connect us to the atom and to the galaxy—to the language of the universe—which is why they are used everywhere in the garden.

BELOW, CENTER: Two solitons going through each other, not interacting (above), and (below) the hump that dissipates versus the trapped twist that can only be eliminated by an anti-twist.

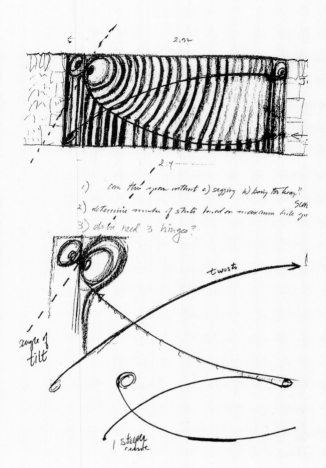

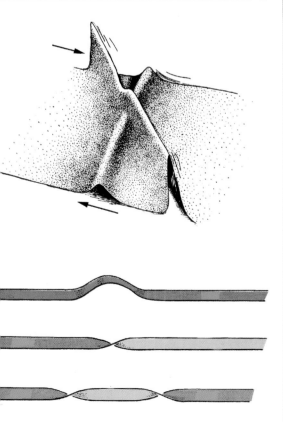

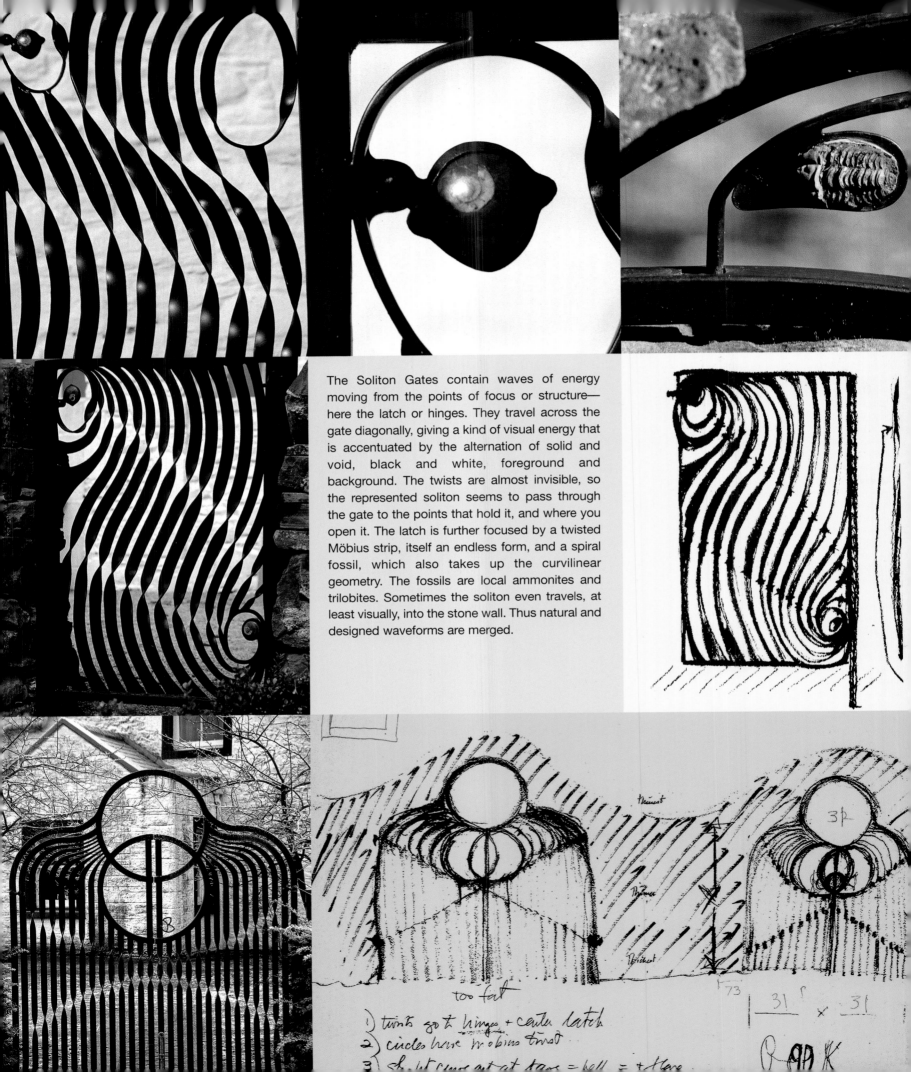

The Soliton Gates contain waves of energy moving from the points of focus or structure—here the latch or hinges. They travel across the gate diagonally, giving a kind of visual energy that is accentuated by the alternation of solid and void, black and white, foreground and background. The twists are almost invisible, so the represented soliton seems to pass through the gate to the points that hold it, and where you open it. The latch is further focused by a twisted Möbius strip, itself an endless form, and a spiral fossil, which also takes up the curvilinear geometry. The fossils are local ammonites and trilobites. Sometimes the soliton even travels, at least visually, into the stone wall. Thus natural and designed waveforms are merged.

too fat

1) twists go to hinges + center latch
2) circles have mobius twist.
3)

A LANDSCAPE OF WAVES

The metaphor of a landscape of waves was carried out in other media, here with different densities of mesh layered to create moiré interference patterns; light waves that add up or cancel each other out.

A RELATIVISTIC QUANTUM PARTICLE   PLANCK'S EQUATIO

PART THREE: WHERE IS THE UNIVERSE GOING?

God and the Equations

Necessity is not always the mother of invention, but in a garden it is usually the spur to build. At Portrack the old, off-the-shelf greenhouse had become too small for the plants Alistair was growing, so Maggie and he designed a new one about twice the size. Involved in work on a book, I stayed out of this design except for suggesting that it be placed on a concrete block base to give it more presence and headroom within. I also designed the potting sheds and Siamese Twins at the back, two oven-shaped volumes to hold the sand and peat needed for bedding plants. To mark entrances to the kitchen garden, Maggie had previously built several robust square pillars on which she placed stone globes given to her by an aunt. We then designed six more pillars to make a transition from the kitchen garden to the mounds, and she asked me to put something on them.

This was a challenge—what is worthy today of being put on a pedestal? Since the first three pylons were near the old "Renaissance" part of the kitchen garden, I thought that suitable subjects would be the Platonic model of the universe, a Renaissance model (Ptolemy's), and a constellation sphere. These would be in bronze, and the other three, next to the new, "present" part of the kitchen garden, would hold the present view of the universe, and be in aluminum. The Bronze Age versus the Aluminum, or is it the Age of Plastic?

Plato believed that God was the architect of the universe, a metaphor pleasing to Christians and architects alike, and that He created the universe from the imperfect material of the four elements, but in the image of perfected eternity, that is, the globe. In the *Timaeus* he spells out this relationship between time and eternity, our changing world and the eternal world behind it. "Therefore [the father and creator] made the world in the form of a globe, round as from a lathe, in every direction equally distant from the center to the extremes, the most perfect and most like itself of all the figures."

Virtually all Renaissance architects tried their hand at globes or circular forms to reflect this perfected, underlying pattern. Seventeenth-century views of the universe, such as those of the German astronomer Johannes Kepler, showed a series of perfect Platonic figures, nested one inside the next, whose harmonies explained the planetary orbits. My Platonic universe was loosely based on Kepler's and made visible the metaphysics that lay behind the work of artists from Phidias to Cézanne, architects from Ictinus

LEFT: The equations that might be on God's mind. RIGHT: "All is spheres and cylinders." Le Corbusier quotes Cézanne's dictum, and then draws "the lesson of Rome" showing that the city is built exclusively from these elements. Platonic metaphysics furnished artists and architects, both Classicists and Modernists, with the idea that regular solids and perfect symmetries underlay the universe, and an art might be built on them, thereby constituting the most perfect culture. However, we now know nature is also fractal and based on symmetry breaking (see page 179) discoveries that are recent and fundamental. This understanding is crucial for a new architecture and landscape design.

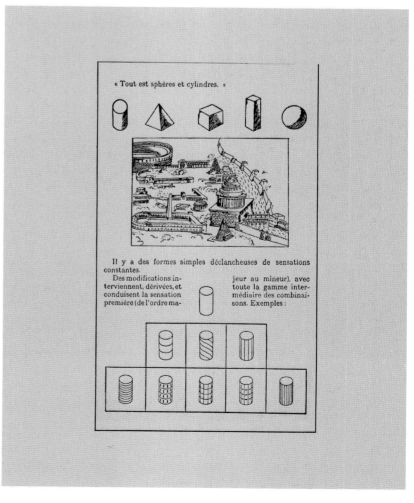

to Le Corbusier. This is the idea that nature is, in Cézanne's words, based on "the sphere, cone, cube, cylinder," the primary forms, and that therefore art and architecture, imitating nature, should be crystallized in these forms. Classical and Modern architecture, not to say Chinese and Hindu, often followed this precept. Although questionable, such venerable metaphysics was followed at this, the Renaissance place in the garden, and the image of God's perfect geometry was put high on a pillar.

Recently there has been much debate about the relationship between science and religion, particularly whether their long, drawn-out Cold War, lasting three hundred years, is still worth pursuing. Many skeptical scientists, such as Stephen Hawking and Leon Lederman, have written books invoking God in the title, a conversion of the atheists explained by pragmatists as intelligent marketing since any mention of the Prime Mover moves sales. Conversely, many clerics, for instance, the Bishop of Oxford and the Pope, enlist Darwin in support of the Deity's work, obscuring the fact that natural selection is cruel and proceeds by the decimation of nine out of ten species. Some God! The Cold War continues *and* abates; old antagonists switch sides with increasing frequency. In the post-modern settlement, however, the new physics not only appears weirder than biblical miracles, it is weirder.

This truth has been the testimony of nuclear physicists since Niels Bohr set out his famous shock test for understanding the atomic microworld in the 1920s: "Anyone who is not shocked by Quantum Theory has not understood it." Quantum electrons jumping from orbit to orbit without going through the space between, or traveling through two different slits at the same time, or changing from being waves to being particles depending on how they are observed: these are just the well-known parts of this weird reality, what has become the "Standard Model" of the microworld. Scientists use such a phrase when they cannot quite prove an idea, but when all the evidence points a certain way. The Standard Model includes even more exotic things, such as quantum particles tunneling through walls like ghosts, and, according to one reading, vibrating the universe into existence out of a vacuum. Some Standard!

Indeed, what we now know about the creation of the universe is also, according to some interpretations, virtually miraculous, as I soon attempted to mirror in several works.

At this time, however, I was not so much interested in the battle between religion and science as how much they could illuminate and criticize each other. Scientists may have uncovered some deep truths of the universe, but they often do not know what these discoveries imply in terms of human experience, nor do they always fashion appropriate metaphors from them. By contrast, theologians may be more adept at teasing out relevant metaphors and attitudes to nature, but these representations are no longer apt to be true. A plague on both their houses—or a chance to think between them?

Partly to address such questions, Maggie and I helped organize several meetings on contemporary subjects of debate. We called them Portrack Seminars, after the house and garden where most of them took place, and before returning to the subject of science, religion, and deep reality, I should explain this background. Some of the Portrack Seminars concerned the global economy and political order, others ecology and spirituality, some were on literature, and all had a post-modern focus. A group of friends constituted the core of what we called, after Maggie's invention, "Restructive Post-Modernism," a phrase meant to distinguish us from the other kinds of deconstructive and structuralist thinkers cutting up the field. Our group included Charlene Spretnak, David Ray Griffin, Richard Falk, and later Ihab Hassan. Later still, Steven and Hilary Rose organized a meeting at Portrack against the reigning fashion of genetic determinism (and evolutionary psychology). The fruits of that last meeting were collected in a book *Alas, Poor Darwin* edited by the Roses. But most of our endeavors reached print, if at all, under individual publication.

My hope was that Portrack Seminars would become a clearinghouse for formulating opinion, collectively. The participants already had other outlets and went to seminars where publication and publicity were paramount. By contrast, we wanted a place to air ideas freely without a sense of embarrassment or ownership, a convivial atmosphere where they could be debated and modified. A backdrop of Scottish hills and rivers combined with unhurried meals might encourage new ideas to emerge: new brain cells would be stimulated by new thoughts plus the liberating potential of drink. The agenda of Restructive Post-Modernism is to provide an alternative to Deconstruction and among its goals two are relevant to the garden. As put in the 1996 meeting, "Reconsidering the Postmodern" held at London's ICA: "[Restructive Post-Modernism] understands that our view of nature, which had been disenchanted by the mechanistic paradigm, can now be seen as self-organizing, dynamic and, in some sense, re-enchanted. . . ." And, as David Ray Griffin put it, following the process philosophy of Alfred North Whitehead: "The ultimate units of the world are 'occasions of experience,' each of which feels prior occasions. . . . Internal relations and some degree of intrinsic value are thereby said to pervade the world all the way down [to the microworld]."

According to such formulations, experience, value, and self-organization do not appear solely with the emergence of human beings—the anthropocentric view of Christianity and Modernism —but are found throughout nature, right down to the level of atomic events. This view is not to be confused with a pre-modern animism, because it denies experience to an aggregation of elements: for instance, rocks do not think, or feel, even if they show beautiful patterns of self-organization. And it is obviously absurd to trace sentience below the level of living matter; but the

quantum paradigm of metaphysics and sciences of complexity have shown the many parallel continuities throughout nature, all the way up from the self-organizing atom whose electrons, in a metaphorical sense, are always making choices. Freedom and value, as I will discuss shortly, may increase as one goes up the spectrum of complexity, but they are already present at the base of reality, and this insight leads to a re-enchanted view of nature. Obviously not all of those attending the conferences held this position, because we were determined to have an enjoyable debate and engage outsiders.

We met near the garden and often walked through it between meetings. Inevitably I engaged them in a dialogue about ideas behind nature. One of our guests, the physicist Paul Davies, had become a friend and, from time to time, we would meet and correspond. Paul had written three important overviews of the basic workings of the universe. The first, *God and the New Physics*, was to my mind not as cogent as the second and third, *The Cosmic Blueprint* and *The Mind of God*. The latter two became fundamental sources for my work and thinking.

Between 1988 and 1992, I was working hard to try to figure out what the basic laws behind the universe were, and to bring them to expression in the garden. Inevitably I asked Paul Davies several questions about the origin and shape of the cosmos, the nature of

Eleven Portrack Seminars on post-modernism took place in the 1990s. This one, on "The Economic Foundations of World Order," in June 1994, was organized by David Ray Griffin. LEFT TO RIGHT, FRONT ROW: Mr. and Mrs. John Cobb, Mr. and Mrs. Robert Hammerton-Kelly, Ann Jacqua, Richard Falk, Sally Sampson, Mrs. Allen, Anthony Sampson, Peter Allen. BACK ROW: David Ray Griffin, Charlene Spretnak, [unidentified], Paul Ekins, Maggie (in door), Sara Parkin, CJ. Other subjects included Post-Modern Culture, PM Religion and Science, Metaphor and Grounding, Post-Modern Cosmology, Political Foundations of World Order, Post-Modern Ecology, Intercivilization—Confrontation and Synergies, Reconsidering the Postmodern, Against Evolutionary Psychology, The Architecture of the New Scotland.

the atom, and what was behind it all. By 1993 I had the idea of using my research to finish off the greenhouse roof, a flat, dull expanse that needed a culmination and contrast to the sky. Traditional finials were out of the question. So, remembering the title of Paul's last book, I asked him, "Well, what is on God's mind? What are the basic laws that run the universe?" There were obvious candidates that I had picked, such as Einstein's equation combining energy and matter, $E=MC^2$, but over the course of several months Davies supplied a more cogent list of about twenty. In the event, the greenhouse roof had room for only twelve.

An obvious question: why make such a thing of the equations? Here a religious sensibility may afford a partial balance, it may critique the off-hand manner with which scientists treat their discoveries, calling the origin of the universe, for example, the "big bang," as if it were simply some kind of shoot-out between constituents no more significant than the acronyms that have been invented for dark matter: WIMPS (weakly interacting massive particles) and MACHOS (massive compact halo objects). From one perspective, equations and words are just tentative, conventional signs to be treated with a democratic skepticism and indifference— here today gone tomorrow. But they also refer to something deeper, that is, the patterns underlying existence and that of everything, even the vacuum or void. Those regular patterns, and irregular ones too, find expression in equations.

Indirectly, they generate galaxies, nature, and us, and for this reason the fundamental laws are like an extended family of aunts, uncles, and distant relatives. Less immediate than living nature, we owe them the kind of respect, curiosity, love, and identification shown to a grandparent. Religious sensibility can educate us in deeper feelings toward the cosmos when, in spite of dogma, it does not alienate us from our progenitor. But neither religion nor science has a monopoly on relating us to nature and ultimate reality. Indeed, as Fred Hoyle has written, it may be scientists who today are more religious in orientation than theologians.

"I have always thought it curious that, while most scientists claim to eschew religion, it actually dominates their thoughts more than it does the clergy." Paul Davies cites this opinion in "The Mystery at the End of the Universe," the last chapter of *The Mind of God*, and it obviously holds true of some scientists at certain moments in their lives, especially when they are pursuing fundamental questions such as the beginning of the universe. Necessarily these investigations may be forever shrouded in mystery and, where mystery reigns, mysticism may burgeon. As Catholics have regretted in a humorous pun, "Mysticism starts in mist and ends in schism," a play on words and an insight into origins that was later to inspire my design. Landscape architects today are employing mist in fountains and it is a natural metaphor for the mystery at the start and end of things.

UNIVERSE EQUATIONS

The equations and geometrical models that lie behind the universe. Einstein's well-known equation combining energy and mass is on the left. Diamonds separate subsequent ones. BELOW: The three globes are in the ancient material of bronze and they depict ancient world-views: a Babylonian constellation sphere, Ptolemy's universe with the earth in the center, and Plato's universe with its nesting, perfectly symmetrical bodies.

RIGHT: Johannes Kepler thought that perfect regular solids underlay nature and the orbits of the planets: the sphere, cube, tetrahedron, icosohedron etc.

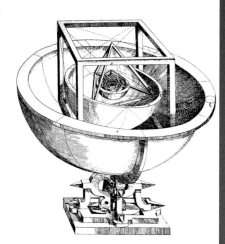

$E = mc^2$

MASS EQUALS ENERGY   LORENTZ TRANSFORMATION RELATING LENGTHS IN DIFFERENT REFERENCE FRAMES

LORENTZ TRANSFORMATION RELATING TIMES IN DIFFERENT REFERENCE FRAMES   LAGRANGE'S EQUATIONS OF CLASSICAL MECH

The Mind of God, Isaiah's notion that God's rational mentation generated the universe, finds contemporary expression on the greenhouse roof. Equations that govern the universe, equations that breathe life into the universe, are conceived as "flames against the sky," designed with the aid of Joanna Migdal and Brookbrae. Different typefaces with varying legibility and expressive form were explored before the flame-letters were chosen.

The name of each equation is given below its representation and each one is separated from the next by a diamond. On the back side, that is, where the equations are seen backward, an ironic or interpretive comment is written. For instance, the equation of entropy, the Second Law of Thermodynamics, saying that all closed systems run down, that the universe itself may end in heat death, has the expression on the reverse: "God plays dice with a closed system, but where there's death there's hope." Disenchanted Catholic bishops, fed up with the Pope, coined the last expression of entropy, and its possibly creative power.

Scientists are decoding the universe; they reveal some of its ultimate patterns and equations but, like any profession or group, they may miss the significance, beauty or horror of what these laws imply.

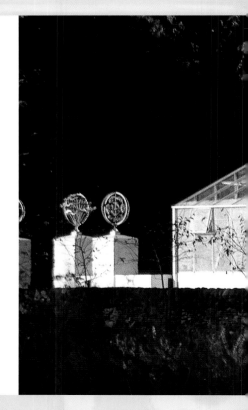

SCHRÖDINGERS EQUATION FOR THE PROBABILITY AMPTITUDE OF A QUANTUM PARTICLE

LAGRANGE'S EQUATIONS OF CLASSICAL MECHANICS

Does the Universe Have a Direction?

If patterns and equations lie behind all things, and the universe shows some order, then it raises the question: is there some direction and purpose in the cosmos that can be discerned? This question has been contested in different ways over the last hundred years. Those physicists believing in the primacy of entropy and chance denied there was a positive direction to history; some biologists, seeing life and growth to show both progress and teleology, challenged the reign of entropy. Physicists responded by showing that all life depended on putting energy into a closed system. The sun gives away heat every second and we feed off a billionth of its giveaway, but it is running down like all closed systems and will self-destruct in 5 billion years.

Recently the entropists have had most of the argument, and also the Darwinians who claim that evolution shows no overall direction—just the adaptation of species to changing environments. Nonetheless, there are physicists, evolutionists, and cosmologists who point out that any conclusions are a bit premature. There may be sources of energy and order from other universes that tap into ours, and energy created as the universe expands. It is obvious that scientific laws, as we now understand them, are both incomplete and waiting for several new ideas to fall into place.

It is these sorts of question I debated with Paul Davies after one of the Portrack Seminars. Paul, who left Britain for Australia several years ago because of the depredations of the Thatcher years and the way science was downgraded in her reign, is different from the way he first appears. Dressed modestly, like most scientists, he sports a close-cropped moustache that gives him a sprightly air. With his youthful looks and eager visage he appears like an alert drill sergeant and sometimes his answers to complex questions seem ready-made. But actually he has thought long and deeply about the fundamental issues, and taken the trouble to popularize ideas that arise from quantum and relativity theories without cheapening them. In 1996, he won the Templeton Prize, the award given for creative thinking on religion and science, an amount of money deliberately set just higher than the Nobel Prize because it's not awarded for such thought. John Templeton believed innovations in religious thinking ought to be recognized, so with some relish he index-linked his honor to always be one step ahead of the Swedish award. Paul won what was then a million-dollar amount, most obviously for *The Mind of God*. In that book as with the others, he musters arguments for the idea that the universe has a predisposition to evolve toward greater complexity. As we walked in the garden, along Maggie's causeway, we explored this hypothesis.

PD: I have always thought that life is not just a chemical freak, not a gigantic improbable accident or just the shuffling of molecules. Or that it is only going to happen in one little corner of the universe and if that's so it might make some people feel special. But the way I see it, if life is just an accident then it would have no universal significance at all. On the other hand, life could be something that emerges pretty well automatically, as part of the outworking of the underlying laws of the universe where the laws incredibly can have some sort of built-in bias.

CJ: Einstein said that "God doesn't play dice," yet the answer here is that "God does play dice," but loads the dice.

PD: That's right and you have to load them fantastically. We're not talking about a slight preponderance toward one thing or another to get the sort of enormous level of complexity that you've got in even the simplest living thing. You can't get that just by shuffling things around randomly, you've really got to have a very strong directionality and bias in the way systems evolve. You have to have laws of complexity in which things like life, and ultimately consciousness, emerge as part of that law-like out-working. Because it's very easy to show that if you just wanted to make even the simplest protein just by shuffling the amino acids at random you would have many, many more planets or stars than there are in the universe and you'd have to go on doing it many times the age of the universe before you'd ever get it at one to make a simple protein. The odds against it are enormous.

CJ: You're not saying that we live in a kind of deterministic universe, where life and consciousness emerge all of a sudden because its programmed in, like predestination.

PD: No, as we discussed many times, it's always a mixture of chance and law. The question is: What is that mix? Is it all chance, as most biologists would say? So it's only going to happen once in the universe? Is it all law, in the sense that everything, not just life, but human beings are biologically and physically pre-programmed? Surely not. It's going to be some middle path.

Or, is the Universe Going Nowhere?

There are many Modern scientists, such as Stephen Jay Gould, who believe that, contrary to Paul's views, there is no overall direction to evolution. Neither individual species nor a succession of species show progress over the long haul, and all species taken as a whole do not reveal any trend such as increasing height or weight. We used to think

LEFT: Discussion with Paul Davies in the garden (from the television film by Trevor Hearing, Border Television, 1997). RIGHT: The Drunkard's Walk.

of ourselves as the crown of evolutionary complexity, but for Gould evolutionary history culminates where it started, with bacteria. There were more bacteria than any other species in the past, more in the present and more in the future, forever and ever. In terms of collective weight, long-term survival, and evolutionary success they outwit us and will outlive us. Compared with them we are a momentary accident, no better or worse than any other species.

Evolution, according to this view, is a "Drunkard's Walk" that leads nowhere in particular. A wandering line, a random motion, a zigzag with no discernible frequency can be represented by the drunkard stumbling down the pavement. The argument goes that, if the universe shows no evolutionary direction as a whole, then such complexity as it does reveal is simply a series of frozen accidents. Here a metaphor helps explain the appearance of progress. Suppose a drunk stumbles out of a bar, with a wall of tightly packed houses that block his movement to one side. On the other side is a gutter into which, given enough time, he is likely to stagger. It is then a matter of probability, and not of design, that in the long run he will fall into the gutter and, being drunk, become a trapped accident. If, over time, all drunks end up in the gutter and cannot get out, then there would be the appearance of a trend or direction of evolution. This collection of the inebriated could be

construed as part of some cosmic design, the result of a progressive evolutionary force, whereas, as Gould would argue, it is simply the result of a random movement away from the restraining wall of houses. Since species are limited by many walls—such as absolute minimum size—they seem to show certain patterns of growth. But these trends are really the result of limits and random variation.

So which view of the universe is right—Davies' or Gould's? The argument continues, and I will show how my preference gets built into the garden. Yet whichever side one favors, one has to pay respect to the other, since we now know both order and chaos are essential to the cosmos. A garden should present this mixed metaphysics, and so there are several places where randomness dominates, accident plays a role, as it does in the arts of love: "A sweet disorder in her dress kindles in clothes a wantonness."

As it happens there is a version of the Drunkard's Walk often found in Chinese gardens, and this became the pretext for Maggie and me to design a pebble and moss path lurching from side to side. In the traditional Chinese garden, designers introduced a meandering pattern as part of a poetic competition. The contest consisted of floating a cup of wine down a zigzag channel. Before it came to the end, the contestant would have to compose a short sonnet or, failing that, drink the contents. Pulled in opposite ways, by literary pride and the pleasure of imbibing, the results were often the same—intoxication—a loss of control that might be creative. This is nicely mirrored by the formal zigzags of the channel. In this way randomness became marked and celebrated in the Chinese garden. The Drunkard's Walk in our garden is, ironically, down a straight and narrow path and the undulations are carried up into gates at either end, that are also constrained by wavy lines. So randomness is hemmed in by order, but present.

The Universe Poised between Order and Chaos

Randomness is not the same as chaos, which can be the result of simple, hidden rules, and what is called "deterministic chaos" is very important to the organization of things. Order often grows out of chaos as a complex pattern waiting to be discovered, a pattern more subtle than a simple geometrical figure. For a long time, Western philosophers and scientists thought that the universe was fundamentally ordered rather than either chaotic or random. The word "cosmos" in Greek means order, just as the word "cosmetic" means putting your face in order. But, since we now know the cosmos includes chaos and randomness, and the computer illuminates both, new opportunities for expression arise.

As I was pondering such thoughts it happened that chaos was close at hand: the garden was under siege by rabbits. We tried to fence them out and Alistair would shoot some. Indeed, British Rail

FOLLOWING PAGE: Models of the universe either side of the greenhouse.

periodically tried several methods of extermination to keep them from undermining the railroad tracks and the trains that sped through the garden ten or so times a day. But in the end, rabbits, as if by biblical command, always multiplied and went forth. One should memorialize the inevitable, so a Rabbit Cabinet for the Waveform Room was skillfully put together by Bobby Dixon to hold dishes and other necessities and to illustrate a mathematical theory.

As every gardener knows, rabbits are like very arbitrary editors of a script, cutting out some of the high points and strangely leaving the low. But are they themselves subject to natural editing? A disease, myxomatosis, has been deliberately spread among them in Scotland and elsewhere and it periodically limits their numbers. But still they rise and decline with a will of their own—or so it seems.

It now turns out there are rules and patterns that describe the way they grow in number and crash. These reveal the way order can grow out of chaos spontaneously, something that can be mimicked by computer simulation. The emergent forms are explained by a process of population growth called "period doubling." Period doubling refers to the doubling of the population cycle, and these cycles reveal some strange oscillating patterns that are as deep and beautiful as any Platonic form. Whereas Western art and architecture have been based on the five pure solids, the new understanding reveals another kind of visual grammar, one more fluid and supple, an order of curves within curves, of statistical patterns, of varying densities and self-similarities. A mathematical formula shows, for instance, how rabbit populations may follow exotic patterns of growth as they are pulled to several strange attractors. These are generated by the formula $X_{n+1} = BX_n(1-X_n)$ and formally this results in sweeping curves that have their own beauty and a strange property—every so often they return to self-similar shapes. The Rabbit Cabinet, which holds dishes not rabbits, makes a feature of this recursive equation and its self-similar forms.

Parabolas and their bifurcations swirl across the surface, so the pattern has that "unity in variety" which is so prevalent in nature. Similar parabolic themes of growth and sudden change are taken up elsewhere in the room, but always transformed. Why highlight such growth, period doubling and nonlinearity? Because most of nature is nonlinear, most of the universe shows the supple and subtle patterns known as strange attractors (used in the formation of the Snake Mound). The beating of the heart, brain waves, the formations of hurricanes and galaxies, all show such order growing out of chaos, a richer mixture of organization and disorder than that codified in traditional aesthetics. Until the mid-1970s, until computers revealed these strange attractors, we could not fathom how such hidden organizational life could arise amid the buzz of chaos. As turned into a cabinet here, the equations strangely resemble birds of prey and the Concorde—neither image part of my intention but a welcome byproduct of the mathematics.

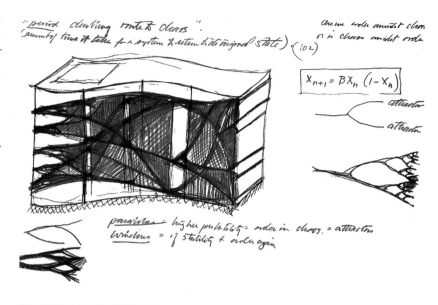

In the last twenty years a new kind of equation has come to the fore: the nonlinear variety, which relays back information into itself. These second-order equations characteristically have terms which compete with each other, such as those in the Verhulst equation: $X_{n+1} = BX_n(1-X_n)$, which describes population dynamics.

Here the two competing terms are X_n and $1-X_n$ because as the first one grows the second one diminishes. The equation is quite predictive of the way populations will double the length of their cycles until they go into deterministic chaos, a chaos that shows some emergent order. This combination of order and chaos is fantastic and counter-intuitive. One can well imagine that, if rabbits keep multiplying, the total numbers might fluctuate as they climb upward (or until owls and ferrets get to work). But why should the numbers suddenly return to a self-similar order with similar patterns?

It is because of the math. It sounds implausible, especially if you have too many rabbits in the garden. Nevertheless, the math entails this fascinating order amid chaos. If one wants to figure the equation out, X_n represents last year's population, B represents the birthrate of the rabbits, and X_{n+1} represents the prediction for this year's population based on last year.

Rather than going through the actual numbers and graphs, I illustrate the results with the rabbit cabinet and its swirling curves. Starting from the left, one can see the four basic strange attractors pulling the total population size to one of four places. Then as one reads to the right and as the female rabbits have more offspring, these attactors bifurcate to eight attractors, then sixteen, and so forth until the mother has about 3.6 on average. At this point the total population could be anywhere within the parabolic swirls; the system has gone into deterministic chaos (that is, a chaos determined by rules). And yet this leads to a certain veiled order. This is indicated by the depth of the parabolic swirls, their continuation across the whole surface and, most surprisingly, the way that, at three points, the three vertical lines, the system returns suddenly to its original bifurcations! Then the previous simple order re-emerges for a very short period, just before it bursts into deeper chaos. But even there, when the populations could be nearly anywhere—illustrated far right of the cabinet—there is still some predictability, some likelihood that will favor certain numbers over others. These probabilities are, again, shown by the parabolas, their depth or thickness.

Lockerbie—Chaos and Catastrophe Never Far Away

Peace and quiet are the two qualities most valued in a garden, a retreat for contemplation. One of the things that Virgil did not have to put up with when he escaped from Rome to the countryside was the constant drone of airplanes, buzz saws, and cars. At Portrack there are the pleasant sounds of nature, and agriculture, the noisy chatter of swallows, the bleating of sheep, the occasional shriek of competing male pheasants. These sounds are punctuated by the rumble of the train, once every three hours, which I have come to like, and the screech of low-flying jets that practise for mountain warfare.

Portrack is in the hilly corridor that young pilots use to train for a landscape like Bosnia. Locals complain to the police and the official bodies concerned when the jets fly below the tree lines but, after a ritual exchange of animosities and promises, nothing is done. The jets regularly take point blank aim at our white house, a good target, and the red-spotted Nonsense in the woods, a subtler

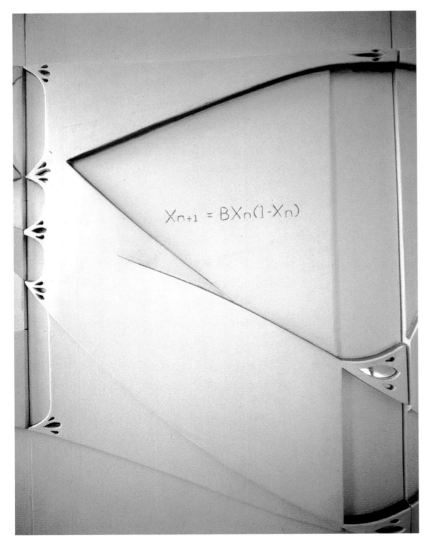

$$X_{n+1} = BX_n(1-X_n)$$

The equation, etched on the cabinet, generates the order out of chaos and the sweeping curves.

one. We telephone the complaints, they apologize, and so it continues. Machines are always audible in the garden today and sometimes they go terribly wrong.

One evening as it was getting dark, Maggie went out to speak with Alistair's wife, Frances. As they were walking in the kitchen garden Maggie saw the sky light up behind Frances' head, in a great yellow and red ball of fire. More extraordinary than this explosion was the way it reached a peak and then suddenly imploded as if sucked into a vacuum cleaner and then the eerie silence of many seconds—Lockerbie is twelve miles away—followed by the roar of the earth. Maggie hurried to the Octagon, where I was working, and said: "I think Chapelcross has blown up!" We then ran to telephone the police to see if the local nuclear power station had, indeed, been hit by one of those low-flying jets. They answered: "We cannot say, but we will tell you it was not the nuclear station. Listen to the news."

They knew, but could not tell us. Curious, the official response to disaster. Efficient, concerned, oblique, opaque.

Lockerbie still has not got over the tragedy of that evening, one that has turned it into a global name for the sudden, arbitrary nature of catastrophe. Although the wreckage has been expunged and the visual scars healed, the citizens of the town still are marked by this fateful event. Everyone carries the memories of it—and subsequent actions and media coverage—in the back of their mind like a constant bad dream.

In the past, especially in the Judeo-Christian era, we might have read some greater meaning into the catastrophe, perhaps a warning sign for the future or a punishment for misbehavior, but today we interpret it differently. Chaos plays an essential role in punctuating evolution, for better and worse. Since the early 1980s we have come to understand several mechanisms that have changed history, radically. One theory, supported by much evidence, is that nature's chaotic target practice, comets shooting randomly at planets, wiped out the dinosaurs 65 million years ago. Another theory, also with many supporting signs, is that this mass extinction was caused by volcanic action in the Deccan Traps area of India. Either way, and it may have been a combination of the two, such unpredictable events are now accepted as playing important roles in evolution. Twenty years ago, in a more Darwinian age, we did not give so much credence to luck—bad luck for the dinosaurs, good luck for us. But now we know, as if for the first time, that catastrophes can restructure history, in positive and negative ways. The crash of the Pan Am jetliner may have been caused by terrorists, but they could not predict it would wipe out a street in Lockerbie. Our lives are played out on this kind of stage: one we construct, and one that is, from time to time, blown away by outside events—"Virtù" and "Fortuna" as they were called in the Renaissance. I was to ponder the balance between these two forces later (see Part Eight, page 234).

Gaia and Limited Purpose

Most of what we know about the last thirteen billion years of cosmic history has been learned in the last hundred years, and the most radical knowledge is very recent. We glimpsed mass extinctions in the 19th century, we had intimations of the origin of the universe in the 1960s (when accidentally we discovered the background microwave radiation), but only since the 1980s did the ideas of evolutionary phase transitions become understood. Now cosmic and natural evolution are seen as proceeding smoothly and in jumps, something I have presented many times in the garden as "the jumping universe," its history in discontinuous stages.

Different models explain different regimes of evolution. For instance, Darwinian natural selection makes some sense of gradual change, while what is called "punctuated equilibrium" by Stephen Jay Gould and Niles Eldredge explains the usual eons of relative stasis that are punctuated by dramatic shifts in the living kingdoms. In addition to these, cosmic and chemical evolution proceeds according to other self-organizing systems. In spite of some claims that the Darwinian model explains it all, we have entered an era when we see many overlapping systems of evolution working in different ways. The most crucial new insight for us concerns the evolution of planetary life as a whole, or what James Lovelock and Lynn Margulis have christened "Gaia." This self-organizing system is something of a miracle because, in spite of five mass extinctions, despite being hit by asteroids and burnt by super volcanoes, the earth has always returned itself to the state of health most propitious for life. The miracle is it seems to know how to heal its wounds (but how could it possibly know anything?).

The idea that the earth is alive and is a superorganism with a will of its own is common to many ancient cultures. Giving this personification a woman's name, Mother Earth, or the pre-Greek "Gaia," makes explicit the animistic metaphor—that all of nature, including nature as a whole, is ensouled. Inevitably modern science threw out this "pathetic fallacy"—as a projection of our intentions and feelings on to nature—as it reduced the living world to the mechanistic interaction of particles and dead matter.

It was not until 1972 that the situation changed. James Lovelock, an atmospheric chemist and inventor, pondered views of the earth seen from space and saw just how unusual the blue planet was. Compared to the other nine planets in our solar system, and the twenty or so we had discovered by the year 2000, earth really is bizarre. Blue water, white clouds, the evidence of life, make the earth a cosmic freak. The more Lovelock compared it with its similar-sized neighbors, Venus and Mars, the more unlikely its qualities appeared. By the mid-1970s his concept of Gaia matured. Along with the microbiologist Lynn Margulis, he formulated what I would call the "Robust Gaia Theory," as distinct from its more modest cousin. As he phrased it in his book *Gaia: The Practical Science of Planetary Medicine*: "Life,

or the biosphere, regulates or maintains the climate and the atmospheric composition at an optimum for itself."

The biosphere maintains the climate at an optimum for itself? This is nearly a teleological view, yet the evidence is compelling. For the last 3.8 billion years the superorganism—or interlocking systems of life, physical conditions, and chemical composition—has kept a host of important dynamics just right for her prosperity. According to this hypothesis, she has cybernetically regulated moderate levels of salt in the oceans, maintained the relative constancy of climate and, most impressive of all, kept the oxygen level where it needs to be for complex life—around 21 percent of gases—over hundreds of million of years.

If oxygen declines to 15 percent, animals suffocate; if it goes up to 25 percent, they spontaneously combust. Could the finely tuned ratio of gases be a happy accident? Or, has some Designer created earth and set the levels of carbon dioxide, methane, nitrogen, and oxygen in just the right proportions? If so, did He patiently stand by and correct them every time He struck earth with an asteroid, wiping out 75 percent of life? Either He is in charge, or He is not; and if not, what is? The facts of the finely tuned earth ask to be explained and, if it is not a God-given miracle, what kind is it? Whatever one thinks of the Gaia hypothesis, some version of it must be true.

Lovelock's more recent formulation, made in 1991, could be called the "Modest Gaia Theory." He explains this in *Gaia: The Practical Science of Planetary Medicine*: "The modern expression of James Hutton's superorganism, Gaia, is the Earth seen as a single physiological system, an entity that is alive at least to the extent that, like other living organisms, its chemistry and temperature are self-regulated at a state favorable for life." The main difference between the Robust and Modest versions is the shift from asserting the biosphere to be "alive" to being a set of "systems," and the addition of the qualifier—"alive to the extent" of favorably regulating earth's conditions for life itself. Modern scientists have been so unremitting in their attacks on Lovelock's teleology that they have forced him to tone down the stronger version several times. Yet it grows back, as hardy as Gaia herself.

Trees make rain, especially in the rainforest; clouds form over the ocean to let through the right amount of sunlight; and a thousand other living and non-living systems experience positive and negative feedback to keep gases at the correct proportion: just explosive enough to make Gaia metabolize but not burn up. The almost perfect balance of these and other gases is almost invariably taken for granted—an absurdity, a stupidity. As the chief of earth's many gifts, it is worth honoring, celebrating, venerating—especially in a garden. With a team of artists, I have constructed a model of Gaia that shows some of these interactions over the earth's 4.5 billion years.

GAIA

These three models depict, from left to right, the Universe, Gaia, and the Atom. Gaia, the earth, like the fluctuating rabbit populations, shows order growing out of chaos. It is a self-organizing system where the order of life, almost four billion years ago, grew out of the chaotic gases, dust, and volcanoes. The scientist James Lovelock invented the Gaia hypothesis to explain how this happens and, because it is so important, we erected an aluminum model of Gaia next to those of the atom and universe. Thus the mesocosm is placed on a plinth between the microcosm and macrocosm.

Gaia, Greek for "Mother Earth," is a supplementary metaphor to "the Selfish Gene," and a more positive one showing that some natural processes of self-organization favor the planet as a whole. It is as if the earth had a purpose: to control the proportions of gases in the exact balance that is best for life. In the drawings one can see how, over billions of years, carbon dioxide and methane (the greenhouse gases responsible for global warming) have been pumped down, while oxygen is pumped up and nitrogen stabilized.

The drawings show several different attempts to present these truths in the most dramatic way; first as an evolutionary vase form, then as a globe with surrounding gases, pumped up and down, and finally as a spiral of history held up by the sun's energy, its rays of light. This is the basic giveaway for us: we live off a billionth of the energy it throws out every day.

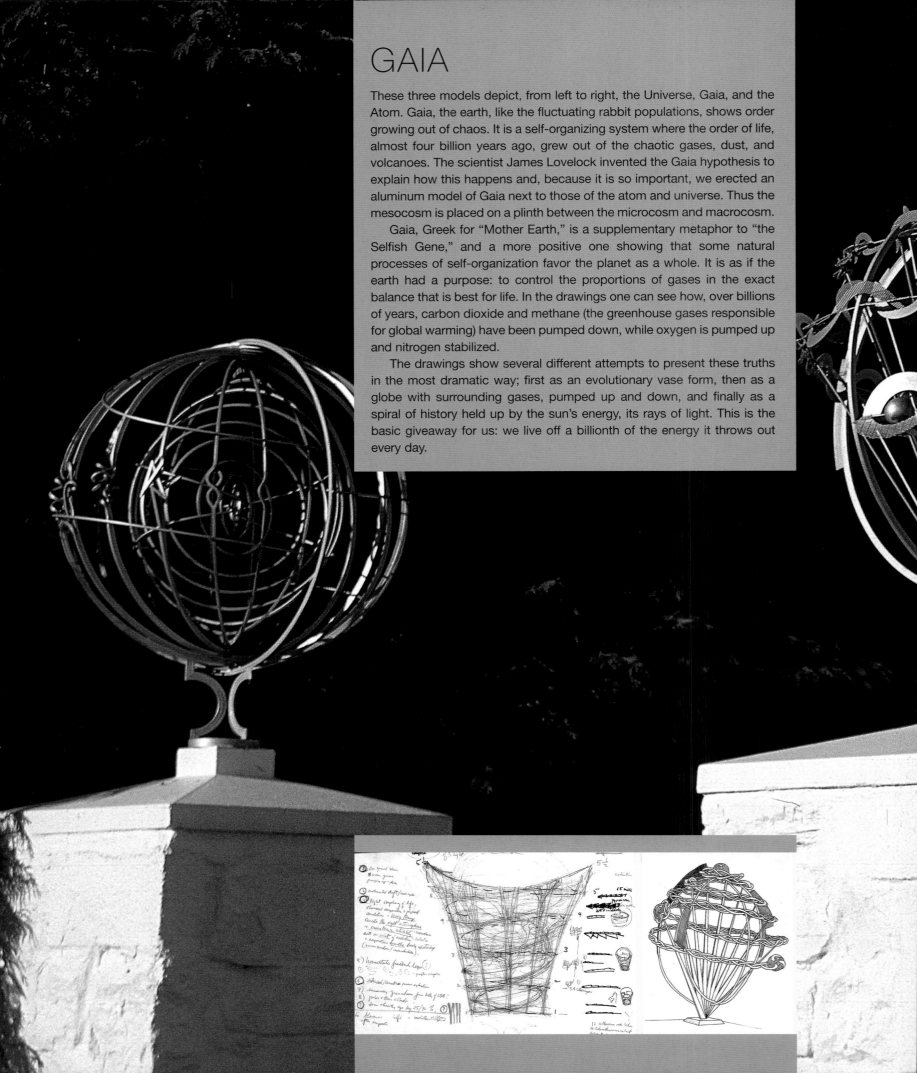

65 million years ago, asteroid strike.
Mass extinction of dinosaurs etc.

TIME LINE   years   Present

4.6 billion   3.5 billion   300 million   65 million   Runaway Greenhouse
                                                                                          Effect

Feedback
cycles of
homeorhesis

Oxygen

Nitrogen

Tight Coupling of:
• Life
• Chemical elements
• Physical elements

Runaway Greenhouse Effect

Pangaea and
continental drift
and rock cycles

Carbon dioxide

Reflective
albedo

Methane

Reading down from the top of the final installation
(opposite), we can see the early, dead planet, then the
origin of life 3.8 billion years ago, then the very
important "tight coupling" between the three main
players: life, chemical compositions, and physical
conditions (represented by the three undulating
metals). The structural members on the four sides
show how Gaia pumped down carbon dioxide from,
roughly, a deadly 20 percent of atmosphere to its
present low of 0.03 percent. (Today, unfortunately, it is
rising again and creating the "Greenhouse Effect.")
Methane is shown falling and leveling out, oxygen
rising up to its crucial 21 percent, and nitrogen
balanced as the major gas. Two more important
events are shown, one of them a continuous process,
the other a punctuation: at the bottom of the model
sunlight rays flare out and increase the temperature of
the earth, over 4 billion years, by 25 percent.

Over 4.5 billion
years the sun
becomes 25
percent hotter

Increase or decrease of:

Oxygen   21%

Methane
                         1.7 parts/million

Carbon
dioxide   0.03%

Nitrogen   78%

Miracle upon miracle, although the sun has become 25 percent hotter, the earth's surface has not—because the temperature is regulated by the planetary system as a whole. Although five mass extinctions have occurred (depicted in the model as if each were the result of an asteroid hitting the earth) the system reasserts itself. Each time, aided by the physical and chemical conditions, life has bounced back.

There are some ironic lessons here that Lovelock and the Gaians have pointed out. Even if today we are at the beginning of the sixth mass extinction, it does not spell the end of Gaia. The earth system is too robust to be killed off—by us, by a million hydrogen bombs, or by their equivalent in greenhouse gases. There is some mordant solace in knowing that if *Homo sapiens* is too pollutant and is snuffed out by Gaia as she jumps to a new level of self-organization, that at least life will go on, and a new robust history will start. Because of our sins we would go the way of the dinosaurs, an echo of biblical morality and a Last Judgment, albeit one caused by Gaia not by God.

In such indirect ways we find morality and ethics built into the universe. Ecological harmony—synergy, cooperation, symbiosis—were working before we transformed them into systems of judgment, customs, or laws. The same, I believe, is true for other affective qualities—love, beauty, and aesthetics. Although the human species takes these qualities to entirely new levels of complexity and expression, they pre-date us and exist independently of us. These, at least, are the propositions I attempt to make clear in the Garden of Cosmic Speculation. The biggest speculation of all is that there is a teleological activity at work though, as Paul Davies' arguments have shown us in the previous section, it should be considered a *predisposition* of the universe to evolve in certain ways. It is not a single, predetermined outcome that is the goal, as the old idea of teleology supposed, but rather a set of tendencies and limitations that guide evolution along certain broad avenues. Teleonomy not teleology. Ecosystems and Gaia are evolving toward greater complexity, ever higher and more stable levels of organization, like the rest of the universe. There is a purpose, or telos, in Gaia as it pushes the interacting variables of chemistry, physical conditions, and life to their limit. This is not a "life force" or "vital fluid" in the sense argued by the Vitalists, but rather the emergent property of all properties.

Trying to Fathom the Atom and Explain it to Clare

In 1994, because Clare was eighty-nine, Maggie wanted to create some permanent record of her for the children. Traditionally Maggie might have commissioned a portrait, but since a close friend of hers was the filmmaker Julie Corman, she decided to record Clare's life and personality in a more immediate and palpable medium. Julie filmed Clare recounting several important incidents of her exotic life in the Far East and India, during the last

years of the British Empire, and recorded a few conversations with the family, and John and Lily, who happened to be at Portrack on vacation at that time. There was another motive behind this filming, never mentioned as such. Maggie had had a recurrence of cancer in 1993 and, though it was in remission, she knew it might come back again. As a memorial and testimony, the filming thus had a possible double role.

At this point I had finished two years of research on the atom and, with several scientists, had constructed drawings of these high-speed, jiggling units of the universe. It was well known that representing an atom visually was, because of its small size and fast movement, almost impossible. Some physicists said the only way it could be done was through such things as equations that might show the probability of an electron cloud being in one place or another. Atoms are probability things. Indeed, atoms and all their various subatomic particles are slippery things whose exact shape and position escape our instruments. By the mid-1980s, one or two had been trapped and "photographed" but this only revealed their elusive, paradoxical aspects all the more. These aspects are collectively termed "quantum weirdness." Partly because of their weird qualities, some of which I will summarize shortly, atoms are obsessively interesting. While involved in the research, I found it was easy to become a misogynist and to fall in love with them.

I tried various ways of communicating my passion to Clare, showing her photos of the aluminum model that had just been constructed and explaining how it would be put down the hill next to the globes of Gaia and the universe—far from the house and well away from the paradise garden she had created. Tact demanded keeping a certain distance and not compromising one garden with another. I gave her photographs of the models and we had the following exchange.

CJ: Clare, I wanted to show you these designs going on next to the greenhouse, the models of Gaia, the universe as a whole, and the atom.

CK: (looking at the model of the atom) I would like them to be explained to me—what's written all the way around the edge? I don't understand mathematics. Why are there these equations?

CJ: Physicists say the only way you can represent the atom is through equations, because in reality it is never still. You can see these parts turn in the wind showing how lively the atom is; it's always buzzing and jumping around faster than you can see it.

CK: It's not a thing, it's a process.

CJ: Yes, exactly, you got it in one, that's what I am trying to show in the garden, the cosmic processes and how we are connected to the universe and nature—what are your views on what we are doing?

CK: Science is to me, Charles, a closed book, it didn't come into my education, which was more musical and not mathematical in any way. Your designs are fascinating—it's all new to me so I don't have any views on it, because I can't contribute anything about what you are trying to do.

CJ: Is what I am doing at Portrack alien to what you have done, or does it fit in?

CK: I think it is alien to what Portrack has been—to me a garden is flowers, plants, shrubs, and trees, nothing whatsoever to do with mathematics, which was not part of my upbringing, but I'm perfectly prepared to try to understand it. And, as I told you four or five years ago, please do things you want to do now, while I am still alive, while I still can take an interest in it—don't wait until I am dead. It's fascinating, far different from what I've ever known before.

As a conscientious mother-in-law Clare was determined to honor my enthusiasms and, as a steadfast Catholic, she was also bemused by the way the new physics presented a world-view closer to her own than the materialist one it was superseding. Quantum weirdness is like the mystery of the Trinity, and other miracles, in that it is inconceivable and you have to take much on faith. The main difference is that it is proved daily by physicists and every time a quantum particle tunnels through a television set.

If you are trying to figure out how the universe is, sooner or later you will come across its basic units, the "atomoi" as Greek scientists called them, those "indivisible bits" that cannot be broken down into anything smaller. What do they look like, or how are we to imagine them? Although no one had ever seen them they were inferred to be *hard* kernels of matter like pebbles or marbles or billiard balls that could not be reduced any further. Newton defined the atom in this materialist way, believing matter to be made from solid particles. He wrote they were as "solid, massy, hard, impenetrable, movable particles . . . even so very hard, as never to wear or break in pieces." "Solid, massy, hard, impenetrable"—one might keep such words in mind because, as I was to explain to

Clare, much of what was discovered in the last hundred years, goes against this materialist picture. She was a listener avid to know there was a scientific alternative to the everyday view of reality.

Modern theories of the atom developed from chemistry and the model that John Dalton proposed around 1803. This was made up of a hard core of attractive force surrounded by a repulsive "caloric" force. Another chemist, Kekulé von Stradonitz, conceived the atom as a sausage with attachments. His model of the methane atom (CH_4) had four hydrogen atoms stuck to protrusions growing from its base. A. W. von Hofmann produced the stick and ball model of the methane atom in 1860, a representation that, with variants, is still used today. By 1874 J. H. van't Hoff had realized that geometry was all-important to atomic structure, and he placed four bonds at the corner of the carbon atom, a tetrahedron in shape.

In the early part of this century, Ernest Rutherford opened up a more mysterious view as he found two important things. First, that

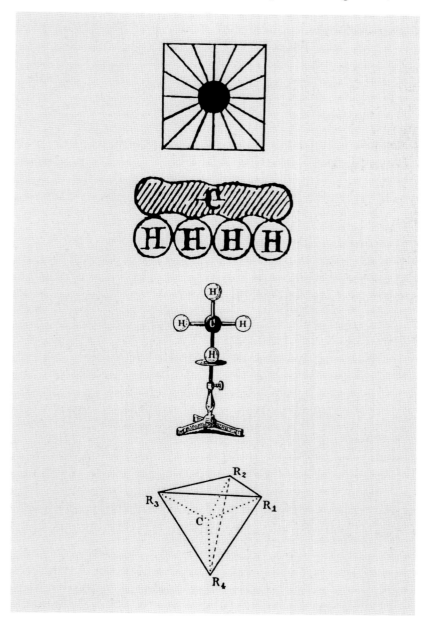

What does the atom look like? Over the centuries this big question about the very little has continued to tease scientists. Four early models of the atom, from the top: Dalton's carbon atom surrounded by the flaring caloric, or "heat" of repulsive forces, 1803; Kekulé's sausage model of methane (CH_4), 1855; von Hofmann's stick and ball model of methane, 1860; van't Hoff's tetrahedral carbon atom with the bonds at the corners, 1874. (After Robert S. Root-Bernstein, "Beauty, Truth, and Imagination" in Kenneth Snelson, *The Nature of Structure*, New York Academy of Sciences, 1989.)

there was a nucleus inside the atom—it was divisible into neutrons and protons after all—and, second, that this was ten thousand times smaller than the electron orbitals that surrounded it. This meant that the atom considered as a whole was 99.9 percent empty space. Thus, by 1911, the solid stuff of Newton was found to be almost a complete void! What was the view of it, or what was a plausible metaphor? "Imagine," I said to Clare, "a marble-sized football in a football stadium and then a jubilant crowd celebrating a winning goal: the jumping, cheering spectators are rather like the electron's chaotic movement jiggling around the nucleus. This image is closer to the truth than the older models that your father was raised with, which had the atom looking like a solid sausage, or a stick and ball, or a raisin pudding." Actually, Rutherford's image was not that of a riotous stadium so much as a solar system. He conceived the very distant tiny planets, the orbiting electrons, as being held in place by the nucleus, a sun, and this was achieved not by the force of gravity but by electromagnetism.

"By the time you were twenty-five in 1930," I went on, continuing my parallel between the atom and her life, "we came close to visualizing this elusive body and its buzzing void through the CPK model of methane and the Schrödinger model." These models show strange clouds of black specks in various orbital patterns. The greater the density of the specks in one area, the greater the probability of finding an electron there: in effect, these were probability models. This "charge cloud model" is real, insofar as an atom is more cloudy than hard. But, and I had initial trouble explaining this paradox to Clare, the cloud even creates part of the hardness; it presents the atom's electromagnetic force. Soon, however, Clare began to see forces and fields as similar to thoughts and feelings, invisible paradoxical things one had to accept on faith, or at least on inference.

"So we learned, by 1930, that the one ultimate thing of the universe is not hard, but extremely hazy, agitated and forceful. An electron only more or less occupies a cloud, until it is measured—and here comes one miraculous part—then it suddenly collapses and becomes a point. This act of measurement is known as the collapse of the wave function," I added, as if this proved the point.

At these moments the Standard Model of quantum physics becomes like the doctrine of transubstantiation, when wine turns into the blood of Christ. One has to accept that it fits in with all the evidence and the other theories, but it still seems bizarre. The strange jump from one thing to another touches the heart of the quantum world, and although the precise meaning of this microcosm is still disputed, all sides agree that it is uncanny. They agree with Niels Bohr's famous test I have mentioned: "If you are not shocked by Quantum Theory you have not understood it." The question that measures understanding and the one I put to Clare is: "Are we shocked *enough* to understand it?"

Here again I had recourse to metaphor. "As you said, atoms are processes as well as things, thus they are very much like your thoughts. These are also processes, like the quick ripples of wind over water, or the spinning of impulses through neurones with a certain rate of vibration. Perhaps thought is a quantum event," I added, referring to an idea that has gathered strength in the last fifty years. While such views of the atom may lead to an exaggerated

ABOVE: The top three diagrams show the Russell–Saunders vector coupling model (1930s), the Corey–Pauling–Koltun (CPK) model of methane by Linus Pauling and cohorts, which fills the space of the stick and ball model, and the charge cloud model of Erwin Schrödinger, *c*.1930, which shows the higher probability of finding the wave function of the electron in the darker regions. Atoms are now seen as probabilistic wave patterns. Our mental set of the tiniest jiggling matter was imposed by the US Atomic Energy Commission in a solar model (bottom) based on the Rutherford–Bohr view of electron orbits whipping around at different levels.

idealism, it also leads some physicists, such as Sir James Jeans, to sum up the ambiguity with the surprising metaphor: "The universe begins to look more like a great thought than a machine." Machines are not so fuzzy and flexible as atoms and thoughts. Maybe the notion of hard matter is an illusion, or at least a disguise for a deeper truth. Here we were back in the territory of Paul Davies and his book *The Mind of God*, which I had given Clare to read.

The Universe as Symphony, the Laws as Harmonies

While I did not try out all the metaphors and views of the new physics on Clare, I attempted one last image because she, like I, had a father devoted to music. The idea is that the ultimate stuff of the universe is like vibrating strings. This image illuminates the

ABOVE: The first three orbits of an electron around a central nucleus. In 1922 Louis de Broglie showed that the orbits of an electron around a nucleus are "standing wave patterns," like that of a violin string vibrating up and down, forming an S-curve with a node point at its center. This single peak and trough forms the first harmonic. The second harmonic has two whole waves, the third three, etc. Only whole waves are possible; by bending the string round on itself, eating its own tail, the possible electron orbits are found. They are here depicted in red. This wholeness of waveform suggests why electrons have to jump from orbit to orbit and are not allowed into fractional orbits. Electrons cannot move in fractional units, hence the Music of the Spheroids, hence the quantum jumps that the electron goes through as it absorbs photons of light, or gives them off. Perhaps on the microscale way below atoms the whole universe is made of vibrating superstrings in whole orbits—a membrane of waves.

fundamentally active nature of the jiggling clouds and particles. Their ceaseless activity, if viewed through a scanning, tunneling microscope, is basically rhythmical. The beats of the atom are syncopated some times and more regular at others. What is more, if the most advanced thinking turns out to be right—and I will look at the idea in conclusion—then the universe is constructed from ultra-tiny superstrings, or even a series of strings tied together into a membrane. According to this recent theory, we inhabit an eleven-dimensional universe and seven of these dimensions are extraordinarily small, curled up into quivering strings. Thus dancing vibration may lie at the absolute bottom of the universe.

Later on I was to explore these ideas even further, and cosmological watching seemed to be steering the garden and my thinking, the universe building itself day by day, discovery by discovery. By the late 1990s the metaphor looked plausible. Everything in the microworld is made from a kind of tuning fork, and all of this matter, up to the size of the atom, is continuously pulsating. Furthermore, pursuing this metaphor, what is called the wave function of the atom is a basic model for still bigger waves such as light waves, ocean waves, piano waves, or the shock waves of an earthquake. To stretch the metaphor we might say the universe is made neither from billiard balls nor from raisin puddings but from music. According to quantum field theory, when the universe is reduced to a single essence it may turn out to be a coordinated symphony of vibrating energy, and its laws would be those of harmonic vibrations. All these arguments became further support for the underlying metaphor of the garden, a landscape of waves. At this stage my attempt at converting Clare to the mysteries of the new physics stopped, and I pursued more philosophical aspects of the atomic world.

Heinz Pagels, the scientist who, in his book *The Cosmic Code*, coined the customary phrase "quantum weirdness" in 1982, singled out three aspects of the microcosm that are weird: it lacks customary objectivity, it is indeterminate and, to a certain extent, the observer creates the reality. All three entail that what we are looking for, and how we look, changes what we see. The notorious two-slit experiment is typical of all the weirdness and, according to the rubric, if you understand it then you have mastered Bohr's challenge—you are shocked enough. Rather than rehearsing the experiment, I will just summarize the results. If one shoots an atom or any quantum particle through two slits cut in a blocking shield, it will reveal that it is both a wave and a particle. This is weird because what we see in the normal world, the mesocosm of our size, is that everything is either a wave or a particle. It may turn out, however, that this great either/or is an illusion and everything is always both. The reason we do not realize this is that, except at the atomic level, the particulate nature of reality is so large that it obscures wave measurement. But you are a wave and I am a wave and the garden is a landscape of waves because of this truth. The second weird truth the two-slit experiment reveals is that

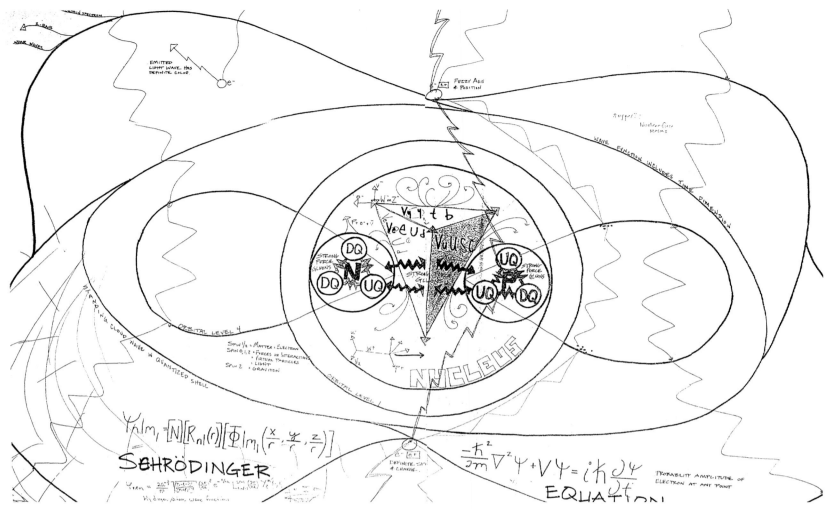

the quantum particle seems to know whether it is being expected to behave like a wave or a particle and, as if this were not bad enough, keeps a memory of the fact as it processes information very quickly.

The two-slit paradox is well portrayed in a Charles Adams cartoon of 1940, a favorite of physicists. This shows a male skier amazed by the path of a woman whose ski tracks have gone simultaneously to either side of a tree. Yet there she is to the male's stupefaction, nonchalantly skiing on, as a perfectly unified member of the species. Here again is the Niels Bohr shock test: skiers may not split in half and go along two paths, but everything in an atom can, and does.

There are many more magical properties of the atomic world to explain why I fell in love with it for a while and explored its possible metaphors. Enough has by now been said to explain why it presented a gnawing challenge: as a fuzzy, vibrating, indeterminate thing, physicists claimed it could not be visualized. But I thought of a trick, and, with the help of students at UCLA, produced some designs called "This is not an atom" after René Magritte's famous painting of his pipe: *Ceci n'est pas une pipe*. These designs became the basis for the model of the heavy hydrogen atom now in the garden. Just as Magritte's title is a warning not to confuse a representation with reality, the model's title indicates that certain false assumptions are introduced by my static abstraction. A film or a moving hologram would be a more realistic presentation; but a static, three-dimensional model has the advantage that one can see and contemplate the complex interrelationships. And I can claim two small victories over those who said it could not be done. First, the electron clouds rotate in the wind, they almost vibrate, and second, the elusive probability wave that always defeats representation is smuggled on to the frame in the form of Schrödinger's equation. That is etched into the aluminum. So, in spite of skeptical physicists, the atom can be modeled.

As one can see from the design, the heavy hydrogen atom is less like the stick and ball model than the solar system model. The "sun" at the center, the nucleus, contains one neutron and one proton, which make up heavy hydrogen, and these two particles are attracted to each other by an exchange of "gluons," particles which constitute the strong nuclear force. The strong nuclear glue, one of the four fundamental forces in nature, is also the significant force released in a nuclear explosion, along with the weak force, the radiation. These are both indicated by zigzag lines in the drawing. Inside the proton and neutron are even smaller things—three "quarks" whose type defines whether the larger whole is a proton or neutron. While we have never seen a quark, we have reasonably inferred them since the 1960s, just as Democritus reasonably inferred atoms and the void in the fifth century BC.

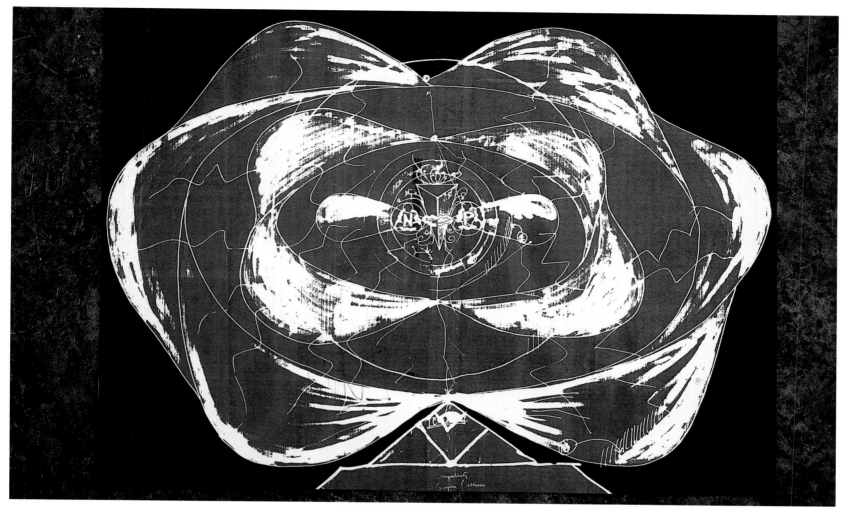

The most important aspect of the atom that my "non-model" shows is the rhythmical path of the electron. In its ground state the electron forms a perfect spherical shell of one wave orbit around the nucleus. When more energy is beamed in, it springs to the two-wave, dumb-bell shape, and then to the three-wave shape, and so on, up the harmonic scale. The electron can only occupy certain positions, as de Broglie discovered in 1922, because of its wave aspect. Only whole waves are allowed, whole tones like a well-tuned instrument.

Three discrete electron clouds are shown, not the ground state, or sphere, because this would obscure the nucleus. Two further aspects are also illustrated: the fact that within the harmonic shell the actual path of an electron is every-which-way. This is shown in the model, on the following page, by the fuzziness of the wire, its smeared-out quality. Observation by a person, or measurement by an instrument, turns the wave-particle duality into a simple particle. This observation-event is called "collapsing the wave function," and it is indicated in the drawing, right, as an eyeball focused on a node (the particle). Every time we measure the position of an electron we turn it into a point, and thereby lose its momentum. The more we know about its position the less we know about its momentum, and vice versa. The same is true of other complementary qualities—wave/particle, time/energy, mass/energy etc. The dualities are known as "conjugate pairs," because a gain in one area of knowledge necessarily entails a corresponding loss of information in the other. This slippery truth is also revealed by the two-slit experiment.

The other aspect brought out in the drawings is the probability of finding the electron in any one place: the darker or denser the pattern the higher the probability; the lighter, the lower. Since an electron does not have a precise position until we measure it—being spread out or "entangled" all over its orbit—probabilities can only be assigned according to Schrödinger's wave equation. In effect, the magic of quantum particles is their non-locality, their multiple existence in every part of an orbit at once, until they pop into one place when observed. In the classical world of Newtonian Materialism, things exist and are definitely either in one place or another; in the quantum world this either/or logic breaks down, multiple things exist simultaneously, and only one comes into being through being fixed by an instrument or observation.

This leads to the often-stated point that, in the microworld, there is an interaction between subject and object, but it does not mean that there is no objectivity, or that mind is stronger than matter. Schrödinger's equation specifies, with considerable accuracy, the probability of how the wave function will develop. Rather it means there is indeterminacy—chance—at the basic level of nature, and that any attempt to measure it—to determine indeterminacy itself—will necessarily change it. Our instruments have a quantum component, as we do ourselves, and they get entangled in the process of measurement. This is why the physicist John Wheeler speaks of a "participatory universe" and why the eye as a sign occupies several parts of the garden.

THE ATOM

LEFT, ABOVE: An early model of the atom. LEFT, BELOW AND RIGHT: The Deuterium atom as built. Seen here to the left of the model of Gaia, and shining with ice and light, the atom seems to glow with energy. Schrödinger's equation, the outer structure, holds it up. Three inner orbits of the electron are seen with their wave (fuzzy mesh) and particle (curved metal) duality. These rotate in the wind, catching the electrons' constant whirl. The nucleus can hardly be seen since the photos were taken when it had rotated at right angles to the picture plane, but it shows the neutron, proton and quarks etc. LEFT, CENTER: The outer shells of atoms have recently been made visible in microphotos. Here, crisscrossed lasers have focused chromium atoms into tiny dots, each just 80 nanometers wide, and the pattern resembles the egg-crate so often revealed in these enhanced and colored photos. (After Jabez J. McClelland, National Institute of Standards and Technology, USA.)

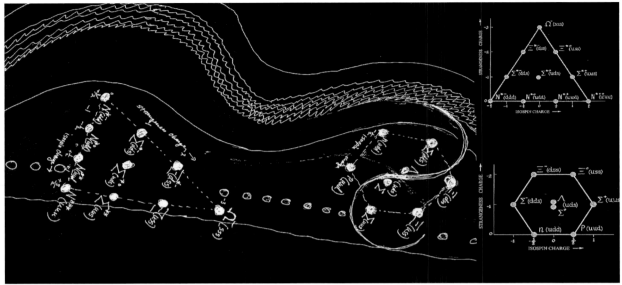

The Ultimate Particles and the Quark Walk

Since the 1960s, the search for the ultimate units produced another kind of weirdness—a no-place or, rather, a mathematical place. When the nuclei of atoms were bombarded to release their constituents, instead of getting tinier as matter usually does, the units started reproducing themselves. This proved disarming, like an endless whispering game of nature leading in circles. Think of how simplification usually proceeds: rocks are reduced to molecules, then molecules are reduced to atoms, and so it goes down to protons, neutrons, and electrons. But then suddenly, as the subdividing collisions went on, it was protons–protons–protons or neutrons–neutrons–neutrons forever. Rock bottom was apparently reached, but what were the rocks—not the protons themselves? The situation was more complex than this, but still paradoxical. When trying to split a proton, or neutron, or any such heavier subatomic particle—known collectively as "hadrons"—more energy is added in collision and that generates new matter (according to Einstein's famous equation $E=MC^2$). The hadron cannot be forced apart, and yet it still has parts lurking inside.

In order to approach this structure in the early 1960s, Murray Gell-Mann postulated a smaller element, the quark. When evidence for it was finally seen, in December 1963, it began to enjoy a conceptual, if not "real" existence. In effect, one ultimate particle turned out to be trapped inside another—according to the math, three quarks hide inside both the neutron and proton. As atom smashers continued their work through the 1960s the "particle zoo," as it was called, became bigger and more and more unwieldy. But Gell-Mann and others presumed there was an order. They realized there were patterns to the explosions, traces inside the cloud chambers that showed various qualities. The elegant swirls and spirals left by the moving particles revealed secrets of weight, spin and other aspects, termed "flavors." These also showed a basic symmetry. The idea that all of nature has a symmetry (but also

evolves, and becomes interesting, through symmetry breaking) provided the basic insight. Gell-Mann, borrowing a phrase from Buddhist metaphysics, hit on a pattern he called the Eightfold Way. Three different types of quark (up, down, strange) hiding inside a hadron could form an eightfold pattern.

They could also constitute families made up of 1, 8, 10, or 27 members—necessarily, mathematically. This mathematical symmetry demanded the existence of a particle called the "omega minus," and so did congruence with other theories. When, after 50,000 photos were carefully searched for clues, the predicted omega minus particle finally turned up in 1963, it supported the quark idea, at least as far as physicists were concerned. This was like the discovery of elements predicted by the periodic table in the 19th century. It proved the inference. A fact is not a fact until it is confirmed by several theories at once.

The ultimate particles started to be collected and ordered so that by the 1980s a Standard Model of irreducible elements could itself be put in a pattern. The standard point-like particle of the Standard Model is the electron. The fact that something like superstrings could be more basic than these may make the word "ultimate" look rather temporary, but such slippery redefinitions have happened in the past. Recall that "atom" originally meant "indivisible," and that misnomer happily survived many subdivisions. So, ultimate particles, according to the Standard Model, may not really be ultimate but, as far as points are concerned, they constitute an impressive rock bottom. After this final reduction they tend to turn into fields or membranes or strings—not hard, stable, points at all.

Ordering Phantoms

This paradox is itself a fascinating discovery worth exploring through a garden. What better place to honor the ultimate pebbles as they transform into fields? "Pebbles" and "fields"—the puns have their relevance too. The microworld of the atom, the proton, and the

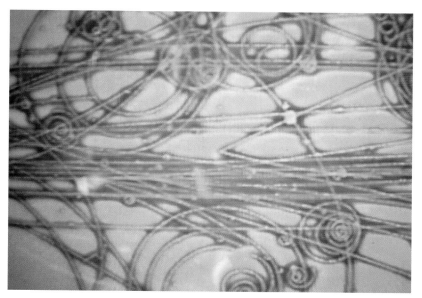

quark is like the mesoworld in the landscape: the boulder, the rock, and the pebble. And the swirls seen in the cloud chamber—evidence of qualities, spins, and flavors—are like the waves and spirals of growing plants. Microcosm equals mesocosm at the poetic level of the garden.

The question then became where and how to present these discoveries and ideas. One part of the garden that had not been looked at very closely for its natural potentials was the meandering stream, or burn, that connected the Water Dragon with the lakes (see site plan, s 36–7). This undulated smoothly, on a very small scale, and became the natural place for a short walk by the burn. John Keswick had planted a curved row of cherry trees here, but several had fallen in two places, and these holes asked either to be filled, or turned into something else. Problems prompted thinking and intervention. Since winter storms usually bring down a few trees every year, and since these leave large rooted stumps that are hard to destroy, the obvious conclusion was to fill in the voids with new stumperies. So the burnside became the place to celebrate the ultimate particles, a Quark Walk.

The first void to the left could be filled with stumps, stacked on top of each other as they accumulated—a totem pole of roots ordered in a tenfold triangle, the "Tenfold Way". The second void could be a more explicit look at the particles and the way their traces are measured in a cloud chamber. Those radiating lines and asymmetrical spirals of the explosion would form a structural net. Eight upright stumps painted red and cut with heads facing north could show the "Eightfold Way." Fencing, necessary to keep rabbits out of the garden, would through its moiré patterns once again show waves of light as a basic reality. In the middle would be a gate of looping particles, where the mowers could pass, and at the edges there could be two sprays. One would fly over pebbles marking the trajectories; the other would fly over the stream. Waves over waves.

The universe discloses its minute elements as traces, not as things. The notion that everything is, in the end, a process, finds expression here, a process of short-lived spirals fizzling out at an attractor point (note the way the spirals zero in to one side). The poetry revealed to us through the cloud chamber is also translated into a spiral steel cable that is unraveled in sinusoidal curves. Below it the measurement, the inference of quarks, is projected as if on to a monitor screen. Black rubber lines on gray pebbles show the path of the omega minus particle. It is a paradoxical trajectory, appearing and disappearing, revealing to detectives the shadows of reality. The phantom quark is seen as an inference, only a trace. Can these fast, jumping, and disappearing shots really refer to things that exist? Can anything be more fissiparous?

The Tenfold Way and the Eightfold Way. Ultimate particles can be grouped in families of 1, 8, 10, 27 etc. Here they mark two voids in a row of cherry trees. Ten rotting stumps in a triangle are surmounted with further fragments as trees fall over in the wind. They create a primitive expressive form of radiating knobs, where the roots previously fanned out.

The Eightfold Way, another family postulated by Murray Gell-Mann, consists of red posts cut at the head to face due north, to the distant view of the mountains and the midnight summer sun. The ultimate units and their constituents are inscribed. For example, TOP, FAR LEFT: a neutron is indicated by an N, and it has two down and one up quarks, that is, DDU. A proton is indicated by a P, and has two ups and one down, UUD. The mass of the quark sub-units are as follows: D quark = $-\frac{1}{3}$; U quark = $+\frac{2}{3}$. Thus N = $-\frac{1}{3} + -\frac{1}{3} + \frac{2}{3} = 0$, and P = $\frac{2}{3} + \frac{2}{3} + -\frac{1}{3} = +1$, or plus one positive charge. The phantom quark can never be seen, but only inferred, and in this respect is like many other cosmological entities including the beginning of the universe. The sprays of particles at both ends of the undulating fence (which is a rabbit and deer barrier) simulate explosions seen within a cloud chamber, and their traces of particles that enjoy a quick life. This implies a metaphysics of process. It suggests that things are turned into events, that being becomes becoming. The black tubing mimics the traces seen in the cloud chambers. Where they spin in opposite spirals a positive and negative particle balance each other; the dashes show energy on its way to becoming matter.

different plane

solid rectangular stone

energy in a different
field - transition

V planes= Fractal point

many small V's

few big, small stuff

Energy
Explosive

Elementary particles

Quarks
u up
c charm
t top

d down
s strange
b bottom

Leptons
νe electron neutrino
νμ muon neutrino
ντ tau neutrino

e electron
μ muon
τ tau

photon

Z z boson

W+ W+ boson

W- W- boson

Force carriers

Higgs boson

g gluon

THE STANDARD MODEL

The Ultimate Particles of the Year 2000. A seat to sit on and ponder the paradox. The Standard Model that every physicist learns shows sixteen ultimate particles—ordered as it is often conceived into a grid of families. The units entail opposites and thus have led to their discovery. But, the Higgs Boson, the seventeenth, eludes detection. This is a little embarrassing: why the number sixteen or seventeen? They seem arbitrary, or bound to be more ultimate in the future.

LEFT: The reflection in the water mirrors the photographs of sub-atomic explosions in an accelerator. These are then analyzed to determine the weight and type of particle. 50,000 photographs from the cloud chamber were scanned before the elusive omega minus particle was found in 1964. RIGHT: A photograph of an explosion coming from the bottom left and fanning out. The spirals indicate the weight of the different particles. Note the energy turning into matter, the dashes turning into positive and negative electrons (e+, e-).

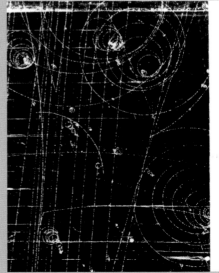

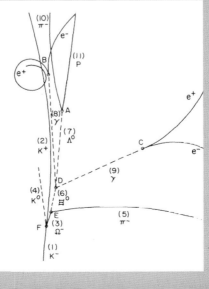

Discovering Nature in an Octagon

The journey from London to Scotland takes six hours, and Maggie and I were visiting about once a month for a long weekend. Whether one drives, or takes a train, or flies to Glasgow and drives, it still works out at six hours. Because of this, and the fact that I can write more easily in the country than in the city, Maggie thought we should move our center of gravity to Portrack. This was a great opportunity for me. While Maggie had her own money, which she looked after, my livelihood comes from writing books, about one per year, and from keeping them in print, about eight at any one time. This does not produce a great amount of money but cumulatively, and with multiple editions, it builds up a steady income. Furthermore, because the post-modern movement was expanding quickly, the freedom to follow these several directions in the peaceful atmosphere of Portrack was most welcome. A result was that I could write six new editions of *The Language of Post-Modern Architecture* and four of *What is Post-Modernism?*, turning them into books with long legs. In competition with the thousands of books on post-modernism appearing every year, they may not have run the fastest, but they have outlasted the sprinters. I called them "evolvotomes" because they could evolve as reality and my views changed, and be easily modified on the computer.

Finally, since John and Lily were away at school, and my two other sons, Cosmo and Justin, were in China starting careers, it made sense to reverse the pattern of our life. Maggie's idea was that we would spend most of the time in Scotland with Clare, and only several days per month in London. Although this plan never worked out completely, it did lead to another building project for me. Clare said, "Why don't you move your London books into the old summer house, The Octagon, and create a new library?"

The Octagon was an 18th-century gatehouse, one of a pair, which her husband John had bought fifteen years previously and turned into something of a folly a hundred yards from the house. Two octagonal gatehouses on an estate near by at Mollance were being demolished, so he and his brother each bought one for a token payment. To underline the gratuity and function of these little gems, they were given the ironic nicknames of Cuddle Cosy and Doodle Dinky. They are well-proportioned, classical octagons that form a perfect foil to a house, and a modest eye-catcher in a garden—hence their traditional nature as follies. Given their small size and shape, however, it is hard to see how a couple could live in them as a pair of gatehouses. Would they run across the road from kitchen to bedroom?

We had the one that was the kitchen. John removed the stove, flue, and ceiling and added another octagonal window, so when I started to conceive of it as a library already it was redundant with eight-sided figures—something like twenty of them. This presented a traditional architectural challenge. Nearly every Renaissance architect tried their hand at designing with regular geometric solids, and many centrally planned churches were laid out as octagons. The problems are notorious. It is hard to enter this pure form—geometrically-speaking the best way would be at the center, through the floor—and even harder to fit asymmetrical functions, such as the liturgy, into it. Yet Leonardo, as other Renaissance architects, was obsessed by these regular solids and determined to invent solutions for them. The reason? They seemed to lie behind nature, as Plato said, as perfect forms from which this imperfect world is constructed. Think of nearly spherical planets, or hexagonal snowflakes, or octagonal crystals. Indeed, as mentioned, most classical and modern architecture is based on regular, repeated geometries. Thus when I took on the project of turning The Octagon into a library a motive was to extend these traditions, acknowledge the obsession.

I doubled and redoubled the octagons in plan, elevation, and details, even designing eight-sided radiators. I added glass octagonal bookcases that repeated the window proportions and mullions, designed an octagonal rug and, above, eight ceiling ribs, and put in an octagonal mirror across from the door, making eight equal window-sections. I divided the books up into eight subject areas and then looked up all the words in the encyclopedia that

start with "oct-" in order to match them. To my delight there were more than sixteen with this prefix, such as octet, octane, octosyllabic, octostyle (a portico with eight columns), October, Octateuch (the first eight books of the Old Testament), octarchy (rule by eight leaders), octagamist (a man with eight wives). Books on nature were located, naturally, under octospore and octopus. Soon I realized that the architectural obsession was a universal one, that octomania existed in every field, and this further enflamed my passion to succeed where Leonardo had failed. Where the chimney was I opened an octagonal lantern and I etched into the cornices above each bookcase the eight general sections and, between them, the eight cardinal points that focused on the landscape (north, northeast, east etc.).

Soon I had accumulated about sixty-four octagons in the room, but then I hit the traditional problems: how to enter the central plan and where to sit and work without spoiling the symmetry. Despondency, failure; I could not, like Santa Claus, get in through the old chimney. Maggie, however, now infected by the octovirus said, "Don't give up, you *must* have an eight-sided desk in the middle of the room." "But where would I sit?" I asked; "in the middle?" "It's too late to retreat," she responded. "Right, I shall design a desk with eight sides and an octagonal hole in the middle, but only four people can sit at it or there won't be any room for storage." More drawings and mock-ups followed, and Bobby soon took to the challenge.

But by then I was convinced of another view of nature and the universe. Platonic forms do not underlie much of the cosmos, and most of nature follows the form recently uncovered by Benoit Mandelbrot: the fractal. Thus I decided on a post-modern hybrid: to combine this contemporary insight with the traditional one and make the pure forms partly fractal, that is, self-similar not self-same or exactly repeated. The result is an interior where the octagon is subtly shifted and fractured. Although it is hard to see at first, the eight ribs on the ceiling actually twist, off the center, and the desk below also has these self-similar angles. All these shifts give dynamism to the pure, static form.

From this time on, much of the landscape design also became more consciously fractal, and I will detour briefly into this recent theory of nature.

An 18th-century octagon, a primary symmetrical form, has been transformed into a library with eight fractal ribs that spin and twist off-center.

In an octagonal gatehouse, which Maggie's father had rescued from destruction, we made an octagonal fractal with self-similar shapes and angles. A central chimney was opened and turned into a lantern with eight-sided splays. Ribs, made from straight sections that twist, are set to the right of the center and on the floor triangular sections of a rug also spiral off-center. This angular momentum gives the static octagon a dynamic twist. The fractal table is constructed from self-similar angles painted in light and dark shades of cream and sand, colors that accentuate the shadows and fractals. Drawers, handles and tabletops that pivot for drafting are constructed from similar angles, giving the table the appearance of a crystal— a typical fractal found in nature.

OCTAGONIA

What are Nature's Basic Forms?

For many centuries, following Plato, many philosophers, architects, and painters thought that the ultimate reality behind things lay in straight lines, right angles, and perfect, geometric solids. If one looks at the surface of nature, however, it is mostly curved, warped, undulating, jagged, zigzag, and sometimes beautifully crinkly. It almost never looks like a Platonic temple or a railroad track. Yet, so deep are the preconceptions of God as Geometer that even Western artists who spent their time painting outdoors—such as Cézanne—are apt to see the world as a proposition from Euclid's textbook. After a lifetime spent carefully observing the landscape of Provence he insisted that "tout est sphères et cylindres." His paintings, like those of the Cubists, may have been better for this, but the mountains and pine trees of Aix-en-Provence are not the regular geometric solids this suggests. So, are there fundamental forms behind the appearances of nature, and, if so, what are they?

Most of nature's forms are continuously changing as they grow, making small modifications on a reiterated program and thus are self-similar not self-same. Representing this dynamic process is difficult for static architecture, as the Futurists found with their monuments to frozen movement. Yet the growing, incremental forms that Benoit Mandelbrot has explained, in *The Fractal Geometry of Nature* (1977), reveal a suggestive approach. As he insists at the beginning of his manifesto, "Clouds are not spheres, mountains are not cones, coastlines are not circles, and bark is not smooth, nor does lightning travel in a straight line." Rather, most of nature is irregular, fragmented, broken—or related to his neologism coming from the Latin word "fractus." Nature does not, except in the relatively rare instances of such things as planets and snowflakes, adopt a Euclidean form and even these are carried out with fractal details. And yet, as Mandelbrot has argued, Western metaphysicians and architects have disdained non-Euclidean forms as "amorphous" and "pathological." Mathematicians damned them, as the mathematician Henri Poincaré pointed out, as a "Gallery of Monsters."

Today the more subtle order hidden within these seeming monsters has been revealed—through the sciences of complexity. Nature's basic forms may be non-Euclidean, but that does not make them unordered. What are called "strange attractors" or "chaotic attractors" (the principles of self-similar organization emerging within chaos) underlie trees and mountain ranges as much as they do the human brain and heart. Because they are the basic forms behind nature, strange attractors became a major pattern for the garden design and their fractal variation became a way of presenting movement and change.

Fractal seats in the garden are made from self-similar elements: sections of a fallen tree trunk wrapped around a tree or concrete spirals sculpted on a metal armature (by Chris Barrowman). The latter has an affinity with the strange attractors of the galaxies, those whirlpools of stars, planets, dust, and gases that send out their arms in coherent but messy spirals. Seven people can perch on this Galactic Seat in a quiet part of the DNA Garden.

NON-EUCLIDEAN FURNITURE

Shatter / Explosion from Centre
Fragments + Lines of Force

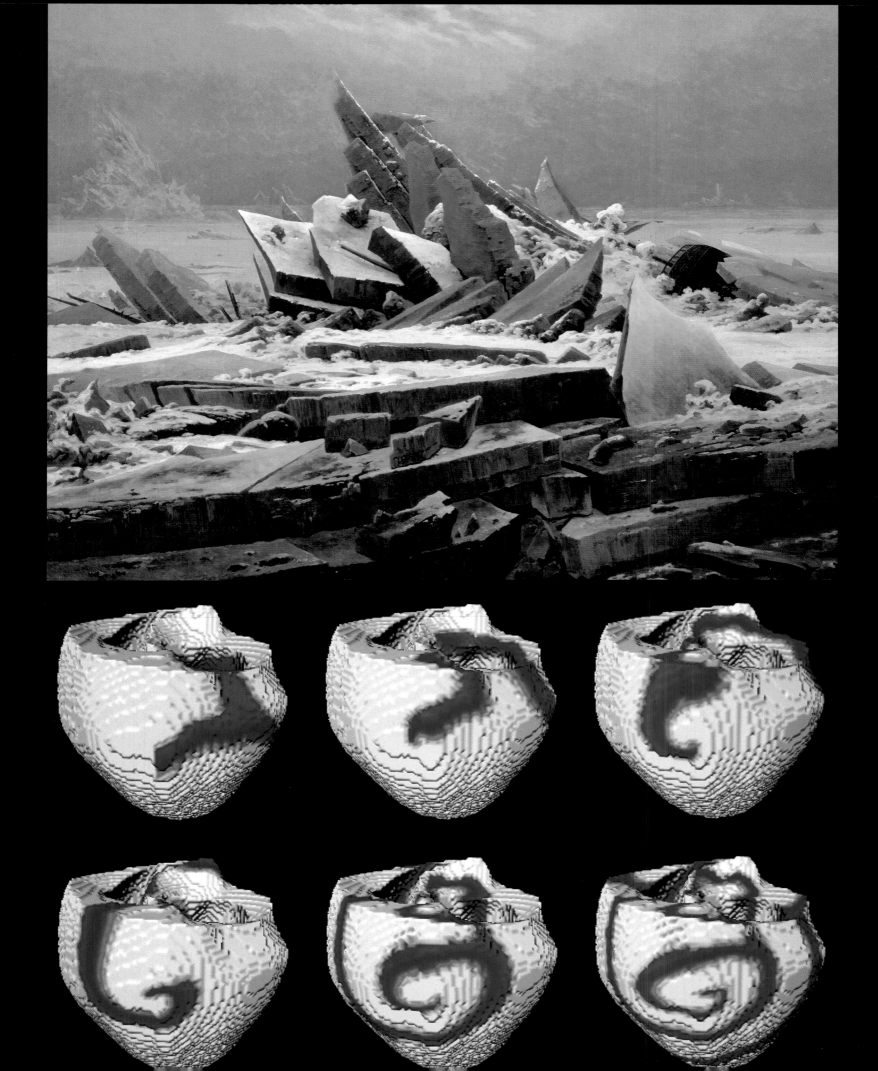

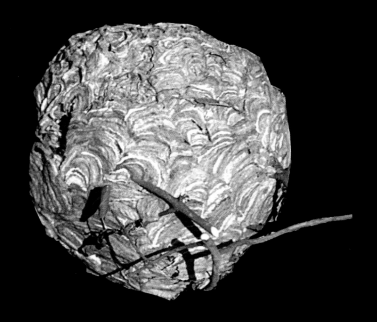

FRACTALS

OPPOSITE, ABOVE: *The Polar Sea* by Caspar David Friedrich, 1824; OPPOSITE, BELOW: a virtual heart showing fractal spiral waves, by Dr. Arun Holden; ABOVE, LEFT: Benoit Mandelbrot's fractal generation, a random Peano curve; ABOVE: Pyrite, a fractal crystal, compared to the fractal geometry of Daniel Libeskind's spiral for the Victoria and Albert Museum, London.; LEFT: A fractal wasps' nest.

Most of nature shows fractal forms of self-organization rather than exact symmetry or complete disorder. Our brain waves and heartbeats cannot repeat identically or else there is a crisis; they have to be balanced finely between order and chaos. The computer model of a heart, visualized from four points, shows the fractal pulse at the top becoming more disordered, toward the bottom.

An Impossible Rug Fractal in a fractal barn. One of the most amazing fractals was invented by Roger Penrose in 1977. Made from only two tile-shapes, a fat and a thin kite-shape, it creates an order within chaos. You can just make out, in the rug I designed for a converted barn at Portrack, a ten-tiled football shape. The figure recurs again and again, but, amazingly, never exactly the same way or in the same clusters.

Ten years after Penrose's invention scientists discovered that nature also had taken out a patent on such fractals—they are now called "quasi-crystals" and they may turn out to be very important. They show the kind of rich mixture of order and disorder characteristic of a growing rainforest, a suitable pattern to keep one's eye and mind continuously engaged. Is aesthetic interest stimulated by fractals—do they enhance perception?

The barn, or "steading" as it is called in Scotland, used to house about twenty cows. Now it is used as a guest cottage and an escape for John and Lily. The ceiling, door details, and window all are also self-similar fractals. I call it the "Rug Impossible" because for a long time the company that made it tried it out on the computer and it always brought up an "error" message. "Of course it's an error," I finally said; "the Penrose tile is non-periodic, it never repeats!" Thus to mass-produce the rug cheaply we had to cheat and repeat the patterns in three-foot sections; but the spirit is kept, the blue tiles do oscillate visually back and forth.

TOTAL N. O. OF SHOTS   59616

SCR/XER   1/1268   2/.852   3/   1   4/1139   5/4087

CPRINT 725/3

TUFT   123   125   SNOW   cp87   cp22
                                 DRIFT

Strip no.   1 of design 23118H. PAT

27" Wide   8x8 Quality   34½" rpt ½ Drop

METAMORPHOSIS

The Fractal Terrace, between nature and culture. Between a stream and the old steading, now transformed into bedrooms, is another main approach to the garden. To mark this transition area and give a presence to the Snail Mound, I designed a slightly curved terrace. The convex curve mounts away from the white steading wall, and perspectival lines veer toward the mound, focusing the view. Thus black and white rectangles take up the architectural theme of the steading, but then progressively break up into fractal forms as they approach nature. The convex curve now made from angled stones then dives into the ground to re-emerge as a large row of triangles—the Teeth Wall.

A double illusion is thus created, one caused by the convex curve and one caused by the perspectival diminution to either side. It is as if the terrace were a small part of a giant cylinder that goes under the ground. Furthermore, the steading to one side looks as if it were dissolving into the ground and then into the grass. In effect, this metamorphosis, written in stone, mediates between the two grand ideas of the universe: that Platonic forms can change into the more universal fractals, or that culture can turn back into nature. Note the way a spiral surprisingly emerges, lower right.

PART FOUR: THE NO-PLACE OF DEATH

One of the great luxuries of designing at Portrack came as a surprise. Maggie and I did not have to be there all the time while daily chores were done and our ideas carried out. A construction site, if you live on it, can wear you down whereas, if you come back to it once a month for several days, or for a few weeks a year, you can approach it with fresh enthusiasm each time. This we did, and our intermittent visits to Maggie's mother thus became moments of intense creativity and pleasure. Every time we returned, as Alistair would pick us up from the station and drive us back to the house, we anticipated what had been done, or how the growth had changed things, or what new projects might be needed. In this sense the gardens were a gift, a present from Clare that brought Maggie and me close together in a complementary endeavor. Usually I would design and she would plant, a division that suited our interests and knowledge.

Because of my inability to learn about plants, particularly their Latin names, Maggie would chide, "For you flowers and plants are a vegetable salad," a quip with some truth. Although I knew something about landscape gardening through many visits to European gardens, my connexion to plants was like that of most architects. I was fascinated by their patterns and organizational structure, but not the things that exercise most gardeners: how individual plants grow and look, how they can be mixed and matched in borders and create traditional compositions. Thus Maggie would go about her work sometimes without even bothering to tell me what she was up to.

We did discuss the red bushes she wanted to plant near the first red bridge, the Easy Way to Paradise, because it fitted in with a symbolic program in which redness led to passion and death. But another decision caught me by surprise. She decided to plant a row of amelanchier leading to the kitchen garden, and then around two sides of its perimeter, framing the Drunkard's Walk. This was an inspired idea, since these small trees create a sea of white froth for several weeks in April, as well as providing red berries for other months. And instead of a solid cover, they give a dappled shade. That is, they were good as a low-level screen and diaphanous wall; they defined the edges of the kitchen garden. The only problem was that

they blocked out most, if not all, of the Dragon Wall and its detail. This blockage can be seen as a virtue, of suggestive veiling, or a vice, of obscuring some beautiful dry-stone walling, and it is both, depending on the season and the amount of foliage on the amelanchier. In any case, I recount this collaboration, and surprise, as typical of the way we worked and of the division of labor.

From the early 1990s Maggie had been taking painting classes with various very different teachers, and she was starting to gain confidence in her own expressive potential. Her skills were impressive. She perfected a scratchy-hairy manner of ink drawing, adapted from our friend Leon Krier, an example of which is her depiction of Cluden Falls (see page 32). She also developed a Renaissance style of painting akin to Botticelli (even using 15th-century methods and grinding her own pigments) and, most creative of all, a free and lyrical watercolor style stemming from her teacher Cecil Collins. Collins, an English romantic with a spiritual and mystical side, freed Maggie from the constraints of both convention and perfection. He had her, together with her close friend Marcia Blakenham, loosen up by holding the paintbrush in her toes, as she painted with her foot. The results were intentionally imprecise, but they had a gestural unity that led Maggie toward a threshold. By 1993, she was on the verge of a breakthrough, a distinctive style, and beginning to take her creative work seriously.

Up until this time she had been constrained by her background. Raised in the traditional manner of the upper class to be a gifted amateur and a wife, rather than a professional, at six Maggie was one of the most accomplished young sword dancers Hong Kong had seen. Her petite feet could piston up and down, as the bagpipe played and the swords swished through the space her toes had just left. At Oxford she starred in several revues as a comic and a vamp, and went on to the Edinburgh Festival to perform in Fringe productions with contemporaries such as Esther Rantzen. But a career in dancing or acting was not encouraged by her parents, and so Maggie developed her other talents. She went into dress design and set up with Janet Cooper a boutique, Annacat (named after their respective dogs, Anna and Cat).

In the spring of 1993, while we were in Los Angeles, she had what she thought was a recurrence of an old, troubling back problem. By the time we had returned to Scotland it had got worse

The Snake Mound in a blizzard.

and then suddenly, in late May, she got a very high fever. After many tests the news came back and it was as bad as could be. She had cancer, and it had spread to the liver, bones, and bone marrow. Many more tests, scans, and consultations later, Maggie found out what the doctors had already told me, privately. As she describes, she heard the news in tawdry circumstances, in a brusque manner, a traumatic event that was to have important consequences and not just for her health. "Charlie and I went to Dumfries and the doctor there said, 'I think you ought to see the doctor who comes every week from Edinburgh.' . . . So we waited in this awful interior space with neon lights and sad people sitting exhausted on these chairs . . . and the nurse said, 'Could you come in?' And then we saw this doctor from Edinburgh, and we said, 'Well, how long, how long have I got?' And he said, 'Do you really want to know?' And we said, 'Yes, we really want to know.' And he said, 'Two to three months.' And we said, 'Oh—!' And then the nurse came up, 'I'm very sorry dear, but we'll have to move you out into the corridor, we have so many people waiting.' So we sat on these two chairs in the corridor trying to deal with this business, having two to three months to live. And as we sat there various nurses who I knew came up and said, very cheerfully, 'Hello, dear, how are you?' 'Well,' managing a laugh, 'I'm fine.'"

While most of the story of her cancer is irrelevant to the creation of the gardens at Portrack, a few aspects are germane and necessitate a detour into personal territory. Negatively, it meant she withdrew from further design but, positively, she decided to fight the disease and with this determination she also threw herself into a new project, one that was to become a passion. This started with her personal transformation from a passive recipient of bad news into an active fighter for her own life. Contrary to the first advice of doctors, she undertook chemotherapy, which got her past the three-month sentence, and then she tried more advanced methods of stem cell harvesting combined with complementary treatments. Her disease went into remission, and she could see hope for the future.

The will to survive may seem simple but often there are complex motives. Apart from the obvious one of staying alive, her main impetus was to live for the children as long as she possibly could. In 1993, John was fifteen and Lily thirteen. Determination to live often stems from beyond oneself, or at least is amplified by others, their love, and urgings. She started to see how her own active involvement in standard therapy, and the many complementary therapies that her readings had suggested, was itself having an effect on her well-being. Together we discussed this abstractly, in terms of the contrast between modern and post-modern methods of hospital practice. The first often treats the body as a machine with a single problem—like replacing a defective battery in a car—whereas the second treats the patient as having a multiple-caused disease, and one that needs combined therapies, in the plural. From our study we knew that cancer was often more like the latter condition, and that is how we approached it.

From her voracious reading of the alternatives Maggie selected about six complementary therapies. As she said on several occasions, these were the ones that were easy, cheap, and suited her personally, such as changes in diet, visualization, massage, and exercise. At the urging of one specialist, she wrote up her experience for a medical journal, and this turned into an article called "Empowering the Patient." Several drafts and a year later, it became a booklet, *A View from the Front Line*, edited by Marcia Blakenham who was, during this difficult time, often as close to Maggie as I was. To understand the main idea, as it led to her future project, it is worth quoting from her vivid and moving essay.

No patient should be asked, however kindly and however overworked the hospital staff, to sit in a corridor without further inquiry, immediately after hearing they have an estimated three to four months left to live. But even after the less devastating diagnosis of primary breast cancer most people need adjustment time before going home to do the washing up. Doctors need better training in how to break bad news. . . . In general, hospitals are not patient friendly. Illness shrinks the patient's confidence, and arriving for the first time at a huge NHS hospital is often a time of unnecessary anxiety. Simply finding your way around is exhausting. The NHS is obsessed with cutting waiting time—but waiting in itself is not so bad—it's the circumstances in which you have to wait that count. Overhead (sometimes even neon) lighting, interior spaces with no views out and miserable seating against the walls all contribute to extreme mental and physical enervation. Patients who arrive relatively hopeful soon start to wilt.

Waiting time could be used positively. Sitting in a pleasant, but by no means expensive room, with thoughtful lighting, a view out to trees, birds and sky, and chairs and sofas arranged in various groupings could be an opportunity for patients to relax and talk, away from home cares. An old-fashioned ladies' room—not a partitioned toilet in a row—with its own hand basin and a proper door in a frame—supplies privacy for crying, water for washing the face, and a mirror for getting ready to deal with the world outside again. . . .

Above all what matters is not to lose the joy of living in the fear of dying. Involvement in one's own treatment is an empowering weapon in this battle. I believe it will be proved in time to make a difference in mortality, but meantime there is a reasonable body of evidence to suggest that patients who eat healthily, keep active and take steps to deal with stress and fear, feel fewer symptoms and less pain even in the final stages of their disease. At a complementary cancer care conference at Hammersmith Hospital, a young girl spoke of how her mother had continued aerobic and dance classes to within a few weeks of her death, delighting in remaining fit and virtually pain-free—"She was," said her daughter with real happiness and pride, "so well when she died."

I have no deep illusions of long survival. . . . I mean to keep on marching down the tail of the statistical curve [of survival rates] and on, into the sunset, and then, when eventually I must die, to die as well as possible.

One can see from this the significance we both gave to the place of architecture in the healing process. Elsewhere, she highlights the importance of walking in gardens and seeing living things while waiting. As she started to develop the idea of setting up a cancer caring center, based on her experience of surviving—by now two years—she visited several "healing gardens" in California with Laura Lee, a nurse she had grown very fond of. The two of them, with me urging them on from the sidelines, began to plot a center in Edinburgh.

In the meantime, Maggie had also started another landscape project. Frank Gehry the architect, who with his wife Berta had been our close friend since the early 1970s, invited Maggie to design the wooded landscape for the Lewis House outside Cleveland, Ohio. This was a project I had seen grow in Frank's office over many years. It had mutated from very modest beginnings—as

the deconstruction of an existing sub-classical scheme—into one of the most grandiose proposals ever put forward for a private house in America. By the time Maggie joined the team in 1993, it consisted of Philip Johnson, Claes Oldenburg, Coosje van Brugen, and a landscape consultant, Fred Olins. Frank used the project to test some ideas that came to fruition later in Prague and Bilbao but his design, as it was then, had a strange anthropomorphic appearance. As Maggie and I joked, it looked somewhat like a stomach, intestines, and other bodily parts, except the images were not explicit and they were more voluptuous and tumultuous than internal organs are. Yet the body images sparked an idea in her mind. What about designing a contrasting rivulet, or line of water, that would snake through the woods? It could be in blue and red and lead the eye and mind from the house into nature. Partly this was to create a mysterious glow going through the grounds; partly it was an artery and vein leading to Frank's heart-and-stomach-shaped volumes.

It was to be constructed from natural materials as well as fiber optics placed under glass and water. And the result, if built, would have added a startling and beautiful dimension to landscape design. This was the breakthrough she made, helped by changes in circumstance and her various studies of different artistic techniques. Her experiments in painting, under the tutelage of Cecil Collins, freed her drawing style of the tight precision that had previously cramped it. Of equal importance was the liberating excess of Frank's unconventional work, and the cultural atmosphere of Los Angeles, far from the constraints of tradition and Scotland. Both inspired her to take risks. But her transformation as a designer was not to be realized; instead she applied herself entirely to the new cancer project.

In the spring of 1995, just as we were leaving Los Angeles to return to London, Maggie had the second recurrence (or third instance) of the dreaded disease. She and I knew the options now had been severely reduced although, as usual, every month brought new approaches of treatment. Eventually, however, on July 8, she succumbed, about two and a half years after her cancer had

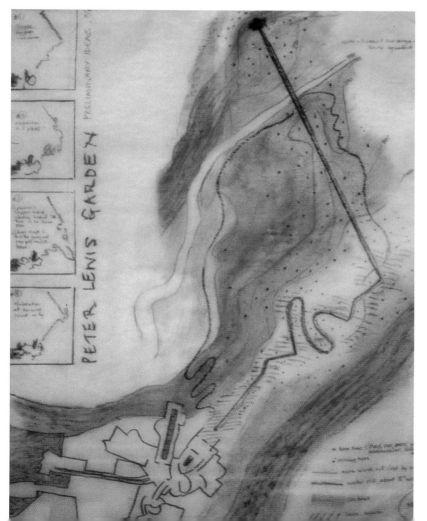

ABOVE AND LEFT: Design for Peter Lewis Garden design, Maggie Keswick, 1993. Blue and red fiber optic rills, the veins and arteries, lead to and from the central organ, the house designed by Frank Gehry.

returned, and more than two years after she had been given three months to live. She did, as she hoped she might, "die as well as possible," keeping up appearances and spirits until the final two days, and even then going to extraordinary efforts to make unexpected visitors feel at ease, as if no one were about to die. Under a dark and rainy July sky we held a funeral in Scotland at the local church, and then a memorial service at Portrack. The only bright moments in a day of Scottish drizzle came from friends who had arrived from different parts of the globe, particularly from America. Their presence gave John and Lily an idea for an unconventional gesture, and so we collected flowers from all parts of the garden. After a few speeches and a couple of drinks the more intrepid took a flower in hand and, in the pouring rain, followed the piper Hugh Drysdale up the Snail Mound, ascended to the top where they looked out across the ponds and then put a flower in a basket. They then descended by the other route, ten feet apart, two files of mourners listening to the bagpipes and seeing some of Maggie's work, particularly the way she had made the ponds curl out of view and disappear. I had not, when designing the double helix of the Snail, ever envisaged it as a place of service, but it worked well that day.

There was one surprise in store for me, which she may have intended, or not. While I had helped Maggie with her idea of a cancer caring center, and the article "Empowering the Patient," I did not know how far she and Laura Lee had pushed the idea. Maggie had asked our neighbor David Landale and me to help set up a center, but I did not fully realize two things: she had written a *Blueprint for a Cancer Caring Centre* that was legally and functionally very practical, and she had raised £70,000 for funding a place in Edinburgh. Given her circumstances in the final months, the document and her organization were extraordinary. I remember muttering to myself on finding this out, "Maggie, you've bloody well done it." With the help of David Landale, Clare, Marcia Blakenham, Derek Douglas, and several others, we managed to get a cancer caring center established at the Western General Hospital. Naturally it was run by the one person equipped for the job, Maggie's close friend in the last years, Laura Lee. She and her team steer the patients in their own self-help course as they navigate the tortuous paths of treatment and choice similar to those Maggie had traversed.

Maggie's booklet for the center, *A View from the Front Line*, was an empathetic battle plan, one patient's report of having fallen out of a plane without a parachute, and a partial map of the terrain lying ahead. It is a view, if not exactly a guide, of the kind of things you can do for yourself if you have cancer, a crisis often exacerbated by overchoice. It argues the case for empowering patients to help themselves and thereby, it is believed, extend their life and enhance the quality of life. These are the goals of what were to become "Maggie's Centres."

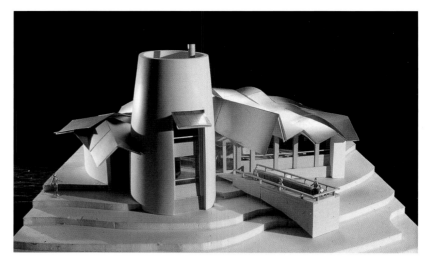

Since it was set up in 1996, the Edinburgh center has proved the ideas and sharpened the organizational model. Laura and her team have developed a potent institution that can be modified for a particular context elsewhere. As a result, other hospitals around Britain have come to us, and now twelve have received funding, both local and national, and are at various stages of realization. Some are being designed by our friends, Frank Gehry, Daniel Libeskind, David Page, Richard Rogers, Zaha Hadid, and other architects. Maggie would be amazed and of course delighted by how her efforts and ideas have taken root. The first building—a conversion of old stables next to the Western General Hospital, designed by the local Edinburgh architect Richard Murphy—has set the standard. His addition also keeps the domestic atmosphere that Maggie felt was so essential to a non-institutional building. After receiving a shattering diagnosis, patients no longer have to sit in a dank corridor and muster up social smiles of "Have a nice day." They can navigate through difficult territory in a peaceful and bright atmosphere.

Prolonging Life

Some day the story of how these centers work, and how the architecture and gardens help their healing activity, might be told. But there is an important lesson that we hope to prove in the near future and it relates, if obliquely, to the work going on in the garden. It is the strong hunch that Maggie's Centres actually extend the life of patients suffering from cancer. Prolonging life and enhancing its quality must be the major objectives of all such centers. How can we actually show they achieve these ends? It looks very hard to prove.

It is true that some studies demonstrate the positive results of patients attending cancer caring groups, but these have not used large or varied enough samples to convince the skeptics. Furthermore, there are questionable claims about the effects of attitude, faith healing, and alternative medicine, and such unsubstantiated arguments muddy the waters. When life is at stake there is nothing more dubious than raising false hopes.

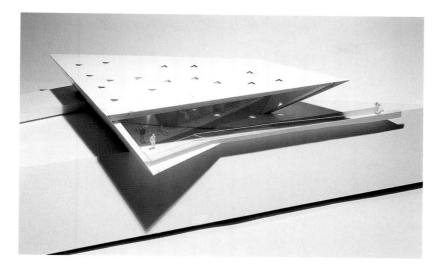

Perhaps, however, our quite different case can be made. I broached the point with Professor Alistair Munro, who works along with the Maggie's Centre in Dundee that Frank Gehry designed. He suggested that the hypothesis might be proved by what is called a Matched Pair Study. This could be started at several centers by following several thousand patients over a few years. Each one would be matched in terms of age, cancer type, background, outlook, and so on with someone not going to a center. A large enough sample of such pairs could be taken to cut out the noise in the study. I strongly believe that the results will support the hypothesis that those patients who use Maggie's Centres will prolong their lives, and for very different reasons.

First, as Maggie's example suggests, the sentence of death can itself hasten the verdict. But by questioning this inevitability, the centers can alleviate the added suffering and stress caused by the diagnosis and thus cancel the negative effects of receiving one. It is accepted science that death can be hastened by willing oneself to die, by knowing that it is inevitable and imminent. Thus those patients so affected can be helped by a stay of execution, and their new-found will to fight can become part of a positive, self-fulfilling prophecy. I imagine this would apply only to a small, if measurable, number of patients, because only a few are actually given a death sentence.

Second, it is also standard science that excessive stress (as opposed to the positive, limited variety) impairs the immune system. Since Maggie's Centres teach patients how to navigate through most of the problems that come with cancer and thereby alleviate excessive stress, these sufferers will do better on average than those who have no such training.

Thus the first two reasons for better outcomes at Maggie's Centres are based on a double negative: they combat the ill effects brought about by the diagnosis and its attendant problems. The third is more obviously positive. The empowering feelings and complementary therapies that patients receive at Maggie's Centres encourage many of them to adopt a benign lifestyle: to change their diet, exercise, relax, and take effective physical action, things that will contribute to their longevity. One might object that such enhancing activities are available to anyone, at any time—a center is not necessary to promote them. True, but it does make them a lot easier and more likely to occur.

Fourthly, Maggie's Centres assist patients to understand the many emergent therapies that may apply in their particular case, and some of these will work, if only partially. Maggie herself was frequently troubled, and elated, by all the supposed breakthroughs

ABOVE, LEFT: Maggie's Centre, Dundee, Scotland, designed by Frank Gehry, 2001. TOP: Maggie's Centre, Kirkaldy Fife, Scotland, designed by Zaha Hadid, 2003. A corten steel and glass pavilion perches over a ravine next to the hospital. LEFT: Maggie's Centre, Glasgow, designed by Page & Park, 2001–2; DNA sculpture by Charles Jencks.

we would read about and some of these exotic remedies do actually bear on a single disease. Generic diagnosis and therapy may work in some cases, but since cancer comes in maddeningly various forms of 250 different strains it often helps if one can sharpen one's focus on the particular type, and then possible remedy. Maggie's Centres help one to find a way through this complex territory of overchoice.

Finally, a certain percentage of patients will be helped even by the placebo effect: the belief that psychosomatic or attitudinal differences or changing patterns of life really do matter. This effect is highly controversial because its reverse has also been shown. That is, those who take no interest whatsoever in their cancer tend to do just as well as those who are actively involved in self-help (and they both do better than the average group). Thus having no interest and having a great interest are both beneficial. But, whatever the causes, it is not necessary to understand all the complex relationships involved here in order to show that Maggie's Centres make a positive difference in prolonging life.

All five effects are bound to work on some patients, in some ways, so that, on average, a significant number can be proven to have lived longer than those who did not attend the centers. Furthermore, an essential role is played by the architecture, gardens and art in supporting the message of transformation through self-help. They amplify this spirit not only in the patients but also in the staff. And for me this conclusion is something of a surprise. For a long time—since the 1960s and my involvement in the post-modern movement—I have been critical of what is called "architectural determination," the misguided claim that buildings shape behavior. However, my work with landscapes and with the Maggie's Centres has convinced me of a more subtle point: architecture and gardens can influence behavior when positively correlated with the activities and ethos of a group. It amplifies that activity. With cancer patients, the ambience can help turn the fight for life into what could be called the Dunkirk Spirit; art and landscape enhance the mood and potential of whatever is already going on.

Wilderness and the Void

As I mentioned in the first chapter, there is a peaceful part of the landscape at Portrack Maggie and I used to come to alone, where we had planned something of a wilderness garden. The remains of the 13th-century Portrack castle are hidden here in the undergrowth, a few stones that were not cannibalized by later farm buildings. Ferns, rhododendrons, and wild bushes surmount each other, daffodils spontaneously sprout from the side of an oak tree that had lost a branch. Parasites, cannibals, ecological succession, growth upon growth. This area we planned to end up as primeval, the first place on earth, where species evolve in rich profusion out of control. The irony of designing chaos was not lost on us.

This was where, after she died, I placed the statue of Maggie, where it would become part of the wilderness and could be seen from a bridge. The Jumping or Fractal Bridge is so called because it jumps across two streams and burrows into the ground with fractal, or self-similar shapes. The stilted curves change their shape to give it a more elastic "jump," and also allow a rowboat to pass underneath. On each side of this double bridge is the type of seat with a wide rail that might be found in a Chinese garden. These heavy rails are used to lean over and look into the water, or in this case to lean against while one has a picnic. From one the bust of Maggie can be seen looking down into the water. I find it hard to write about Maggie, adequately, and even harder not to speak about her, but what can one say that is sufficient?

It is such perplexities, the inadequacy of language, that I discussed here with my close friend, the architect Daniel Libeskind, when he was visiting Portrack in 1997. He was refugee from Lodz in Poland, and some of his family were murdered in the Holocaust. His work on the Jewish Museum in Berlin deals with the unutterability of death and the void at the heart of life. Indeed this museum that commemorates the 200,000 Berlin Jews that died has a large void that marches down the center of a zigzag, a void to which one always returns but on which one cannot walk. The zigzag itself, another kind of Drunkard's Walk, is also used to symbolize the unspeakable nature of mass extinction. Its lurching from side to side shows the pathway of the 20th century as lost, and the incomprehensibility of death. We talked about the way our design both here, and in Berlin, dealt with death and the mystery of the "plenum vacuum."

CJ: I sited the statue of Maggie here because it is the quietest most unassuming place, and also because we had decided it was a place of death that creates a riotous growth.

 **DL:** This is a place of emptiness and fullness, in a sense that the issue of death is not something you can really decide on.

CJ: In Berlin you treat it as unnamable, unexplainable.

DL: Unexplainable and not containable in the logic given of spaces.

CJ: Or of words.

DL: Yes, or of words, or of numbers.

CJ: Something you cannot figure out.

DL: You can't figure it out from the outside and you have to be inside of it—we are all inside of it anyway.

CJ: Did you put in the center of the Jewish Museum a void because it was a mystery, or was it something at the center so that you cannot escape it?

DL: The museum really has no center, it is postponed. There is no one final space you can get to, the building is continuous across the void, only a cut which runs across all time chronologies. The emptiness, the void, is not on the same track as time.

CJ: One of the great discoveries of physicists is that the plenum vacuum, the void, might have created the universe. How could everything come out of nothing—it boggles the mind. The plenum vacuum seethes with activity, the full vacuum, the empty space in outer space which cosmologists tell us is full of potential activity, of particles and anti-particles coming into and out of existence every microsecond, with one imbalance perhaps starting our universe. Is there any parallel there between the void as you see it and your void in the Jewish Museum?

DL: Well, without being facile in making comparisons to scientific thought, the building deals with the contemporary, the orientations and disorientations, visitors have to find their way across the triple route system in the underground, which is not just given, but has to be found by walking through it . . . and the light in it.

We also discussed the mysterious way death can lead to life, the cycles of decay and rebirth in nature, and the creative destruction of capitalism. All these find parallels in the quantum foam of particles coming into and out of existence every microsecond. The void, a no-place, a mystery. Words about the dead are like graves and monuments, markers of memory we hope may be adequate in some way while knowing they will not. In reviewing a book on Holocaust monuments before he designed the Jewish Museum, Libeskind noted the failures of explicit symbolism and rhetoric in dealing with issues that outstrip them. The paradox of wanting to speak and having no adequate words haunts this book on garden design.

OPPOSITE: The wilderness area and the bust of Maggie. I asked my sister, Penelope Jencks, to rework a bust of Maggie she had done in the early 1970s and placed it in this, the quietest part of the garden, the area of death, destruction, and regeneration. LEFT: With Daniel Libeskind, on the Jumping Bridge, filmed by Border Television, 1997.

The Jumping Bridge and Quantum Foam. The bridge jumps over two streams and dives into the ground. It is made from fractals that tilt against each other.

One theory about the origin of the universe is that it started out as a runaway imbalance between particles and their opposites, anti-particles. According to the Uncertainty Principle the void, or vacuum, is always seething with pairs of such virtual particles that jump into existence, from nothing, and then are annihilated by their opposite. Perhaps the origin was an imbalance that inflated very fast? In any case, the bubbling, quantum foam, as drawn here after Kip Thorne, has a fractal self-similarity like superstrings. This theme is taken up later at the base of the Universe Cascade (see Part Seven, page 198).

JUMPING BRIDGE

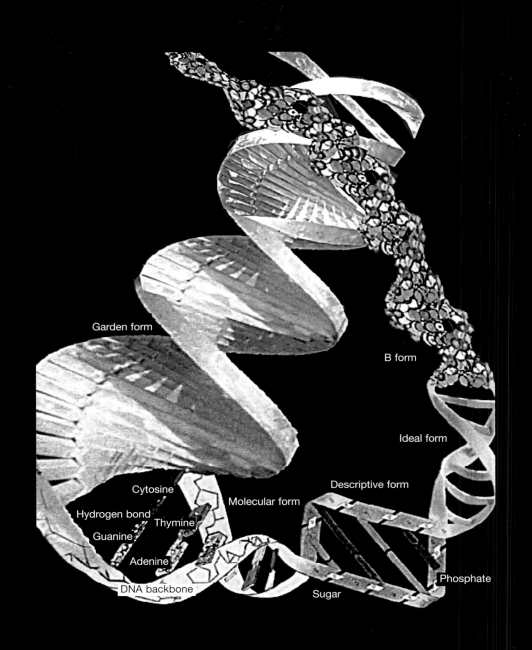

Garden form

B form

Ideal form

Descriptive form

Molecular form

Cytosine

Hydrogen bond

Thymine

Guanine

Adenine

Phosphate

DNA backbone

Sugar

PART FIVE: THE SIX SENSES GET THEIR DNA

"Take one's pain to nature," is an old nostrum. Nature spreads it out and is big enough to absorb and delineate incomprehensible feeling. After Maggie died, I started to pick up my ideas where they had been frozen. Perhaps it was never in doubt, but from this time I vowed to complete the gardens Maggie and I had started. I owed it to her; in a way, through death, she started to become my muse and I would carry on enjoyable discussions and arguments with her memory.

Many things were unresolved, particularly the kitchen garden, which was a quarter finished, exactly where we had left it when we had that argument over whether some paths should be in brick or stone. I had hoped Maggie would finish the design and I had suggested, when we came back in April 1995, that she try out two new grammars: some snake-like paths versus some fractal hedges. We did several snakes-and-ladders designs that had a lot of energy, but they were impractical since the hedges would shade, and dwarf, the vegetables we wanted to grow. Nevertheless, in principle we had settled on a new grammar, a dramatic counterpoint to the grid of stones and bricks.

It was this opposition I was playing with in my mind as I tried to imagine what structure might go in the center of each of the six rectangles. What dynamic shape might hold some creepers or roses? One day I read an article by Matt Ridley in *The Times* about what might be properly celebrated at the turn of the Millennium. He wrote that while the century's two greatest scientific discoveries belonged to the worlds of quantum and relativity physics, it was Jim Watson and Francis Crick's discovery of DNA, in 1953, that was the equivalent breakthrough in our understanding of life. Of course, he was right. DNA, that molecule with the unpronounceable name of deoxyribonucleic acid, is, in a sense, the atom of life's organization. Its four letters—A, T, C, G (representing the four molecules adenine, thymine, cytosine, and guanine)—underlie every living thing: plants, animals, fungi, even single-celled amebae. The letters always pair up so that they bond together nicely; A looks for a T and C seeks out a G. In combinations of three pairs, a codon, they code the words that write the sentences that

make the book that is a person. They do this by unraveling messenger RNA from the center of each cell, "messages" that are then "read" by ribosomes and transformed into protein.

At the time of writing, December 2002, a most extraordinary breakthrough was announced. After both the human and the mouse genome were sequenced and compared, it turned out that we share most of our DNA, these words of life. The implications are radical for the treatment of inherited conditions such as the predisposition to Alzheimer's disease, paralysis, and diabetes. One spelling mistake in 15,000 letters of a gene can cause cancer. Inevitably, during her illness, Maggie and I followed very closely all the work on gene therapy, and later, at meetings at Maggie's Centres, it was pointed out how the Genome Project will alert us, in the future, to fallibilities that lurk somewhere in everyone's inheritance. The discoveries concerning the mouse genome were celebrated because they herald the time when we will be able to edit out the errors. At the same time, another conceptual breakthrough was announced. The vast stretches that were called "junk DNA," without apparent purpose, turn out to include the master set that controls the basic genes. For instance, if we, like the mouse, have a group that codes for a tail, then with us the master set turns this basic set off. The recent discovery was justly celebrated because it shows the great extent of these editing and plot-making genes. They are probably greater in number than the elemental units of construction. To continue the analogy with books, it is as if Mother Nature wrote in two kinds of mode, with "highly conserved" sub-assemblies—heart, lungs, kidneys, brain etc., comparable to the archetypal themes in literature—and composes them with "more variable" master assemblies that specify their arrangement in a specific organism—the plot of an individual book. As a result, although we share 98 percent of the sub-assemblies with the chimpanzee and almost as much with the mouse, we are not 98 percent like either mammal, thanks to those genes that used to be dismissed as "junk."

Such discoveries constitute a fundamental lesson for our time. DNA and RNA are the basic words of nature and therefore suitable elements for us to celebrate in a garden. Also fitting is the double helical structure of DNA, something I had already used on the Snail Mound, because it affords a beautiful climbing frame for plants.

The representations of DNA stylize several of its pertinent qualities and here grow out of each other.

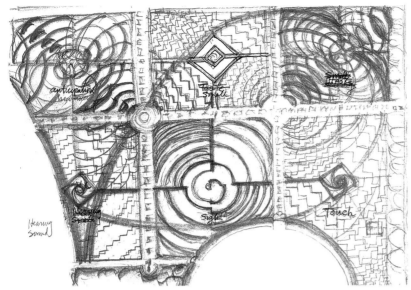

I set about researching DNA and to my delight found that, fortuitously for the existing plan, it unwound its messages from the center of each cell. Fantastic, what luck, I already had six rectangular areas, each with a central section. QED, I could put six different DNA where we had anticipated the six senses and grow things up them and have them send out messenger RNA into what suddenly became six symbolic biological cells! It all fell into place: DNA in the nucleus of the cell, where it really exists, and the cell walls or membranes represented by the existing boxwood. Such are the small victories of symbolic design. An iconographic program is a loaded gun. It helps aim design in some ways and rules out other targets, and this teleology spurs one on to greater creativity. Another analogy brings out the virtues of symbolic design. It is like unearthing an archeological site, hot on the scent of discovering gold or a Rosetta Stone, convinced there is something pre-existing waiting to be dug up, not invented. Then when things fall into a plot, a result of luck and symbolic intention, it is the gift of telos, a rare creative moment that happened a few more times, as I shall later recount.

Soon I had decided to show DNA in some of its different incarnations: ugly when tightly coiled and beautiful as we commonly know it, stretched out in a smooth double helix. Here I faced some choices so typical of symbolic design. What should I abstract, what represent, what suppress and what express as the essence of the molecule? Textbooks were consulted and the five or six common ways of depicting DNA were sketched and tested against different materials. At first I thought concrete blocks or oak blocks might form the curved coils, the sugar and phosphate molecules that hold the four letters in place, and these could be represented by galvanized metal bars with a twist in the center, the hydrogen bond that unites the letters. Sketches, sketches and more sketches followed, then small models in foam board and large, full-scale models in styrofoam.

Through these simulacra I was gaining confidence in the expression, but I wanted to tighten the design with appropriate detail. Once when I returned to Portrack, I invited friends, the biologist Nancy Lane and Steven and Hilary Rose, both knowledgable about DNA, to spend the weekend and help me with conceptual design. They fine-tuned some of the points I had not grasped and suggested further building blocks of life, some plants such as rosemary that might well serve either as the ribosomes, or the proteins of the cells.

Not for the first time did I find scientists ready to give their expertise, and not even asking to be paid for it. Exploitation? Sure, but willingly granted. Why, I have often mused, do scientists often share their knowledge so generously? Like architects they have a professional tradition that encourages joint authorship, sharing, mutual creativity. There is a utopian and ethical side to this and then, with the garden, the obvious pleasure they find in transforming first nature into second and third nature. They, as much as I, become involved in a fascinating game. Can one find, or invent, the points in common between function, form, and the icons of science? It is a game of truth and transformation played for high stakes. You cannot cheat with DNA or the atom, add an electron just because it is better looking or more functional for your purposes; and yet you cannot merely illustrate the textbook clichés either. You have to criticize the metaphors of science where they are lax and celebrate the truths where they are exceptional.

What recent discovery is more important, more amazing than DNA, the molecule of all life? But how precise and clumsy its name is: deoxyribonucleic acid. And how pedestrian are the diagrams that illustrate it for the schoolroom. As teaching models these horribly colored wobbly plastic children's toys may be fine, but as celebrations they sag, as pathetic as the DNA clichés that Damien Hirst has copied from a catalog and presented as art. Think if the Greeks had discovered the ultimate truth of DNA—would they have depicted it like a synthetic noodle?

About the time that scientists were helping me, November 1997, I also started working on model building with another close friend, Madelon Vriesendorp, the wife of the architect Rem Koolhaas. One advantage of design over writing is that it can be a collaborative exercise where opposite ideas can be bounced around separately, then combined. She, with a surrealist sensibility and skill at translating zany ideas into colorful images, would bring me strange presents—a six-inch concrete eye, painted vertically; plastic green fingers with long red fingernails, and other body-parts that suggested the importance of the senses. Some of these were used later in ways unforeseen at the time. For instance, I had the green/red fingernails cast into aluminum talons for one generalized sense, and she painted her giant eye on to a plastic dome to crown the Sense of Sight. Madelon was a tonic and spur during some lonely years and, with Rem, kept me pushing the edge of the Garden of Common Sense further and further out.

By then, of course, it had changed from being a kitchen garden to a Physics Garden to one based on the Six Senses and then the DNA. Each layer added to, rather than negated, the previous one. Equally important in constructing what had now become a compound metaphor were the carpenter Bobby and the blacksmith John Gibson.

John, a soft-spoken Scot, is like Bobby, a perfectionist who is not afraid to take chances and try something new. He started work at Portrack on the Soliton Gates and through them had perfected the art of twisting metal so that it bent both smoothly and quickly. The smooth bend gives the gentle continuous curve, what they call "sweet" in southern Scots, while the quick turn, sometimes under heat, makes the metal fail and this sudden rupture results in a beautiful new detail, the symmetrical twist. This is Catastrophe Theory in action again. When metal fails suddenly it usually results in a chaotic ruckle with bulges and depressions happening any which way. Not so with John's masterful control. He learned this

method first on small square section bars of steel, then worked up to larger dimensions of aluminum—2-, 3-, and finally 4-inch sections.

The first DNA model built was the Sense of Touch, constructed out of oak and galvanized tube. Before starting we examined various models of DNA and I explained the significance of the structure and the molecules to Alistair, Bobby and John. The way the letters A, T, C, G are encoded in triplets, the way the messenger RNA swirls out of the cell nucleus, the way a double helix folds together. They listened tolerantly, if somewhat ironically. My focus was on what the content and expression of the twisting shapes might be, while they were trying to figure out how to get oak helices and steel cross bars to spiral up in a diminishing curve. The what and the how had to grow together. So it has been with other collaborations.

Four plans for the DNA Garden. The first plan shows interfering waveforms spreading from the center of each cell, the nucleus from where the DNA uncoils.

The next plan shows the paths laid out in their final form, the messenger RNA coming out of the nucleus and unzipping and being "read" by the ribosomes (blue and orange) and the linear planting rows that undulate on the curves of the coils.

The third planting plan, 1998, shows the extended code of the cells including the mitochondria (red tubs of flowers) and "torque fields," where different species interpenetrate. Here also the two central cells are conceived at a different height than the other ones: the higher is given to Sight and the lower to Smell. Visually strong keystone species morph in color and shape along the diagonals, forming a backbone for the smaller or transient species.

The final plan, "Cosmic DNA," an axonometric drawn with Liane Wilcher, emphasizes the metamorphosis further. Species of similar color, or different versions of the same species, blur one into the next in a seamless way. These plants, worked out in discussions with Louisa Lane Fox and Alistair Clark, are perennials chosen to give a continuous color background for the annually planted vegetables. To the right seven colors of heather morph into each other below the amelanchier. All is metamorphosis.

Because the small homosote models I made could fail in different ways, we had no idea if the Sense of Touch would stand up, concertina, or sag to one side. In the event, the two double helices sagged only a bit. Bobby brought the oak swirls to a tightly coiled ring at the top—the ugly form of DNA that we wanted to mimic—and John made a thin, triple-twist support for the aluminum hand. This now waves in the breeze beckoning visitors. It oscillates back and forth above the thorns, thistles and nettles that grow on one side, and the lamb's ear and dock weed that grow on the other. Thus the Sense of Touch is heightened by prickly and soothing plants, those that assault the fingers and those that assuage the pain.

This worked well enough to make the idea of five more DNA structures plausible. The questions were where to locate the other senses, and what the Sixth Sense would be. The last question had a literary if not scientific answer—it is anticipation, the so-called female sense of intuition, the ability of women to pick up subtle moods that supposedly escape men. Surprisingly, there are many more senses, including those in plants and animals. Fishes, for instance, have a sixth sense known as the lateral line, an area running down both sides of the body. Receptors here perceive shifts in the current and they allow the fish to pick up close moving signals, both as predator and prey.

Aristotle numbered the human senses as five, a definition that stuck especially in the popular mind. But recently scientists discovered we have several more, such as a sense of balance (located partly in the inner ear) and movement, the kinaesthetic sense. Furthermore, internalized senses register the amount of salt and sugar we need and, as if we were oversized but insensitive shrimp, we discern a vague sense of air and water pressure. We have, considered abstractly, about fifteen senses that transduce electromagnetic signals from one medium and send them to parts of the brain. The human being is a buzzing sensorium tuned to the electromagnetic spectrum of the universe. Thus the first plans were conceived as a series of overlapping and interfering waveforms.

These were further refined by the DNA curves, as they unwrapped from the central nucleus. A few more conversations, with scientists Mae-Wan Ho and Peter Saunders, led to a post-modern interpretation of the way cells communicate with each other. They are not just passive recipients of DNA, or vehicles for selfish genes. The fact that cells exchange information with each other all the time, and do so to keep alive, led to the idea of locating the *ambigrammi* at these junctions. These are very appropriate signs of information exchange—words that can be read two ways. Thus the cells and DNA now communicate across the whole garden, even on the diagonal, giving a pattern of linear waves. As can be seen in the drawings, the different colored species create a new style of Linearism.

Transduction, the Miracle of the Senses

Every perception of the external world entails an extraordinary translation event. First, an energy wave—in the case of light, an electromagnetic wave—hits a specialized receptor cell. In the eyes these are rods and cones, 126 million rods and 4 million cones, the former responsible for peripheral vision, the latter for focused, sharp vision. When photons of light hit these receptors, they transduce the energy, turning it into electrochemical energy of another form. Such transduction goes on in all the senses, in effect translating the language of the universe—energy waves—into the language of the nervous system—electrical impulses. These travel through nerve bundles to the brain. The transducer cells are magicians that turn shorter wavelengths of light into purple and blue, and longer ones into red. They can discriminate 200 gradations within this continuous spectrum of wavelengths.

In the ear, tiny hair cells are stretched and strained by energy in the form of sound waves, and these transducer cells translate mechanical energy into electrical signals—music or noise or poetry. All receptor cells are sensitive to differences in energy levels, intensity and quality.

In the abstract they can be conceived as fingers waving in the breeze, antennae picking up signals, then turning the stimulus into another language to be passed to a nerve bundle, and then to an interpreter, the central nervous system, and then to the brain. Finally the perception is to be decoded and understood by the mind. This five-step process is abstracted in the Sixth Sense.

LEFT: the hydrogen bond—a twist—and the four letters A, T, C, G. INSET: Working with John Gibson on DNA. ABOVE: Senses generalized. Sense impressions come through a receptor, here fingers, and are transduced into nerve impulses resolved by the brain and mind.

DNA MODELS

The first idea was to build the double helix in steel and lightweight concrete and to metamorphose the blocks into ice crystals, which would become tightly curved at the top. In the end these ideas led to the use of different materials, but the expressive nature of the curves and coiling remained.

Sketches were made exploring the way the DNA unravels into RNA when it breaks out of the nucleus, and alternatives tried for showing the letters A, T, C, G, and the hydrogen bond between them, as abstractions. Again these ideas were modified, but still an important step toward a solution.

Madelon Vriesendorp and I made five or six models for the aluminum DNA that expressed its dynamic, flying nature and explored the possibility of walking under its supporting coils.

CULTURAL DNA—A REBUS

All the paths are divided up into rectangular steps with symbols of the four letters, A, T, C, G, etched in the concrete. Pairs of letters are joined in threes, called codons. The genetic code has an obvious parallel with language, so why not show this in one part of the garden?

The result is the rebus with the following codons in three pairs: "You See Before U unlock the wheel of time a great chain of rings . . . R U open 2 see fantastic links or do U call a spade a spade . . . Great power chains one 2 excess so wrench open yr mind's eye and jump . . . see file record a date 2000." FOLLOWING PAGE: View of the DNA garden.

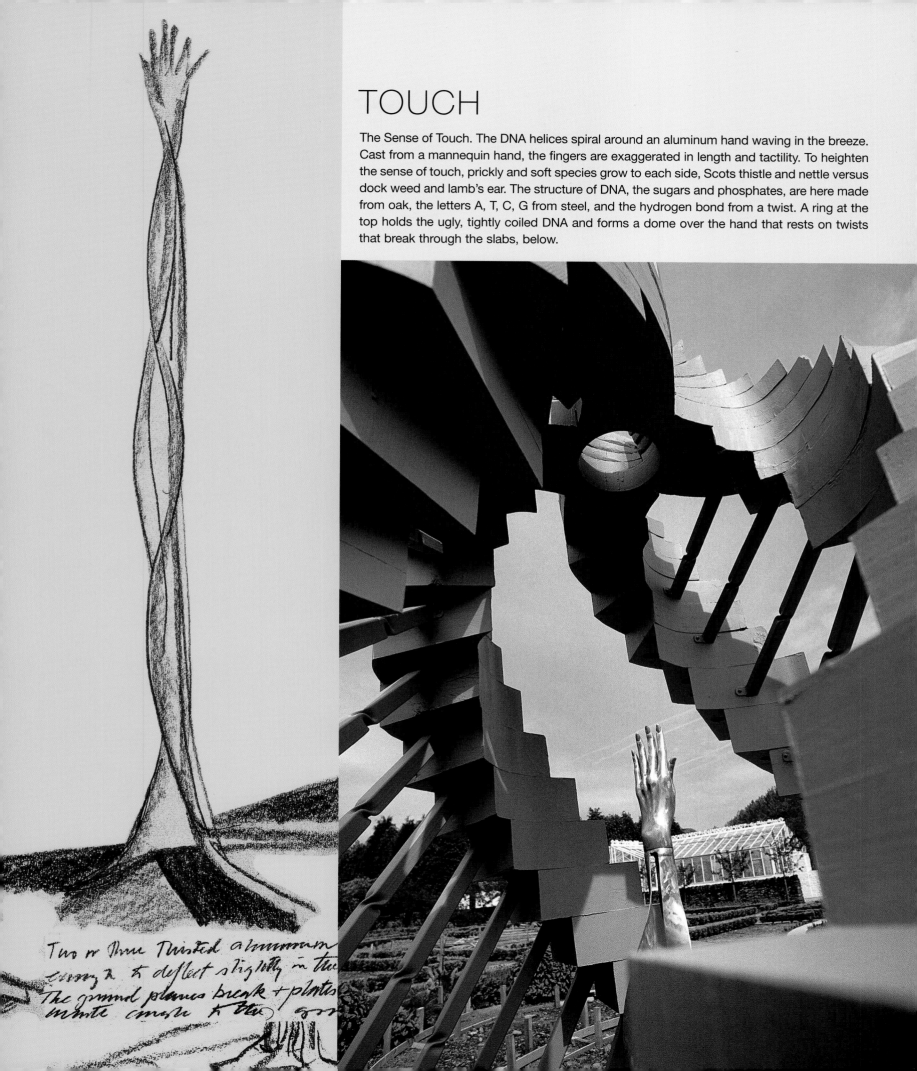

TOUCH

The Sense of Touch. The DNA helices spiral around an aluminum hand waving in the breeze. Cast from a mannequin hand, the fingers are exaggerated in length and tactility. To heighten the sense of touch, prickly and soft species grow to each side, Scots thistle and nettle versus dock weed and lamb's ear. The structure of DNA, the sugars and phosphates, are here made from oak, the letters A, T, C, G from steel, and the hydrogen bond from a twist. A ring at the top holds the ugly, tightly coiled DNA and forms a dome over the hand that rests on twists that break through the slabs, below.

TASTE

The Sense of Taste sends its unwinding coils leaping over the paths, structural supports that twist and frame the sky. They spiral down to an large aluminum mouth on one side and tongue on the other that are embedded in two types of very tasty wild strawberries. Braising or scoring the aluminum enhances the highlights by making them patchy or contrasting with dark spots. The letters A, T, C, G are again separated by the hydrogen bond created from a twist, now quite a beautiful detail that results naturally from bending the section under heat.

SMELL

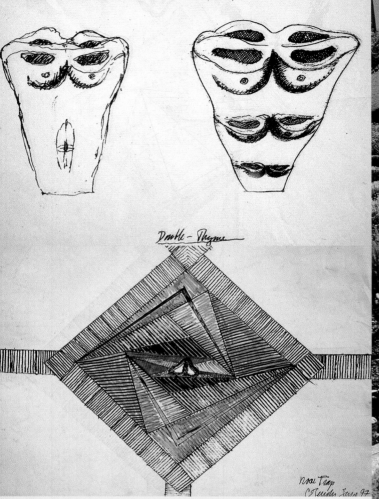

One descends into the ground on a splayed double helical path stepping over four kinds of thyme to smell the giant nostrils of a double nose put back to back. The fragrance wafts upward from each step.

The fortuitous encounter of an upside-down double nose and the pun "Double Thyme" leads to the phrase: "A Nose By Any Other Name Would Smell As Sweet." A conclusion? The discovery that two joined noses equals a fiberglass female torso. This illustrates the general scientific principle recently enunciated by complexity scientists as a truth of emergence in the universe. The Nobel laureate Philip Anderson put it succinctly in a famous 1972 article. In contrast to the Modernist dictum "less is more," the principle of emergence is "more is different." When things are combined more meaning emerges, a most benevolent principle behind the universe.

An ear gently swings in the breeze, emitting various sounds—clangs and tinkles. Suddenly the wind catches the parabolic reflector and gives it a spin, and snap go the chimes below.

This oak-sided DNA rises above white flowering anaphalis and when the oak finally weathers and turns silver the whole composition, including the stones, will have a common silver-gray tone. Also planned for the future is another parabolic reflector, a hundred yards away, aimed precisely to exchange sound waves with this one. When this is finished one will be able to whisper across the garden. Waves of vibrating air are transduced into sound through the middle ear—another miracle of the senses.

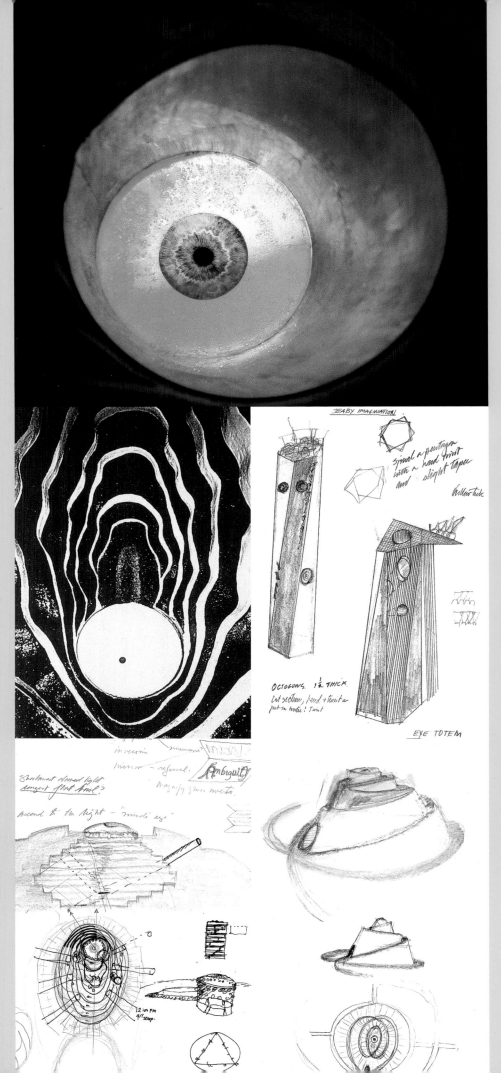

ZEABY IMAGINATION

Sqread a pentagon
with a hard point
and slight taper

William tick

OCTOGONS. 1½ THICK.
Cut section, bend + twist or
put on water! Turn!

EYE TOTEM

SIGHT

The DNA Garden needed a high point from which to view all the senses, and so here the double helix is a grassed mound. "More is different" again. The "more" becomes another surprise: around the back, hidden from view, is a black cave-like entrance to a secret grotto, a place of escape into another world.

One enters the womb-like space. Horizontal lines of black and white dazzle the eye as they metamorphose from the base to the top, from straight lines to undulating folds. What strange objects appear in the gloom? Light cannons, tiny telescopes, are oriented toward the morning and evening sun. Small holes aimed at high noon project an "M" on to the wall at certain moments of the year. Two seats, with optical vibrations below, have eyes on the top. If one discovers how, these tops can be rotated, revealing more hidden pleasures and words—or sat upon for private conversation. An eye totem is straight ahead which also pivots. It is punctured by several peepholes revealing further messages and optical illusions. One then finally sees into the lantern through which light spills and discovers the eye-dome, the theme in the garden of reflection, of looking back on the universe and its history. The dome as an eye on the cosmos has a long history. This grotto has so much more than meets the eye.

I once asked Maggie, "What is the Sixth Sense, the female sense of anticipation?" She raised her hands in front of her face and, wiggling her fingers slowly, answered, "Intuition is sensing the winds of change, the way things are going, the mood of the moment, and how it will affect the future." Here a woman, cantilevered off an automobile spring so she gently bounces in the wind, contemplates her open brain and the impulses coming into it through her antennae, the fingers. These are also cantilevered on springs so they too undulate in the breeze—as do the passionflowers and love-in-a-mist. Waves in synchrony and counterpoint.

Intuition is not a normal sense, nor limited to women, but the idea that it could be presented through moving fingers grasping at a thought just out of reach was a favorite notion of Einstein. He referred to brilliant scientific intuition as "fingerspitzengefühl," a feeling at the tips of one's fingers, and believed a developed sense of this anticipatory sensitivity was essential for scientific inquiry.

This sculpture reveals sense impression in general. Impressions hit a receptor—eye, finger, tongue—which then feeds impulses to the brain. These then have to be processed by the neurons and memory and made coherent, and finally questioned by the mind. The act of sensing and understanding thus goes beyond the instantaneous single action that one feels. Intuition is counter-intuitive: while it appears to be quick and spontaneous, it actually takes effort, calculation, and memory.

LEFT: The DNA Garden, prior to completion, showing the RNA paths. RIGHT, ABOVE AND CENTER: The completed DNA Garden. RIGHT, BELOW: DNA sculptures at Maggie's Centre, Glasgow.

ABOVE: This DNA sculpture, at the Centre for Life, Newcastle 2000, was commissioned by Matt Ridley. RIGHT: This version, at Cold Spring Harbor, was commissioned by James Watson, the co-discoverer of DNA. BELOW, LEFT: At the opening with Tom Shakespeare, James Watson, and Matt Ridley. BELOW, RIGHT: A sketch of DNA for Maggie's Centre, Glasgow.

PART SIX: ULTIMATE METAPHORS

Questioning Modern Metaphors

Since building a garden takes so long I must return to a previous stage in the design saga. Soon after we had finished building the landforms, the Snail and Snake Mounds, Maggie asked me to design a transition between the house and the hollow right outside, the dip in the landscape that leads to Crow Wood and the Nonsense. From time to time this area had been grazed by cows and sheep and it was therefore bounded by an ugly barbed wire fence. In the future we wanted animals to continue grazing there, and thus needed a wall high enough to keep them from getting next to the house, particularly roe deer that can jump six feet. So, bearing in mind the basic metaphor of a landscape of waves, and thinking in particular of the surprising properties of the soliton, I went about merging several waveforms to form an undulating wall. From the house side it became a modified ha-ha, that is, a drop in height not visible from the house. The illusion seems to make the landscape come right up to the building, while the actual drop keeps the animals away. According to the pun one is supposed to come upon this sudden drop in earth with surprise—"Ah-ha!"

Working on these waveforms while also studying aspects of quantum physics made me think about the ubiquity of waves: light waves, water waves, quantum waves of all types, even the supposed gravity waves: gravitons. As previously mentioned, if waves are, like particles, the ultimate stuff of the universe, they should find primary expression in a garden. Yet, for Modern thinkers since the time of Newton, particles have been the primary reality and, as his view of the atom shows us, materialism has dominated our metaphysics, and metaphors about the universe. Primordial material, in his words, was "solid, massy, hard, impenetrable, movable particles . . . even so very hard, as never to wear or break in pieces." By contrast, for us, the complementary aspects had come to the fore: the self-organizing, mostly empty atom of whirling waves. That new view might be true of the microcosm, but what of the macrocosm, the galaxies, and the universe as a whole?

Consider the importance of our world-view. The images we use to describe ourselves, nature and the cosmos come back to haunt us. As Virgil said, "We make our destinies through the gods we choose." First we construct mental pictures and then, through feedback, they construct us. If, as Richard Dawkins has written in *The Selfish Gene*, we are conceived as robotic vehicles for genes, we may—even knowing this is a literary conceit—be encouraged to think that our genes are in control. We make our destinies through the metaphors we choose and, if Modern ones are often mechanistic and reductive, how should we construct new ones based on our new understanding of reality? This question continued to nag me as I got to work on some terraces to be placed between the two soliton waves.

I should reiterate that functional and philosophical questions were equally absorbing. Not only were the walls necessary to exclude animals, but so too was a place to eat outdoors in the summer months. The tables and chairs used for dining would have sunk into the damp soil by two inches by the end of the meal. So function demanded a solid terrace and bench for drinks and sitting. Another benefit of multiple motives? When function, formal composition and reference come together, a resonant symbol is created where the meaning fluctuates ambiguously from one level to another. Unlike gratuitous or simple design it can never be exhausted from one perspective.

The supper terrace was sited on a flat plateau by the trunk of a large sycamore tree Maggie had played under as a child, with a swing on its largest branch. From here in mid-June one can see the sun set almost due north and it rises only an hour later. Summer sunsets over the Dumfrieshire hills are the most propitious time to experience the garden as it turns a dramatic red and black-green. The terrace was designed to appreciate these moments and, because it was fairly close to the main house, Clare was worried when I told her it was also going to celebrate one of the most interesting, recent discoveries: the existence of black holes and the way they might be major actors in creating and destroying large parts of the universe. She imagined that the design would compete for attention with other things in the landscape or be too modern or ugly. She never said any of this, but I could read it in her eyes and so I set about designing a terrace that was a discreet black hole.

The ha-ha consists of soliton waveforms that pass through each other offering unbroken views of the landscape and connecting it to the terraces. Apart from being a functional feature, it constitutes a sudden and surprising "symmetry break" in itself.

"Black Hole" is Almost a Good Metaphor

As Einsteinian physics has it, "matter tells space how to curve," and the denser the matter, or the greater its gravity, the more it tells space to curve. Under normal conditions we perceive space as flat or extending in straight lines, but actually, around a massive object such as the sun, it is bent considerably, and around a black hole both space and time are swallowed into a vortex altogether, eaten up, destroyed. Most metaphors derived from science are either mechanistic or inept, but "black hole" is fairly good. All matter and light near this whirlpool are sucked in, so it is black, and the force of the implosion creates a tear in spacetime, so it is a "hole."

How are these metaphors of whirlpool, of space being ripped apart, and blackness translated into a design? On approaching the terrace one sees at first a wide curve, the "event horizon" of the black hole. Beyond this rotating disc of supergravity, matter and light cannot escape. This sharp curve and the further cuts in the landscape that a rotating black hole would make are represented by thin black ridges set against the green grass. Then, as one descends into the terrace and is literally pulled at an oblique angle by the tilt of the earth, by gravity, one looks down and sees space being stretched apart. Scientists say that if we could actually fall into a black hole we would be spaghettified; that is, we would become an elongated string of spaghetti and our legs, closer to the zero point, would be stretched much further than our head.

This bizarre possibility is not shown in the terrace, but the stretching of space is represented. The aluminum grid is warped and stretch-marks are etched in it as v-shaped grooves. These also make the metal slip-resistant, a necessary safety precaution because the warp of real gravity pulls one down toward the vanishing point, just as it would inside a black hole. While the warped grid shows space being stretched, it also shows time being compressed. As one heads for the zero point, the units of Astroturf and aluminum get closer and closer and closer. Finally one reaches the singularity of the black hole—the point of total disappearance—and steps over this nothing, this absence. According to some theories one might even travel through a wormhole and re-emerge into another spacetime, that of a white hole. This, if it were possible, might be accompanied by the rush of continuous creation in another, baby universe. Such are the amazing, but current, speculations of scientists, and one is meant to contemplate them as one steps over the void and reaches the dining terrace.

Recently more and more black holes have been found, and some physicists hold the uncanny idea that the universe as a whole can be conceived as one. As I will discuss, there is probably one at the

The Black Hole Terrace radiates black cuts through the landscape. Theoretically a worm hole (right) may lead to a White Hole or one universe to another (above, right).

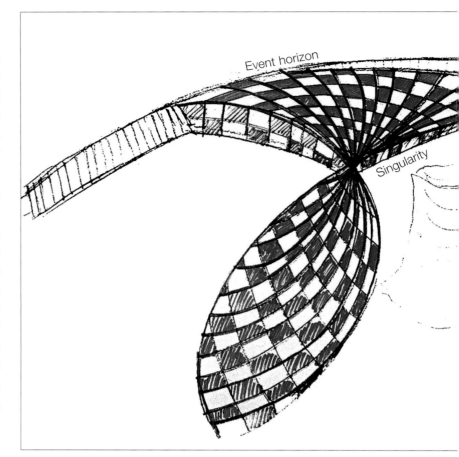

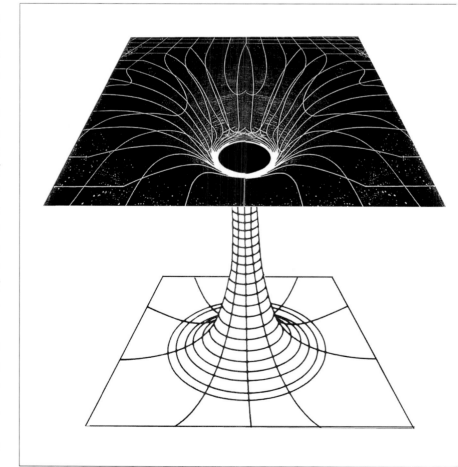

Event horizon

center of every galaxy and they play a seminal role in galactic formation. So the black hole as a total universe, or as the creator of galaxies, turns these enigmatic objects into something more than the playthings of science fiction or even their usual metaphor of being a dark void. They become as basic as the atom, as essential to creation as Gaia, and so invite further speculative naming.

Recent descriptions of black holes are extremely provocative. Judging by the evidence from quasars (quasi-stellar objects that emit an abundance of radio waves), they are key for the creation of cosmic bodies at all scales. Since the 1990s black holes have been found at the center of galaxies, with a size and weight proportional to that of the galaxy. For instance, at the center of our relatively small galaxy, the Milky Way, is a black hole with a mass 2.5 million times that of the sun; but at the center of the bigger Andromeda galaxy, near by, is one of 30 million sun masses. They are massive and controlling. Even the speed of the stars circling at the outermost galactic edge is controlled by the size of these monsters. They are all-powerful, generative, and, one wants to say (although it would be absurd), omniscient. When they are very big, spinning fast and ripping space apart in a feeding frenzy, scientists call them supermassive black holes, as if adding super to massive would make them much too big to think about. And their contrary properties are very hard to comprehend. At one and the same time they are absolutely massive and invisible, creative *and* destructive.

But the paradoxes do make one reflect on their importance and challenge the metaphors used to describe them. When very young, at the beginning of the universe 13 billion years ago, they formed at the center of a gaseous cloud. As they grew in size, eating the material around them, their rotational speed heated the surrounding gas and ignited stars into existence. The force of their energy can be gauged by the fact that they hurl stars, near the riotous core, at the amazing speed of 500,000 kilometers per hour, and their rotational effect can be felt even on the outermost stars of the galaxies. They tie the whole system tightly together. In effect, their birth and development actually creates the galaxies, stars, and by extension the planets, like a fecund whirling dervish spewing out children. But then, as if this mixed metaphor were not enough, in a further feeding frenzy the increasing rotational energy drives the inner stars away from the center. At this point the black hole has nothing to feed on, and becomes dormant. It continues to spin silently at the heart of the galaxy until maybe, like our own black hole at the center of the Milky Way, it starts feeding again, turning nearby stars bright hot as they are swallowed into the mouth of the vortex.

"Swallowing, destroying, black, invisible, creating like a mother?" Should we rechristen this pregnant void as a monster goddess, or an invisible mother? Because she brings all large bodies

into being might her appropriate name, and metaphor, be not "black hole" but "invisibilia"?

What would be the point of this? No one any longer, as the church used to do, tries to enforce the naming of events or, like the French Academy, establish usage. But, in the small world of a garden, we can speculate on what might be a conscious decision, the choice of image and name that bring out the salient characteristics of some basic actors in the universe. The black hole is a protagonist, a main agent of change.

Next to the dining terrace black hole is another one, naturally functioning as a seat and serving table. The patterns are canonic. The outer circles are a swirling spiral of stars that rise, characteristically, toward circular lips that surround the vortex. Here is a stream of deadly particles, the invisible central maw—all aspects photographed recently by the Hubble space telescope and thought to be typical of large black holes. It could be invisibilia, the nourishing eater of all things, whose stream of energized particles has been seen to shoot out into space a plasma jet some ten thousand light years long. This

potent source is here presented by an aluminum spiral that spins a beam of light up to the branch of the overhanging tree.

While the terrace was under construction, it was fortunate that the theoretical physicist Lee Smolin happened to be staying for the weekend. Lee is a subtle and synthetic thinker willing to build radically new structures on top of old standard models in order to pull them together. Ceaselessly looking for the unification of quantum theory, cosmology, and relativity theory that has eluded scientists since Einstein, he has the slightly detached melancholic air of a man who knows how much patience this search requires, and that it may not be rewarded soon, if ever. His training at Harvard, and professorship at Penn State University have made him something of a realist. At the same time his romantic drive is also apparent, the pursuit of the ultimate theory. This is sometimes called the Theory of Everything, or TOE, and, while it certainly does not live up to its name and encompass all things, it does seek to unify the physical forces. The pursuit of this theory is an eternal passion, a Platonic affair of the heart.

We had several discussions concerning black holes and the way they might play a fundamental role in creating new universes, ones that are tuned just right for a universe balanced on a pencil point, and the emergence of life. At this stage of his research, in 1997, he was applying Darwinian ideas of selection to cosmology.

CJ: One of the most extraordinary things about this universe is how well balanced the parameters are, the constants and the laws.

LS: This is very surprising but it seems to be the case. People have discovered that if the parameters were slightly different the universe would not have atomic nuclei in it, so there would not be stars. There also would not be atomic physics, and the enormous variety of different forms of matter. It seems this variety really does depend on the constants being tuned quite precisely in nature and we do not understand that.

CJ: When people look at this exquisite balance today, they think it is either a put-up job (i.e. God created it) or some laws created it. You are giving another explanation.

LS: There ought to be an explanation which is rational and scientific and that means one of two things. The first is that consistency determines everything and the problem of having a consistent unification of quantum theory and relativity is that the different forces can only go together in one way, in which case that must be right. That's what most of us have thought: that we are looking for a single unification to solve everything. The alternative, with Superstring Theory and Quantum Gravity, is that there may be many possible unifications, but they don't go together very well.

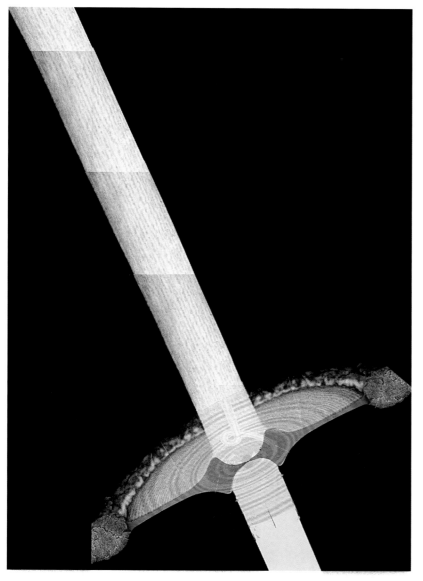

OPPOSITE AND LEFT: Rotating black holes that are actively feeding and spinning fast have a characteristic shape that has been studied by the Hubble telescope. An outer galactic whirlpool of stars centers on a bowl shape. This rises on both sides of the accretion disk, and beyond its lip a jet of electrons emerges, shooting almost at the speed of light. The strong radio waves coming from the center probably indicate a feeding frenzy.

At the center, and invisible, is the supermassive black hole, creating in energetic rotations the supernovae, stars, planets, and heavy chemical elements that make up life; at the same time it is constantly devouring gas, matter, and stars. A new metaphor for this Janus-faced entity—invisibilia? The way spacetime is ripped and stretched and the stars are hurled about is shown in the landscape. The tail of the galaxy rises out of the ground, and leaps across to the center, which rises in a bowl and then focuses on the aluminum spiral. The latter two elements serve in the garden as a chair back, table, and structure for a growing plant. ABOVE: Discussing the salient aspects of a black hole with Lee Smolin, 1997, as filmed by Border Television.

Consistency is not strong enough. So in some real sense there is a choice that has to be made and if so, and the universe is all there is, the universe must itself have made that choice. So we have to understand how it is that a system can organize itself to make a choice. We don't want to say that there was a choice imposed from the outside by God.

CJ: So you are trying to find an inner choice, that the universe self-organizes itself in such a way to choose the best parameters—these almost miraculous parameters. How does your theory explain that?

LS: The only part of science where something like that is well understood is in biology. We understand how a choice that is made in the system can lead to the organization of the system, to greater complexity, and so the idea that I have been working with is to try to mimic that logic in cosmology. That logic needs reproduction, and variation and then selection, so that those things which reproduce themselves more often are more prevalent. This last step is just a logical tautology.

CJ: So what mechanism are you proposing?

LS: A number of us have looked at various different ones, the one that seems to work best, at the moment, uses the notion of a black hole.

CJ: Why?

LS: It's an old idea, going back to the 1960s, that black holes may actually lead to the reproduction of new universes.

CJ: You are saying there are many other universes around?

LS: If this idea is right then our big bang is the result of the collapse of a black hole in another region of space and time, and every one of the black holes in our region of space and time which evolved from the big bang that we see leads to another such region.

CJ: So big bangs come out of black holes, in effect?

LS: According to this idea, yes. And this, by the way, is an idea that goes back to Johnny Wheeler and other people.

CJ: You are saying that these black holes lead to new baby universes, and that everywhere we look, we are discovering more black holes and perhaps at the center of every galaxy there is a black hole?

LS: There seems to be a black hole at the center of every galaxy. But there are probably many, many more than that because whenever a very massive star comes to the end of its life and burns out its nuclear fuel it explodes as a supernova, and a certain proportion of those supernovae leave a relic which is a black hole. That could be many more than just the number of galaxies. If you make a rough estimate of how often that has happened since our big bang it is something like a billion billion times.

CJ: Ten to the eighteenth power.

LS: Ten to the eighteenth power.

CJ: 1,000,000,000,000,000,000. There are that many black holes?

LS: Yes, it's a reasonable guess.

CJ: In our universe alone. Each one of those can lead to a new universe, is that right?

LS: Yes, it's scary, but yes.

CJ: And what happens in those new universes?

LS: This is where you need variation. If you want to mimic natural selection in biology, you have to say those new universes that have been created have laws and parameters which are very similar to ours but not precisely the same. There have to be some small mutations, some small changes.

CJ: But why should they be small?

LS: For the same reasons that mutations have to be small in biology; otherwise you don't get the accumulation of what people call "frozen accidents" leading to greater complexity.

CJ: There is a kind of gradual evolution, one universe leading into the next, like generations of species.

LS: That's what this theory says.

CJ: So there would be a clustering of baby universes, one after the other?

LS: Yes. If there are universes choosing laws that lead to greater production of black holes, then after a while those universes will proliferate and overwhelm in numbers the others. It's a simple idea.

CJ: It's a simple idea, but it implies that in the future everywhere will be a black hole.

LS: No, because they create the space. An important idea to grasp, and it's one of the important ideas in relativity theory, is that space is not something absolute. Space, in Einstein's relativity theory, is an aspect of relationships amongst things. So there is not a fixed amount of space. Space can be created, and is created. This accounts for the expansion of the universe.

CJ: But you are saying that there is a kind of internal selection for universes creating more black holes.

LS: Just by the numbers. You have some population and you pick one at random: is it more likely to have come from one that had many, many progeny or from one that just had a few progeny? It is much more likely to have come from one that had many, many progeny.

CJ: There is a kind of runaway self-selection process that will create universes with more black holes and more black holes. How does that relate to life?

LS: It is a very interesting fact that part of why our universe is so good at making black holes is that it has organic chemistry in it. Because, to make stars massive enough to lead to the formation of black holes, it turns out that you have to have clouds of dust that are very cold. Only if the matter is very very cold will it clump enough and accumulate enough matter to become the massive stars that we need. Furthermore, the refrigerant that cools those clouds, which are called giant molecular clouds, is carbon monoxide and dust which is made from carbon, and from ice as well as other things. So it turns out that the same organic chemistry on which life is based is what plays a major role in ensuring that the universe does make continually massive stars, and therefore makes galaxies. That is a very interesting coincidence. It means somehow that the universe has some chemistry that life can take advantage of, that life needs, because the universe already needs that chemistry for its own reproduction. If this theory is right.

CJ: The other thing is that if massive stars end as black holes and explode as supernovae, we know that the supernovae actually seed the heavier atoms that chemicals and then life are based on. So without supernovae you would not get life at all. So these implosions and explosions are double birth processes! They not only lead to baby universes, but they lead to matter becoming more complex and then to life.

LS: Yes.

CJ: So it is a very generative process. You are talking about cosmogenesis on a certain level.

LS: On a certain level. The organic chemistry—the carbon and the oxygen that one needs for these processes—come from supernovae. By the way, look at the energy which drives this process. This is a system that is way out of thermodynamic equilibrium, which is developing structure. The energy that drives the system also comes, to some extent, from the supernovae.

CJ: So you are getting a lot of "order for free" here?

LS: Yes, as Stuart Kauffman calls it. You have a system that fits the classic requirements of what we call self-organizing systems, a system that is pushed far from thermodynamic equilibrium, which is maintaining itself in that state. There are sources of energy flowing through the system that lead to the creation of organization. That scenario also seems to apply as much to the processes and the discs of spiral galaxies as it does to the understanding of ecological processes, and the origin of life.

CJ: That is extraordinary. You call your book *Life of the Cosmos*, and in that sense you are putting forward a metaphysics that the cosmos is like a living entity? This is not unlike ideas in the past, under Aristotle. In pre-modern times many people believed the universe was alive: you are not saying it is alive but it is like life.

LS: It's *like* life. By the way this idea has been foreseen by philosophers, for instance the American pragmatist, Charles Peirce anticipated this idea in the late 19th century.

CJ: The implications are that human beings are much more like the cosmos than we thought when we conceived it as a dead, inert, materialistic thing. In other words the cosmos becomes much more like us. In that sense it has radical and philosophical implications.

LS: I think to begin with Darwinism is radical and we are just in the process of beginning to assimilate Darwinism. And if I can say so, everything you are creating in the garden is an aspect of this.

So, Lee Smolin's intriguing idea is that every black hole may create a new baby universe with slightly different laws, until, through a process of Darwinian selection, one such as our own has the laws balanced to such an exquisite degree that it looks as if it were designed by God, or as if it were a miracle, or as if it were alive. Of course these are speculations and metaphors, but they have a certain plausibility and they pose the big questions from a new perspective.

It is beyond dispute that for complex life to have evolved a series of highly specific and unlikely conditions must be fulfilled and it is this notion that is dramatized in the terrace. If you look closely at

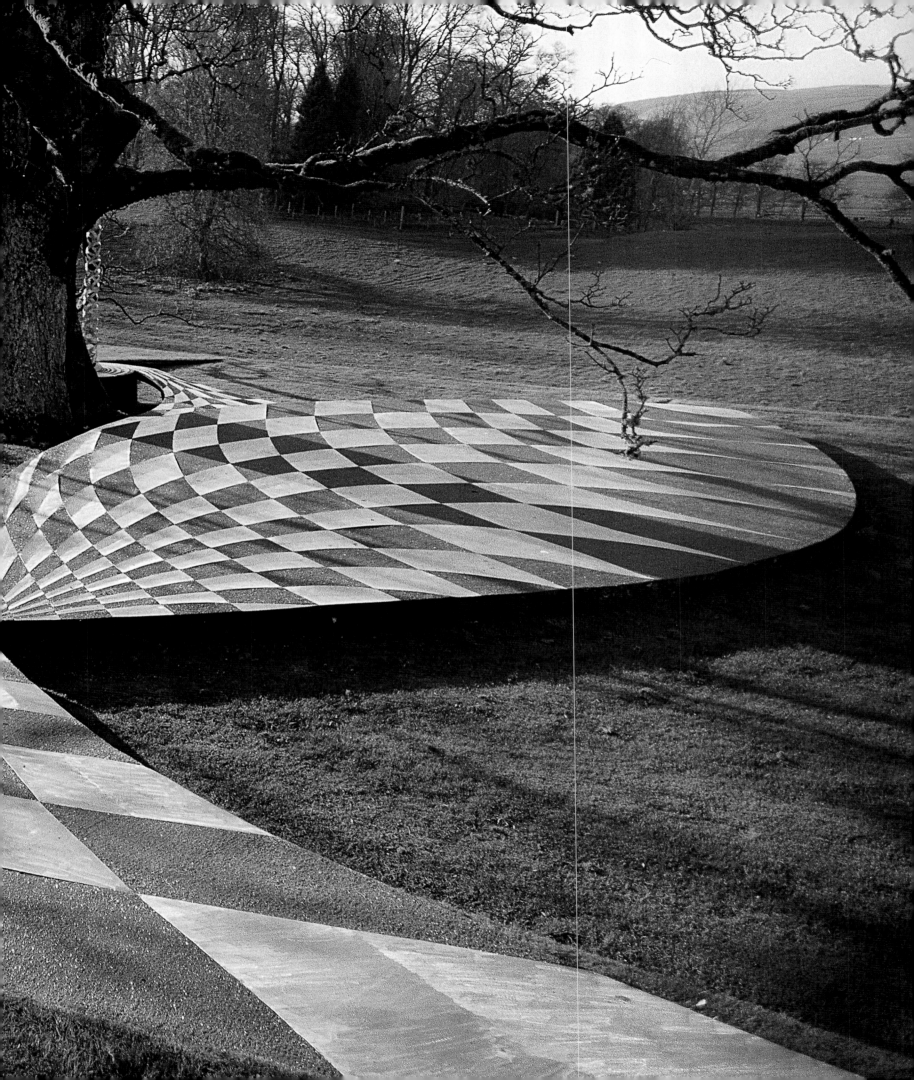

the two warped grids you can see that they are similar to each other, but not exactly the same. Slight variations leading to slightly different laws result in more black holes and more baby universes, until the laws are propitiously balanced just right for life. So here in the terrace the notion of positive cosmic evolution is coincident with the fractal aesthetic and the function of supporting table and chair legs. The meanings relate in a seamless manner, creating an ambiguous, resonant symbol that keeps the mind and eye actively interpreting.

However, my own notions of cosmic evolution, or cosmogenesis, are less Darwinian and gradualistic than Smolin's and are based on a different kind of metaphor, one that does not rely so heavily on natural selection. But before showing how I explored these ideas through the garden, I must recount another sad event in the changing fortunes of Portrack and our life as a family.

Change of Fortune

One night, I was returning to Portrack by a late train with Lily and John. We arrived to find Clare lying on the floor upstairs on her back, unable to move. Apparently, in excited anticipation of the visit, she had gone to arrange a coming-home present in Lily's room and, as she was stepping up a half-landing, thought of something more to be done. In her indecision, she had fallen backward and broken a hip, at over the age of ninety a life-threatening and completely incapacitating event. So into the hospital she went, for one of many further stays, hospitalized and in great pain, but with a renewed will to live. After an operation, and when she returned home to Portrack, she built up her strength, and muscles, by walking on a Zimmer frame. She would perambulate at the top of the garden, with a nurse, and explain what she had gathered about such things as the Black Hole Terrace. I was delighted at her change of heart. Initially skeptical, she embraced its meanings with the zest of a convert, and was particularly good at describing the theoretical possibilities of this strange object: how in crossing the event horizon one might be pulled in and stretched out—human spaghettification: as amazing as any doctrine of transubstantiation.

In early February 1998, after a bout of 'flu or a heavy cold, her already weakened heart started to fail. I was called back to Portrack and arrived at night to find Clare clinging to life, barely conscious. John and Lily came the next day and with their presence she began to rally. We took turns sitting, talking and reading to her, John reciting nonsense verses from Lewis Carroll and Edmund Lear. For a week she held on, but then her very strong will succumbed to the inevitable and she died, literally in my arms, exactly at 12:00 midnight. She ended her life much as she had lived, with a certain nobility and dressed in style, like Maggie: stoic to the last and putting a brave face on things. In her ninety-two years she had

experienced several worlds to the full, and in that sense her passing was less tragic than Maggie's. I reflected on this as I went the next day to register her death officially. Having gone through three years of probate with Maggie's estate, and the endless rounds with lawyers and bequests and possessions, I thought I knew most of the ropes. Thus I was shocked at the response of the Scottish Registry Office: "She cannot have died at 12:00 p.m., it is not legally possible because that is not an official date, neither one day nor the next." Inwardly, I gave a chuckle at how funny both Clare and Maggie would have found this loophole of legal immortality, reminiscent of how Clare's marriage was unofficial because the order of her many names was not repeated correctly. We would have shared the brilliant poignancy of bureaucratic idiocy at such a time. Pedantry of such stupendous proportions provides a welcome kind of distraction and fury. To legalize the matter I fudged the moment as 12:01.

As a result of Clare's death there were many changes at Portrack. It became a weekend house for me or place to visit from time to time, and the housekeeper Heather McLune and her family had to leave since there was no more daily work to be done. There was just one more significant change at this time. A new person had come into my life, curiously, someone who had known Maggie many years before, in fact been in the same school with her and had her as a part-time teacher of English. Louisa Farrell, or Louisa Lane Fox as she is now, arrived just as Clare died, and together we have continued to shape the gardens of Portrack, carrying on the program, or modifying it, as we see fit.

A garden is probably never finished, because of changes in life, because things grow and die before the initial idea can be completed, and because one should change one's mind in response to what has happened. Preservation of buildings has some justification, but the idea of a preserved garden is much less easy to achieve and is likely, unless a great deal of money is spent, to create the appearance of a pickled skeleton, as the paradise gardens of the Taj Mahal have become. With gardens, life gets on with life, death is a catalyst, and one learns new things—the universe develops both through slow evolution and sudden punctuation. Such had been my experience and such were the theories I was to engage with more explicitly in the garden.

Breaking Symmetry

It is a truth generally acknowledged that symmetry, of one sort or another, is a desirable goal of design. Vitruvius in the first century BC summarized Greek attitudes and means for achieving symmetry, and Renaissance architecture was built on these canons. Wholeness, balance, harmony of parts, and bilateral symmetry, particularly that of the human body, were proffered as the ideals. Vitruvius described the model that was to become canonic for two thousand years. A

man, lying on his back like a sacrificial specimen and moving his arms and legs in an arc, could generate the perfect circle and square. His lesser parts (nose, eyebrows, hand, foot) would also reveal multiple other harmoniously related details. Symmetry meant order, pattern, repetition. Above all it meant the proportional relationships between pleasing forms: the absolutely regular curve of a circle, or the sides of a square one to one, or rectangles one to two, two to three, and so on up the scale.

Arguments for symmetry were based also on analogies. The physical and metaphysical justifications rested on the pleasing musical sounds created by vibrating strings, where reinforcing harmonies came from ratios of the same lengths: e.g. 1:1, 1:2, 2:3, and so on. The underlying overtones reinforced each other, resonated in frequency.

By the 17th century, Western architecture was based on these principles. But with their very success doubt set in, caused partly by proportions that were overly repeated—predictability undermined the argument, strange proportions became more attractive. Metaphysical doubts and empirical research also killed the Vitruvian settlement. And so more complicated forms of symmetry were sought, ones that provided greater challenges. These included the asymmetrical symmetry of Rococo ornament, Art Nouveau compositional patterns, the dynamic symmetry of the Modern Movement, and the intricate forms of rotational and translational symmetry evident in such practices as tiling and Islamic architecture. Such were basic variations on the theme, all attempts to explore simultaneously the underlying nature of reality and refreshing forms of a new kind of beauty.

Recently another insight has occurred that casts the whole question of symmetry in a different light. Oddly enough it has grown from theories concerning the birth and development of the cosmos. At the beginning of time, so the Standard Model goes, the universe started in a state of supersymmetry. Everything was in a featureless, uniform state of perfect harmony, the sublime beauty of what we mistakenly call nothingness, or what is really the plenum vacuum. Then, with an imbalance of particles and anti-particles, the whole business started. Asymmetry, as it were, created the universe! The rest of history, from this formal perspective, is just further breaks in perfection, the continual evolution through jumps in organization. The analogy is with phase transitions, which are so familiar: the way a gaseous cloud can cool and change suddenly into water vapor, and then cool further and change suddenly into ice. The history of the universe follows similar breaks in symmetry caused by a drop in temperature. It starts in a hot plasma state of pure energy and, after cooling, jumps into matter. Symmetry breaking, phase changes, jumps in organization caused by changes in energy, are now understood to play an essential role in evolution.

This raises a fundamental point. If symmetry breaking creates the *interest* of the universe, if the variety of matter, rocks, landscape, and culture is a result of symmetry breaking—then this process should be put on a par with symmetry making. Perhaps Vitruvius and aesthetic theory are only half right and the physics and metaphysics behind design should feature phase change and metamorphosis as well as regularity. From this new perspective, the simple symmetries of classical design relate to the beginning of things but not to their development. We need an aesthetic that features, at once, the basic harmonies and their extension, shifting, and complication. This idea was explored in several media.

Symmetry and the breaking of the word "symmetry"; symmetry as positive–negative and negative–positive.

One of the ambigrammi in the DNA Garden uses the word symmetry in both a symmetrical and a symmetry-breaking way. First the word is cut in the stone so that it flares out at either end like a bow tie, and then it is doubled in plan to create an ellipsis of negative space between both words. Since it can be read upside-down and either way, the resultant patterns form a triple symmetry. But, also, since one figure and ground are the inverse of the other—positive–negative reversals of each other—the symmetry between them is subtly broken. One is meant to trip over this sign and to ponder its paradox: that symmetry and breaking symmetry create a more complex and interesting set of symmetries.

Consider the most minimal description of the history of the universe. In the first epoch there is only energy; then, with cooling, that shifts into matter, then life, then consciousness. It is hard to get any more basic. Each epoch shows a jump in organization from the previous level, and is a symmetry break. Of course, it is only a small part of the previous structural level that is undergoing the transition, not the entire regime. There is still much energy around from the original hot plasma soup, the fossilized evidence of the origin discovered in the early 1960s as microwave background radiation. Likewise only a small part of matter jumped into life and only a small part of that into consciousness. But each of these organizational events marks a developmental step, a process worth picking out and emphasizing. If one takes a human or cultural view of the cosmos, these four levels stand out as most important. They, and countless other ones which happen at different scales, comprise cosmic history. And living nature's way of evolving, as Stephen Jay Gould and others have shown, is to undergo sudden punctuations—not just the continuous, gradual developments predicated by Darwin. So, living nature and inanimate matter both evolve through shifts, phase changes, catastrophes—as well as continuous variation.

The question, as with the black hole, is one of presenting recent insights, of accepting part of contemporary science while challenging its metaphors and reductionism. For instance, the Standard Model of creation, held by most cosmologists (and even underwritten by the Pope), contends that the universe started in a big bang and that, following this logic, it will end apocalyptically either in a big crunch (gravitational collapse) or in heat death (dissipation). Much of the universe is said to be dark matter we cannot see, termed WIMPS (weakly interacting massive particles) or MACHOS (massive compact halo objects). According to these metaphors the universe is an adolescent melodrama. Its origin is an oversized firecracker, its end a catastrophe, and the major protagonists are alpha or beta males. No wonder people are alienated from science.

There is a widespread tendency in our culture to simply accept the reigning words of scientists when even they have not given

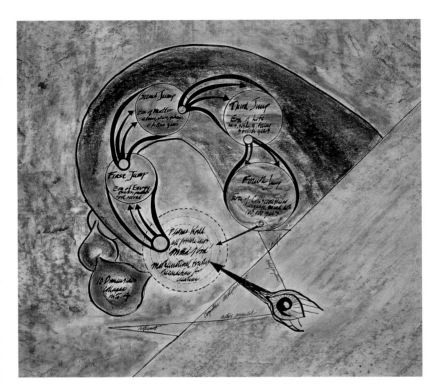

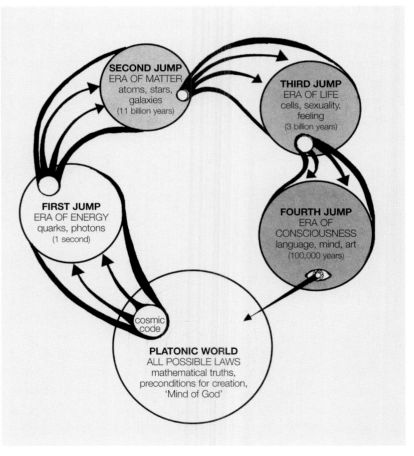

The universe in four basic jumps. The perfect symmetry of the beginning is broken by energy, then that symmetry is broken by matter, then by life, and then by consciousness. Each break is from a small area of the previous regime. The eye of consciousness looks back on history, and the cosmic code behind it all.

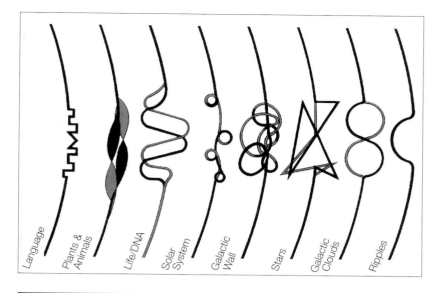

Language   Plants & Animals   Life/DNA   Solar System   Galactic Wall   Stars   Galactic Clouds   Ripples

these figures of speech much thought. The phraseology "big bang," for instance, was coined in the 1940s as a negative epithet aimed by one cosmologist at another and unfortunately the insult was gratefully accepted as a compliment. It stuck, as vivid words have a way of doing; but that is no reason for leaving the matter there, since new insights about the birth of the universe will no doubt soon emerge. Where scientists produce alienating metaphors, there lies a fertile territory waiting to be explored.

No matter how aggressive reductivist metaphors are, and most scientists adopt them without reflection, they are not very cogent. The origin of the universe was not "big," but smaller than a quark; it was not a "bang"—no one heard it. It was not like the explosion of a firecracker, but actually the inflation of space. In fact, because it was the very fast stretching of space between plasma and matter, according to inflation theory faster than the speed of light, the origin of everything should really be seen as the "Hot Stretch." In a similar dialectic, all metaphors that ground us to the universe are partially open to rethinking—constrained by the evidence, but not fixed for long. To rephrase Virgil, we make the choice of our metaphors, and then they choose our future. It is the designer's role to get them right—or, at least, more convivial, less adolescent.

In the first model I conceived the universe as a holistic globe spiraling out from a center, like a wave gathering momentum. In another design, discussed later in depth, it is presented as an expanding trumpet, with thirty cosmic jumps marked as steps. A similar narrative, based on the same evidence, can be portrayed in a third metaphor. In the garden terrace embraced by two different soliton waves, the four basic jumps are dramatized in a pattern of grass and pebbles. This, the Symmetry Break Terrace, is a warped ellipse that culminates in the leap of consciousness: a growing hedge that flies over the wall and continues around the house.

Thus three different solutions—ellipse, globe, and trumpet—are all compatible with the Standard Model of the universe, and are alternatives to the metaphor of the big bang. This reveals a freedom of choice which, given the ubiquity of the normal phrase, is not generally understood.

The universe in eight jumps, conceived as a globe inflating from its center. Actually we do not know what the universe as a whole looks like, but here it is conceived as jumping from stage to stage while being held together by the four forces: gravity, electromagnetism, and the strong and weak nuclear forces. These are the spiraling curves that, radiating from the center, actually hold the circular hoops in mid-air—a visual metaphor of dynamic unification. The eight jumps are made as articulations in the aluminum hoops. The model was constructed by Joanna Migdal of Brookbrae and placed next to those of Gaia and the atom.

On the Symmetry Break Terrace, the history of the universe is conceived as four breaks in symmetry. To the left is the origin, the era of energy, inflating in straight lines. With cooling, matter suddenly emerges (the shift is marked by the jump in pattern that focuses on opposite trees). Matter, according to Einsteinian theory, bends spacetime, here shown by the curve of the grass and pebbles. The third jump, life, is seen in the oval bowl focused on a tree, and the fourth, consciousness, by the hedge that leaps the wall. Breaks in symmetry are sudden shifts in pattern. LEFT AND OVERLEAF: The Symmetry Break Terrace and Black Hole Terrace and hedge are part of a giant soliton wave that wraps around the house.

The Universe Project

Many individuals live quite happily with a kind of animal faith in things as they are, or live with various kinds of belief-systems that were worked out generations ago. These systems and feelings give structure to life, but today they might not be followed with much faith or passion. "Weak belief," as the philosopher Giattano Vattimo has pointed out, characterizes our time and, as another post-modern philosopher Jean-François Lyotard has put it, the reason may be because we live in an age of skepticism towards all metanarratives. Metanarratives not only comprise such things as the account of the universe in the Book of Genesis, but the story of Western progress, the emancipation of women, and the rise of egalitarianism, that is, the narratives that drive society forward. These accounts of where history may be going, or its meaning, orient individuals as much as societies, so when they are called into question, or only half-believed, a form of cultural entropy sets in. People begin to lack confidence and direction, artists and architects lack a goal beyond their own success. Such pervasive doubt is caused by many things: pluralism, the increasing complexity of life, relativism, and above all, the rise of a global economy that exploits every belief for its market potential until it is drained of credibility. Science, too, has played a corrosive role. With a skeptical attitude towards the finality of any theory, it also has undermined the belief in any metanarrative, even the one that supports its own continuance, the conviction that science can be progressive or neutral or long lasting.

Perplexity and cynicism have thus come to characterize the age. But this depressing situation also has led some visionaries to seek another grounding outside conventional religion and science, in an unusual place. They have looked to the most pervasive and all-encompassing event there is, the universe as a whole, its unfolding, its cosmogenesis. Many people are loosely involved in this project, such as the scientists I have been fortunate to work with: Lee Smolin, Brian Goodwin, Stuart Kauffman, Paul Davies, and Roger Penrose. They have written important books, such as *The Life of the Cosmos*, *At Home in the Universe*, and *The Cosmic Blueprint*, that describe key aspects of the way the universe unfolds. But more explicitly involved with metanarrative are the authors Brian Swimme and Thomas Berry, some of the first to see that the history of the cosmos could provide a spiritual grounding equivalent to the Book of Genesis. They wrote an important book called, simply, *The Universe Story*, published in 1992. Yet, while having a grand vision and opening the field to poetic treatment, the result suffers from an uncertain tone. It fluctuates between scientific description that is matter-of-fact and a somewhat religious phraseology that is stilted or out of date. The narrative of cosmic history turning into global and then contemporary affairs seems a genre doomed to fail. And yet, as Berry argues, our age is the first to recount this tale with any accuracy and depth, and therefore the initial steps are bound to be tentative.

As it is transformed and improved over the next years, it is likely to become more convincing. Like the account in such myths as Genesis, the story is inherently dramatic and relevant for human understanding and, unlike them, it is also true in a literal sense. The linear sequential narrative is, for instance, common to both the Judeo-Christian view and the history of science, the Old and New Testaments and the progressive discovery of chemical elements. It is possible, as Berry avers, that the story of the universe will become the metanarrative for global culture, for theists, atheists, and agnostics alike, and that all philosophies will have to defer, in some ways, to its message. Barring the selective control of media in some countries, it is no longer possible to insulate a culture from this story because it seeps through so many channels. Even though, in the year 2000, banal versions of the narrative were concocted for millennium celebrations, the message had an impact. The question is not whether it will triumph, but how well its poetry and truth are portrayed. Obviously, its Homer, or even its Spielberg, has yet to arrive.

Accepting this point, I nonetheless became involved in the universe project and looked for a place in the garden to pull the metanarrative together. The Symmetry Break Terrace and aluminum globe were the first, small-scale attempts. But there was a larger

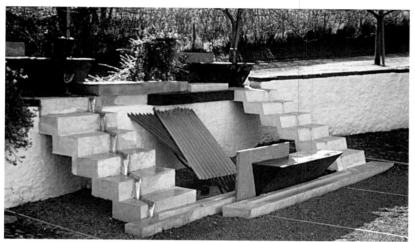

area, a key part of the site, that remained to be completed. Looking out from a high point of Portrack House, one can just see the top of the Snail Mound, the place where one has a panoramic view over the bottom gardens, and these two points create a major axis. My first design was a zigzag path on this axis that overlooked a white pebble maze. The maze was to be a reduced plan of the whole garden. The idea was to create a synopsis. Thus, in traversing this path, one would emulate the typical experience of reading a post-modern novel in which an enigmatic version of the whole story is wrapped up in a miniature vignette to be decoded like a puzzle. Umberto Eco and other writers had made a point of how these labyrinthine mysteries were like the branching paths of thought, and had a structure similar to both the detective novel and the brain. What better than to look down on a white "brain-maze" of pebbles set against a green lawn—visually the contrast would be stunning—and then as you reached the ground to walk through the maze. If you could crack the labyrinth you could figure out the whole garden and, appropriately, walk further along the axis up to the Snail Mound to survey it.

But the slope suggested a much more dramatic possibility, its use as a meandering staircase and cascade, a modest version of the Villa Lante where falling water might perform different tricks. Although, given the flow of water, a grand waterfall was out of the question, something more than a trickle was possible. I set about testing an idea in miniature. The first model was a small fountain made from different concrete steps and seats with channels cast on the diagonal. This was called Water in Chains, because it continuously recycles the same imprisoned water, around and around.

This concrete structure showed that we could build a more ambitious staircase along the same lines and achieve some quality, if not the perfection of either professional contractors or traditional Italian stonemasons. Thus we were on our way to constructing what I had already thought about many times in the abstract: a structure that would portray the story of the universe. And having a symbolic program in mind brought serendipitous benefits, as it often does.

OPPOSITE: An early plan of the garden's axes and viewpoints, 1991–6. A series of axes unite views and high points or trees. The main axis is between the Snail Mound and the Lookout from the house. When I explained to one visitor that everything has more than one meaning, he said, "Oh, I see. There—with the necklace, cheek etc.—is the portrait of Margaret Thatcher." (Drawing with Madelon Vriesendorp.) LEFT: Water in Chains. A small mock-up of a cascade tested the idea of water channels stepping down on the diagonal. Water spills from the left bowl and pulsates as it hits the horizontal cuts while, on the right hand cone, it travels down spiral cuts. In the center it emerges from a horizontal slit and then courses down zigzag channels of metal. The seat in front has an enigmatic rebus made from a chain, file, and letters. Decoded it underscores a meaning of the fountain: "U R N [CHAINS] 4 U R D [FILE] D."

PART SEVEN: THE UNIVERSE CASCADE

The Universe in Jumps

By some coincidence that makes life particularly interesting, it turns out there are deep affinities between the microcosm and macrocosm. The discovery of these links can be delightful. As we stumble across similarities of patterns at all scales, we discover not only that the universe is a unity, but also the relationship between the unknown and the already familiar. This is what Einstein called the great mystery of the universe: the fact that it is comprehensible. We can map the uncanny on to the everyday, the counter-intuitive on to the commonsensical. Of course something is lost in these parallels—all analogies contain an area of untruth—but the similarities are illuminating.

One of these parallels is the way jumps in evolution, indeed shifts in the history of the universe, mirror the steps of a staircase. In the early 1990s, following Roger Penrose's idea that the history of the universe could be conceived as a light cone coming from an origin point, I imagined cosmic history as a flaring fan, or trumpet. Two more ideas were added to this model: the notions that a balance of the four forces holds the universe together as a unity and that the cosmos unfolded as a series of symmetry breaks, as I have explained above. Here was one of those delightful parallels: breaks in symmetry are like discrete levels; evolution in nature is like the climbing of a ladder of organization, with definite steps and platforms. Since I had been developing this model of the universe for ten years it was natural to apply it to a most crucial part of the garden where it was fitting: the side of the hill. There, a main axis connected the highest garden mound with the house. The slope would provide a good angle for a cascade. So mapping the evolution of the universe became an obvious strategy.

Several models were designed. Some had spirals of planting that leaped over the steps; others with aluminum gongs that, filling up with water, would make sounds as they fell down (see page 196). None of these solutions materialized, but the main idea of the "jumping universe" as a cascade of steps was finally built. Ironically, and typically with design related to science, just as the model was being finished in 1998, cosmologists announced an important development: the universe was not the 15-billion-year-old structure hitherto conceived, but probably only 12–13 billion years old. Others may not have been holding their breath for this piece of news, but for me it was interesting that we were closing in on the origin of all things, a fact that brought the universe much closer to our reality. When one co-creates with scientists and they discover basic truths, the relationship with cosmogenesis becomes all the more immediate. Usually we take for granted things as big and seemingly permanent as our world. When we see it unfold or jump, or when we see a cosmic event such as the comet smashing into Jupiter, abstractions come very much alive. The universe as a single, creative, continuous event becomes palpable. A dramatic shift in knowledge creates the same close relationship.

Rocks, Minerals, and Concrete

After deciding what shifts of the universe are important, and basic, one has to settle on a medium of representation, something that is flexible, contemporary, durable, and monumental. The choice was obvious. Since I had been collecting rocks for many years, particularly some from China that had what are called bullet-holes, I decided to present each jump in organization as a billowing stone. It would rise upward from a sculptural base that would also identify the particular epoch of history at that point in the cascade. Industrial materials, and letters, would contrast with traditional artifacts of nature: cross-coding of media. What better than the artistic wonders of the cosmos—crystals, fossils, and rocks eroded into extraordinary clouds—to explain the cosmos? Real nature would signify nature's history, second nature (or culture) would add to the picture and third nature (or the garden) would be the context = nature cubed.

From time to time there would be a seat near a rock, at which to ponder its strange beauty and the view. Ascending the hill, one would be forced to go slow, both by the water channel cutting through the steps—forcing one to take care—and the difficulty of interpreting

According to Genesis, God, the architect of the universe, laid out the four elements, specifically the "void" at the center which was the earth "without form"; the heaven, or "firmament," surrounds this blob; "two great lights, the greater to rule the day, and the lesser light to rule the night; he made the stars also." The metaphor of God as an architect, who designs all cosmic elements including the laws, helped create a personal and rational relationship to the universe that inspired Western thought and cosmic passion.

each stage of the jumping universe. Again it was the idea that experiencing a garden should take time, that multiple meanings should slow down transition while they sped up appreciation. Obviously the Universe Cascade was not a staircase to run up and down—a hidden path behind the trees served that purpose.

And so we got to work. First, Bobby Dixon built the formwork to each section of steps. Then, after placing the reinforcing rods and mixing the concrete, Alistair, Doug, Neil, and Andy formed a tenuous bucket gang perched on the side of the hill. Carefully stepping over spikes and other impediments, they poured the sludge into the shuttering, gray concrete at the bottom and white where it showed. The greatest problem was placing the huge rocks precisely on their bases, and doing this before the concrete went off. A local farmer came to our aid with his forklift truck, block and tackle, and three slings. For the largest rocks it would take two days of adjusting the angles and rebalancing the weight before the correct center of gravity could be found. The weather had to be right, not too much rain, no frost, and enough time for a whole pour to be made. Only then would the attempt be made. At any moment disaster might strike: a stone might roll down the hill, a sudden downpour ruin the surface, a midnight freeze disintegrate the concrete. In effect, this was a kind of action sculpture, art against time, a race against the elements. Started in the winter of 2000, the Universe Cascade was finished in the winter of 2001 and never built at an ideal time or under propitious conditions.

But such hardship contained hidden gifts. Since building progress up the 35-degree slope was slow, I could design each platform in detail while the one below was under construction. Also, Louisa and I could go rock hunting on the River Nith and elsewhere, building up a considerable collection of different specimens to use on the cascade. This search for interesting stones became an enjoyable pastime in itself, one that amused the fishermen we came across and, as far as we could see, much more rewarding than waiting for salmon to bite. It deserves celebration and a new appellation, "rock fishing." Combing the rivers and beaches for distinctively shaped and colored stones is a superior form of distraction, especially if one has a project in mind. We picked up small red jasper stones to use as highlights, lots of greywacke eroded by the river into fish or phallus shapes, and various types of quartz and gneiss. Most strange was a white-blue-green stone that gives off a horrible smell when cleaned. This recommended itself for use at the stage when the universe was a plasma soup, very near its beginning. Most diverse in appearance was a conglomerate or puddingstone, a mixture that could be used as a sign of nature's plenty. Also distinctive was an ancient yellow and black rhyolite found on the seashore, something whose smoothness suggested it be used as a seat. The most sought-after specimens were, of course, the Liesegang rocks, those natural signs

ꝓ·LVMINARIA·IN
FIRMAMTO·CELI

of the self-organizing process of the universe I mentioned at the outset. Also called Goethite, they are quite hard to find, perhaps one in five hundred thousand on our stretch of the Nith. Their rarity makes discovery all the more rewarding, a focus for any expedition. But even when we did not find them, the afternoon hunts became their own kind of reward and a pleasant form of exercise. In this manner we managed to assemble about fourteen different types of rock, and, with these local artifacts in hand, planned an assault on the universe.

Recounting the story of the cosmos with rocks and objects is like writing poetry with semaphore flags, an approximate affair. Detail, narration and nuance are severely limited by these media. In terms of drama the best one can hope for is a mixture of evocative phrases and cartooned ideas, something approaching the art of mosaic combined with Japanese rock arrangement, Constructivist collage, and word art (epigraphy). There are places where it reaches considerable quality. Outside of Palermo, on a small Sicilian mountain, is the cathedral of Monreale where mosaicists have depicted the biblical story of creation. Here cosmic bodies of stars, sun, moon, earth, and living nature, become stereotyped but powerful in their primitive expression. Perhaps at the time the artists worked on these mosaics the biblical account of creation had been standardized, but in order to piece together the plot today you have to embark on a research project, and splice together different accounts from astrophysics, Complexity Theory, biology, and philosophy. Then, after comparing the evidence, one has to decide what reduction of the contentious facts makes sense and is really important. In particular, I had to reduce cosmic and terrestrial history radically to twenty-five of the most fundamental jumps, because that was the number of platforms that could be accommodated within the flare or trumpet design.

What follows is a narrative, step by step, platform by platform, beginning at the beginning of time. Twenty-five jumps to the present, and one into the future, a universe of forked paths, progress and regress, of two steps forward and one step back.

OPPOSITE, TOP LEFT: Shuttering work for the Universe Cascade constructed by Bobby Dixon, above, while Alistair works, below. OPPOSITE, TOP RIGHT: Limestone bullet-hole rock from China flaring toward the top is strung up so an aluminum base can be fashioned. OPPOSITE AND ABOVE: Rock-fishing leads to various temporary compositions: a spiral of granite eggs, mud fossil tablets, vertical pestles placed in holes eroded by the constant motion of a pebble, and a mound of Liesegang rocks. LEFT: Mosaic of God creating Heaven and Earth, Monreale Cathedral, 12th century. A narrative of the earth story starting with cosmic history surrounds the central nave. The Genesis story, here depicted in the primitive medium of stones, leads to later accounts and then to the present evolutionary theory of the universe.

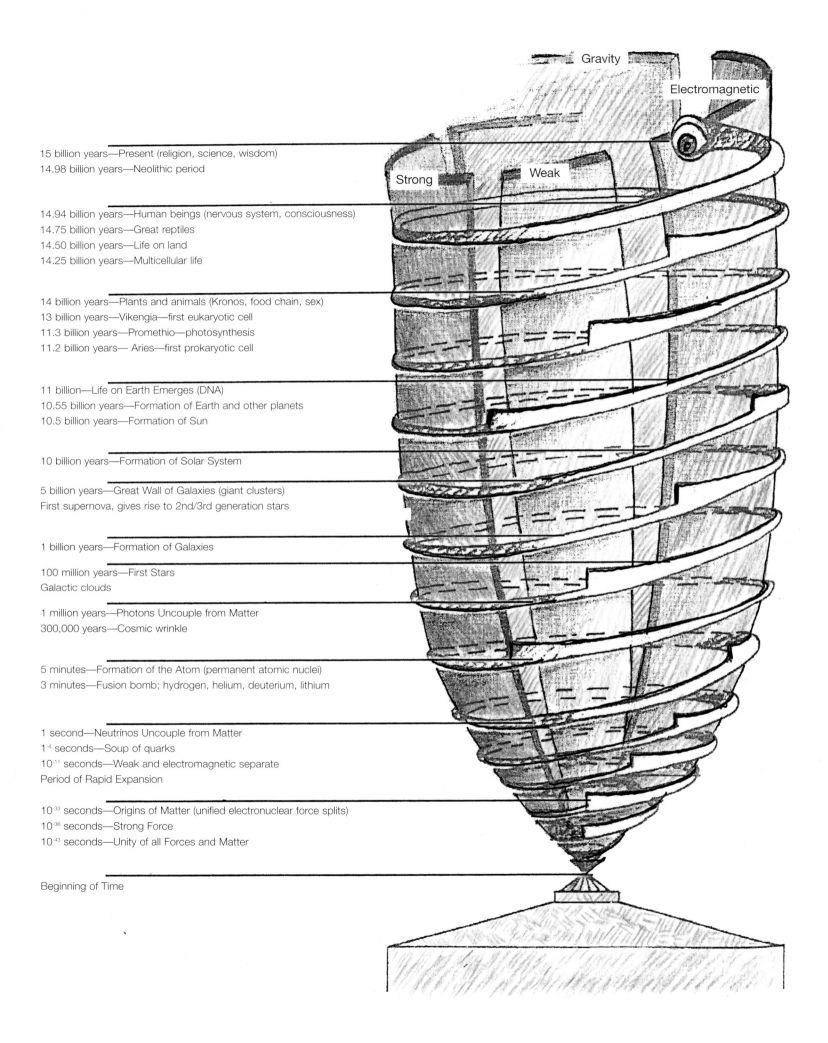

Gravity

Electromagnetic

Strong

Weak

15 billion years—Present (religion, science, wisdom)
14.98 billion years—Neolithic period

14.94 billion years—Human beings (nervous system, consciousness)
14.75 billion years—Great reptiles
14.50 billion years—Life on land
14.25 billion years—Multicellular life

14 billion years—Plants and animals (Kronos, food chain, sex)
13 billion years—Vikengia—first eukaryotic cell
11.3 billion years—Promethio—photosynthesis
11.2 billion years— Aries—first prokaryotic cell

11 billion—Life on Earth Emerges (DNA)
10.55 billion years—Formation of Earth and other planets
10.5 billion years—Formation of Sun

10 billion years—Formation of Solar System

5 billion years—Great Wall of Galaxies (giant clusters)
First supernova, gives rise to 2nd/3rd generation stars

1 billion years—Formation of Galaxies

100 million years—First Stars
Galactic clouds

1 million years—Photons Uncouple from Matter
300,000 years—Cosmic wrinkle

5 minutes—Formation of the Atom (permanent atomic nuclei)
3 minutes—Fusion bomb; hydrogen, helium, deuterium, lithium

1 second—Neutrinos Uncouple from Matter
1^{-4} seconds—Soup of quarks
10^{-11} seconds—Weak and electromagnetic separate
Period of Rapid Expansion

10^{-33} seconds—Origins of Matter (unified electronuclear force splits)
10^{-36} seconds—Strong Force
10^{-43} seconds—Unity of all Forces and Matter

Beginning of Time

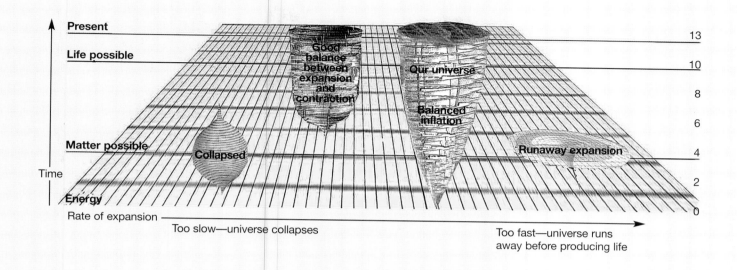

Present
Life possible
Matter possible
Time
Energy
Rate of expansion
Too slow—universe collapses

Good balance between expansion and contraction
Collapsed
Our universe
Balanced inflation
Runaway expansion
Too fast—universe runs away before producing life

13
10
8
6
4
2
0

THE JUMPING UNIVERSE

What does the universe look like? The question implies we could get outside it, and have a god's-eye-view because, from the inside, it would appear as it does now—infinite in all directions. Nonetheless, there are conceptual models based on time traveling in one direction (along the Y axis) that make a certain amount of sense. These stretch the balloon shape of an expanding universe into various kinds of vase shapes, an idea derived from Roger Penrose's model of a light cone. In order for us to exist, the universe must have only three manifest dimensions plus time (the additional six or seven dimensions postulated by superstring theory, as we will see, are small and not manifest). Lucky for us too is that cosmogenesis is old enough to have cooked the heavy elements like oxygen, and of a certain size. Furthermore, if it were too old the star called the sun would have run out of energy. In fact our mere existence places certain restrictions on the size, shape, and time dimensions. It demands that they be fairly close to what they are. It takes a universe 13 billion years to get us here. This insight is known as the Anthropic Principle.

But how to model it all? In the vase model, left, the universe is presented as a spiraling evolution held together and delicately balanced by four forces: gravity, electromagnetism, and the strong and weak nuclear forces. Again we can be thankful for these fine balances that make the universe a unity and come together just right, and remain balanced for 13 billion years.

The origin, in hot supersymmetry, evolves as it cools and undergoes further breaks in symmetry (the jumps). The trumpet, or flare, or flower of steps marks twelve major, and twenty-two minor, jumps. Although not everyone will agree with the ranking (is sex really less important than Gaia?) the stages are fairly common to many historical accounts of the cosmos. I have taken the liberty to run cosmological and natural history into each other and select what most people deem important.

In May 1999, after taking meticulous measurements for eight years, The Hubble Space Telescope Key Project Team announced that the birth of the universe happened between 12 to 13.5 billion years ago. They sampled Cepheid variables, cosmic yardsticks, with four different methods to come up with their results—which agreed. Allan Sandage, using different assumptions, placed the age closer to 14.5 or 15 billion years. But ten years previously the difference of opinion was bigger: it varied from 10 to 20 billion. Imagine a difference in answers as big as the thing itself! We are continually getting closer to answers about the birth, but will no doubt find more spectacular reversals in interpretation, and surprises, as we approach this ineffable point.

Look at the universes with different expansion rates, above. Those where gravity is too strong collapse in a "big crunch" before life can evolve, those that expand too fast "fly apart" and do not produce stars that can cook the heavy elements like carbon. Ours (center right) is in that tight range of "just right" universes where the forces of expansion and contraction are finely balanced—again an example of the Anthropic Principle. (Multiple universes, after Stephen Hawking, *The Universe in a Nutshell*, 2001, and *Scientific American*, January 1999.)

OVERLEAF: Two views of the Universe Cascade.

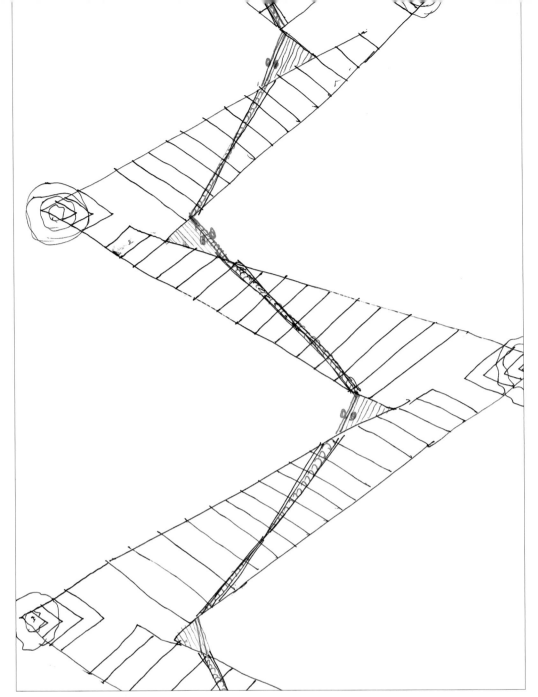

OPPOSITE: A wooden model of the Universe Cascade shows water falling diagonally across steps, and the translation of the major jumps into platforms, seats, and rock monuments. RIGHT, AND BELOW: Drawings show various solutions including a spiral of planting, aluminum water gongs to mark the sudden phase transitions, the dynamic opposition of planting and steps. BELOW, RIGHT: The eye of consciousness reflecting back on cosmic history. Is the universe a giant computer, are we the perceivers who interact with it and bring certain quantum events into being? Quantum cosmology is beginning, in the year 2000, to overturn fundamental assumptions, as it did in 1900. Electrons, photons, atoms, even molecules come in "information bits" and their waves are "collapsed" through perception.

Aye, the eye, the I does matter, matter for thought.

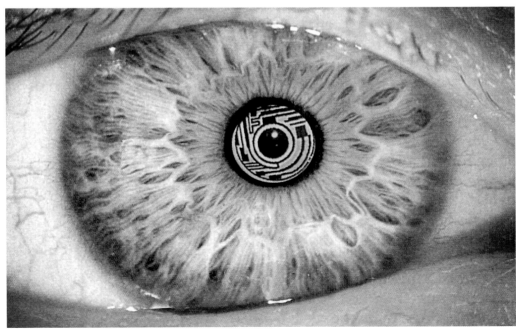

25
13 billion years
Present, Future
Eye, Reflection, I

24
12.9999996 billion years
Modern economy

20
12.935 billion years
Catastrophe

21
12.975 billion years
Feeling, Society, Gossip

16
11 billion years
Symbiosis

17
12.47 billion years
Life types explode

12
8.5 billion years
Earth and planets

13
8.55 billion years
Moon stabilizes earth

8
50 million years
Galactic clouds

9
100 million years
First stars

4
10^{-6} seconds
Matter

5
1 second
Neutrinoes

2
10^{-41} seconds
Inflation

22
12.999948 billion years
Consciousness

23
12.999995 billion years
Civilization

18
12.5 billion years
Animals, Sex

19
12.856 billion years
Color, Music, Perfume

14
9.1 billion years
Life

15
9.2 billion years
DNA

10
2 billion years
Supernovae

11
8 billion years
Solar System

6
5 minutes
Hydrogen and Helium

7
300,000 years
Light

3
10^{-35}–10^{-33} seconds
Unified forces split
10^{-11} seconds
Electroweak force splits

1
0
Superstrings

THE UNIVERSE CASCADE

0
ORIGIN—ULTIMATE MYSTERY
SUPERSYMMETRY— SUPERSTRINGS
QUANTUM FOAM—PLENUM VACUUM

At the beginning of time there was a unity of the four forces, matter and energy. Time and space do not pre-exist this point, but are brought into being to become, not the background stage, but rather major actors in the cosmic drama. Perhaps the universe arrives as the white hole of the black hole of another universe, or a collapse of eleven dimensions into four, or the result of a quantum fluctuation. Or maybe it is made from infinitely small superstrings, the collisions of membranes, or something else. We will be closer to an answer in twenty years, but the origin is likely to remain the ultimate mystery, the ground of being.

Whatever its cause, it is not a big bang since it is infinitely small, silent, hot, fast-moving, and it creates energy in the form of plasma. Here the hidden mystery is conveyed by steps descending into a reflective murky surface of water the depth of which is beyond seeing.

Quantum foam, the smallest rock and ripple, water reflecting stairs, bundled-up tiny dimensions, a Calabi-Yau space.

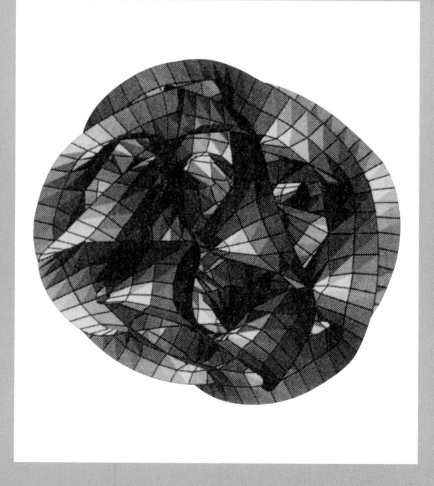

2

10^{-41} SEC
FINE-TUNING–INFLATION–SPACE STRETCH

For a very short period, according to the Standard Model, the universe consisted of a quark soup, an energy plasma of up-quarks and down-quarks, the fundamental stuff which we can never see because it is now trapped inside protons and neutrons. After the origin a most important event took place, and without it there would have been no future: the very hot and fast stretching of space. The universe expanded from the size of an electron to that of a grapefruit, and did so faster than the speed of light. This fast stretch is called, in an understatement, "inflation," and it had one great result: it smoothed out and finely balanced the forces. Among the many that it tuned precisely were the forces of expansion and contraction. This delicate balance was the first miracle. A trillion-trillionth faster and the universe would have exploded apart into a series of pluriverses, a trillion-trillionth slower and the force of gravity would have long ago squeezed the universe to death—we barely made it. The balance was just right, to a degree of accuracy of one over ten to the 59th power, that is, with an accuracy of 0.0 . . . (58 zeroes) . . . 1. Such odds make biblical miracles look more likely. That is why some scientists say, "the universe looks like a put-up job"— as if designed by a Swiss watchmaker.

Inflationary steps in a zigzag swoop.

10^{-35}– 10^{-33} SEC
UNIFIED FORCES SPLIT
10^{-11} SEC
"ELECTROWEAK" AND "STRONG" FORCES SPLIT

After inflation, the next great surprise is that the unity of the universe broke up. This is the first symmetry break, a model for all later ones and, like them, something that gave the universe interest and diversity. Within the first second of the origin event, the four basic forces, which hold everything together, evolve out of one, unified superforce: the force of gravity, electromagnetism, and the two forces within the atom—the weak and strong force—all four emerge as a surprise. First gravity splits away from the other three. Then with further expansion and cooling, the electroweak force splits from the strong force and at 10^{-11} seconds it further splits into the weak and electromagnetic forces. So, by then, the perfect unitary symmetry was broken by the stretching and cooling of the hot soup.

10⁻⁶ SEC
MATTER!—UPDOWN QUARKS CLUMP

The next surprise—if anybody had been watching they could not have predicted it—was that the soup cooled further and parts of atoms were formed. Rapid cooling permits the invisible quarks to clump into protons and neutrons.

UUD=protons, DDU=neutrons, both indicated by rocks eroded by small sea creatures.

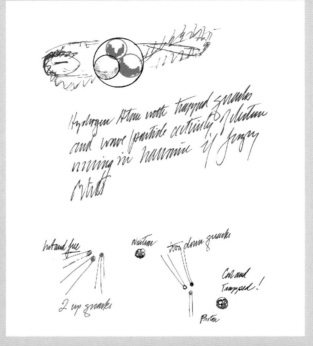

1 SEC
NEUTRINOES IN HOT FOG

Neutrinoes emerge, the most plentiful things in the universe, perhaps constituting part of the dark matter. Charged electrons and protons prevent light from shining, it is still too hot for complete atoms to form.

6

5 MINUTES
HOT PLASMA SOUP OF HYDROGEN AND HELIUM —SIMPLE ATOMS

First come the simplest atoms—hydrogen and helium—then deuterium and lithium. Today their ratios in the universe partly confirm the standard evolutionary model.

Bluey-white sulfureous rocks fished from the Nith.

7

300,000 YEARS
LIGHT!—PHOTONS UNCOUPLE

Eventually, photons uncouple from matter. There is light, and transparency, the space between. This cosmic ripple was first observed by COBE in 1992.

Water splits photons and matter.

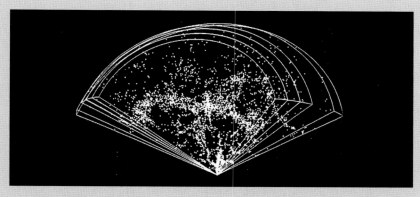

8

50 MILLION YEARS
GALACTIC CLOUDS

Galactic clouds form, along with galaxies, perhaps by the explosive force of a supermassive black hole. The clouds condense out of debris and gases that form "top-down" from the initial expansion and/or "bottom-up" through collisions of gassy material combined with the work of gravity on the accumulated bits. After another billion years several basic structures have emerged. The three main galactic types are the spiral, elliptical and irregular conglomerate. Force and form, gravity and spiral, give some direction to cosmic evolution, cosmogenesis. Then, after another 4 billion years, the biggest pattern in the universe forms: the Great Wall of Galaxies. What is going on, what force works at this scale, or is the pattern simply the result of a previous event? Bubbles and bubble-voids exist at the scale of the universe as a whole; its overall shape is another mystery.

LEFT TOP: The Great Wall of Galaxies, the largest structure in the universe except for itself. (Diagram compiled by Margaret Geller, 1989.) BELOW: A spiral of Liesegang rocks.

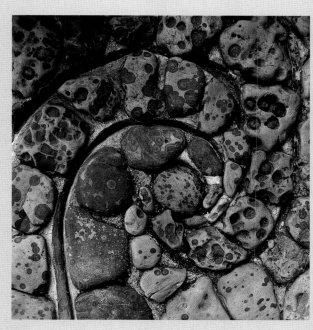

100 MILLION YEARS
FIRST STARS

The first stars are turned on, lighting up as enormous hydrogen bombs which have the strange property that they do not disappear, but self-organize in a fine balance between explosive reactions, nuclear fuel, repulsive forces, and gravitational force. The first generation of stars form in the center of a galactic cloud, a place of violence, extreme heat, and crushing gravity. Then the cloud begins to move, to rotate, and a flattened disk emerges which leads to further concentrations of gases and elements. These movements, shock waves, and condensations lead to later stars, younger stars such as our own, that form further out in the rotating arms. Further from the center, movement is slower and thus a spiral is naturally formed.

Meanwhile, at the center of the stars elements heavier than hydrogen and helium are formed.

Liesegang rock cut in two reveals similarity between microcosm and macrocosm. Liesegang rings are concentric bands of alternating colors usually found in sandstone, formed from iron oxides when oxygen-bearing water diffuses in through the sandstone. Water with more or less oxygen thus creates more or less rust. Two hundred and seventy million years ago, when the area was a Permian desert, these drops of iron pulsated from a central core in cycles of weathering. Images of star formation, from the Hubble Telescope, one in the back of this collage. (Jeff Hester and Paul Scowen [Arizona State University] and NASA.)

2 BILLION YEARS
SUPERNOVAE

Until this point, in terms of complexity, the universe was a little dull; it takes a series of unexpected catastrophes to make things more interesting. Some stars run out of nuclear fuel, collapsing under their gravitational weight, thereby forming many of the complex ninety or so elements we know from chemistry, those elements we breathe, such as oxygen, and those that make up most of our bodies, such as carbon. They then rebound and explode, so through this catastrophe, their death, they give birth to greater complexity—one direction to the universe—and, ultimately, give birth to life itself. As a cosmic act, destructive creation is a theme, along with entropy, of the universe story and it appears several times on the cascade. While there is a progressive direction to history, from less to more highly organized, it is marked by waste and spectacular setbacks. Hence the rhetoric of tragic optimism and ironic celebration conveyed in the collisions and juxtapositions.

LEFT: Ling-bi rock and colored rocks from the Nith with a central Liesegang. LEFT, BELOW: The Eskimo Nebula, photographed by the Hubble telescope, shows a bright face of pulsating gas blasted out by a supernova at 1.5 million kilometers per hour, and a surrounding parka of colliding orange gases. (NASA)

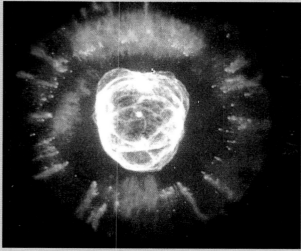

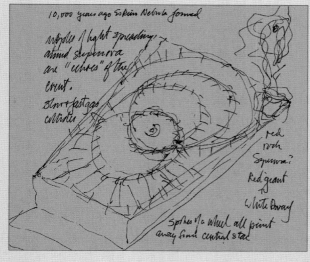

11

8 BILLION YEARS
THE SOLAR SYSTEM

A disk implodes and forms the solar system. Two thirds of the distance from the center of our galaxy, the Milky Way, in what is called a minor suburb, there crystalizes a disk of matter around a spinning star. This position may be important precisely because it is not near the center of action—where things are hot, violent, and destroyed by a voracious black hole. Perhaps only in galactic suburbia is there a habitable zone where planets can form and remain amenable to life. If this is true it would make our peripheral place rather special, a charmed part of Edge City.

In any case, gravity gets to work and pulls the disk of dust and gas toward a center. Then, because of a perturbation, the disk gets a rotational direction and spins like a whirlpool or a galaxy. Soon, a gas jet explodes from the center, but when the mass is great enough it shuts off and a star is born: our sun.

Five-stage evolution of the solar system from gas and dust pulled together by gravity to a spinning star with a central gas jet to a disk with condensed planets.

8.5 BILLION YEARS
THE EARTH AND PLANETS

When the sun stops spinning, the planets coalesce and settle into planar orbits. Bombardments by planetary debris increase their size. Jumps 11 and 12, taken together, show a progression from simplicity to complexity, a kind of teleonomy that arises from basic forces, such as gravity, and basic structural patterns, such as spiral rotation. Crystalizing evolution, in this sense, has a very broad direction and drama.

Black ling-bi rock and polished globe as Mars with its accretion of red jasper rocks. The orbits of Mercury, Venus, Earth, and Mars evolve after collisions of planetesimals (planetary debris). This is creative destruction at work. Black and red are the conventional colors for earth.

13

8.55 BILLION YEARS
MOON TUNES EARTH—PANGEA
—THE GREENHOUSE EFFECT

As the earth cools, the heaviest element, iron, sinks to the center and remains molten, forming a magnetic core. In rotation, this seething mass radiates a large magnetic shield around the globe that protects it from deathly solar winds and other destructive cosmic particles. Our sibling planets, Venus and Mars, do not have this liquid core and its magnetism, and are unable to sustain life. A planetesimal hits the earth, causing its axis of rotation to tilt and the moon is blasted into orbit. This is an extremely important event. The lunar satellite stabilizes the earth's axis at this angle, creating the seasons and, most importantly, keeps it from flipping, a chaotic motion that would decimate life. At this time the earth forms the oceans, the landmass known as Pangea, and our atmosphere.

Venus and Mars evolve in opposite ways, the former creating an atmosphere that is too hot for life, the latter too cold. In contrast, the earth creates a more temperate atmosphere through the greenhouse effect, which is achieved principally by the regulation of the amount of carbon dioxide in the atmosphere. The "carbon cycle" reaches an initial balance with the subduction of tectonic plates, volcanoes, and the weathering of rocks.

14

9.1 BILLION YEARS
LIFE!

The single cell, the prokaryotic cell, and then photosynthesis occur. The first cells, without a nucleus, may have formed in the seas, perhaps with the aid of an energy source, such as lightning, or an undersea volcano, a hot vent of gas. That is, it took more than 9 billion years to create the conditions for life, the first small bacteria. These started the Gaian cycles that sustain the conditions that are best for life—another form of telos without a final teleology. Feedback within Gaian cycles even becomes literal: one cell's waste becomes another cell's food. Mutation creates diversity, interdependence grows, death leads to more food for greater life. The result poses moral problems with a new principle: everything eats everything. At this stage only single cells devour each other; afterwards they invent a way of turning the sun's photons into food, photosynthesis.

Life eats life. The prokaryotic cell, the simple form of life, is represented by holes formed in the rocks by the constant abrasion of small pebbles. Water emerges from the right breast of the figure, water the substance of all life.

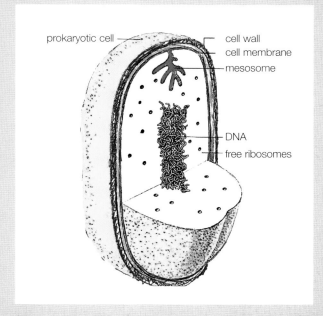

prokaryotic cell — cell wall — cell membrane — mesosome — DNA — free ribosomes

15

9.2 BILLION YEARS
DNA—GAIA

DNA, the small molecule for the universal code of life based on a double helix, and the large scale Gaia come into being sequentially. The molecular code is based on four letters, a double helical structure, and "words" that come in codons of three paired letters. These create a way of replicating cells and, along with mutations, a way of changing patterns, piecemeal.

With the origin of life, the earth as a self-organizing system, Gaia, starts to develop locally, then after millions of years, globally. Through its many cycles it balances the atmosphere, pumping down carbon dioxide, pumping up oxygen to its present level of 21 percent of the gases, and regulating other conditions such as temperature to create the best conditions for life. Gaia, like galactic evolution, seems to have a direction and purpose, creating a delicate balancing act across time. With DNA allowing many new life experiments, Gaia finds those interactions that push diversity to critical points. The history of life and ecosystems shows a constant build-up toward maximum saturation, until external or internal perturbations destroy the balance.

The DNA double helices, on two corners, spiral toward a green rock, Gaia.

11 BILLION YEARS
SYMBIOSIS

It took nearly another 2 billion years for the next big idea to come along, the first compound cells, with nuclei. Another new principle of organization is discovered by the universe: symbiosis. It allows prokaryotes to form more powerful and interesting alliances, new superorganisms.

Many types of evolution are at work in the living world: cosmic and chemical evolution, natural selection on random mutations, accidents of planetary evolution, asteroid impacts, and runaway volcanism. Luck, genes, planning, self-organizing systems all play different roles. There is not one law of evolution that is superior to another. Tragedy strikes thousands of species with a meteor impact; they are unlucky to be in the wrong place, but this allows a new set of species to flourish and to take over the territory. This is destructive creation once again, and at all scales.

A limestone bullet-hole rock sits on aluminum twists, a symbiosis of opposites, while green shards of fused glass have been formed from old wine bottles, another type of symbiosis. The seat is made from contrasting pairs of black/orange rock from the sea.

17

12.47 BILLION YEARS
THE CAMBRIAN EXPLOSION

In the Cambrian Period, 530 million years ago, life types explode in an extraordinary outburst of different types of life, body plans, and phyla. These include the first shellfish and corals, Burgess Shale fauna, and many skeletal organisms. Why should life have become so suddenly inventive? Two recent theories are suggestive. At this time, the eye evolved, escalating the competitive strategies of prey and predator, bluff and armaments, hence these impressive displays—the aesthetics of war—that emerged and are visible here. Secondly, the runaway growth of cyanobacteria created a surge of oxygen in the atmosphere, giving evolution a massive boost.

The five major forms of life are presented by opposite rock types. Clockwise from lower left: prokaryotic cell, eukarytoic cells, flora, a real fossil trilobite, 270 million years old—the phylum headed toward the next stages, evolving animals, below. (Stephen Jay Gould, Wonderful LIfe: The Burgess Shale and the Nature of History, W. W. Norton & Co. 1989.)

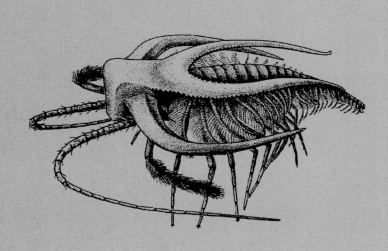

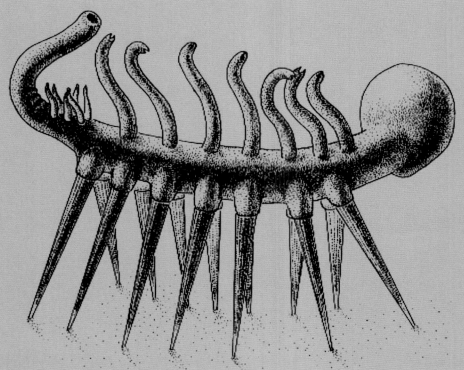

18

12.5 BILLION YEARS
ANIMALS—SEX—MASS EXTINCTIONS

Multicellular life evolves a few species of intermediate size: the plants and animals that emerged roughly 500 million years ago. Sexual reproduction not only gives these organisms pleasure but, by shuffling parental genes, can lessen genetic damage to their offspring. The higher species, sex, and a developed nervous system are three new aspects of evolution that seem tightly interrelated. Given the complication of social species, not to mention competition and jealousy, greater brainpower was necessary to compute the innumerable relationships.

A waterfall of mass extinctions punctuates evolution, thus allowing new relationships to emerge. Five or six events are noted under the water, starting with the first, 505 million years ago. The most devastating marked the boundary between the Permian and Triassic Periods, when roughly 92 percent of species were lost, 245 million years ago. The one that killed off the ammonites was the mass extinction 65 million years ago. They had bounced back from four previous events. In late 2002, some debris from the mass extinction of 214 million years ago was accidentally discovered in a cliff face in Bristol, England. Some bits of shocked quartz and vaporized rock that condensed into emerald-green droplets were evidence of a comet's impact that took place thousands of miles away. An impact crater in Canada, 65 miles wide, marks the extinction event as much as the related debris found around the world. The energy released by the explosive crash might have pushed the tectonic plates toward their present-day continental positions. If so, this destructive event would become, after the origin of life and its explosion in the Cambrian Period, the third most significant event for evolution—yet another example of destructive creation.

Ammonites punctuate the waterfall extinctions. Four large ones frame, in death, an Orthoceras, killed at the end of the Devonian Age. Mass extinctions punctuate the climb in biomass and biodiversity.

505000000

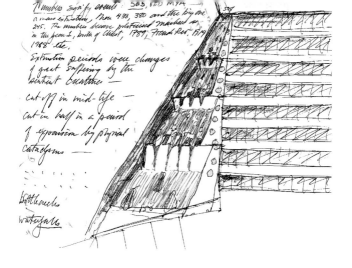

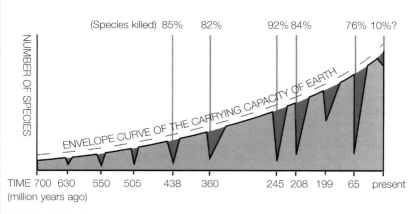

(Species killed) 85%   82%   92% 84%   76% 10%?

NUMBER OF SPECIES

ENVELOPE CURVE OF THE CARRYING CAPACITY OF EARTH

TIME 700 630 550 505 438 360   245 208 199 65 present
(million years ago)

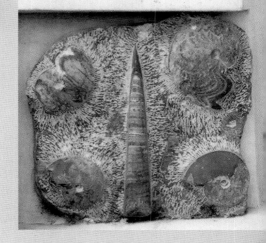

505000000

438

308

245

208

19

12.856 BILLION YEARS
COLOR—MUSIC—PERFUME

Birds and flowers, color and perfume emerge. Until this moment, life on earth had been too green, and without song. Colored plumage and tinted petals heightened the sense of sight. Birdsong turned sound into an aesthetic delight; the scent of flowers accentuated the pleasures of smell.

Sensuality accentuated against a green backdrop, the omnipresence of photosynthetic plants.

20

12.935 BILLION YEARS
ASTEROIDS AND VOLCANOES DECIMATE LIFE

Catastrophes change the course of life. Volcanoes in the Deccan Traps, India, erupt and add much carbon dioxide to the atmosphere. At the same time, a meteor strikes the Yucatan Peninsula. These events kill off major species—such as the dinosaurs—that dominated the earth, thus allowing new species a chance to flourish—such as horses, small rodents, and primates—our ancestors.

A mushroom cloud, a spectre, and a shadow of Mother Destruction, the Indian Goddess.

21

12.975 BILLION YEARS
FEELING—SOCIETY—GOSSIP—BRAIN

Monkeys, apes, and chimpanzees have complex feelings, primitive intelligence, and even rudimentary culture. Along with these direct ancestors, as well as a few other primates, we find complex social behavior, a developed brain, and a set of feelings. Chimpanzees have the mental capacity of four- to six-year-olds and can solve new problems with creative insight. Like crows, they can look at a possible food source and suddenly see how to use a tool to get it. They groom each other and form gangs with complex hierarchies that they have to remember and negotiate. They work in alliances—early examples of NATO and ASEAN. Being immersed in complicated and conflicting relationships (the age-old conflicts between family and desire), they develop complex feelings to sort through these perplexities. Some evidence exists that elephants and chimps feel loss and mourn their dead. For domestic and sexual reasons, bower birds and termites build architecture, which is both functional and symbolic. In any case, a sentience analogous to our own has arrived some 15 million years ago showing that creatures responding to the cosmos may work out similar structures to deal with it. Given enough time, a "complex adaptive system" will evolve habits, traditions, and a culture. To figure out the universe, nature will produce culture.

Old and new brain in four types of red rock.

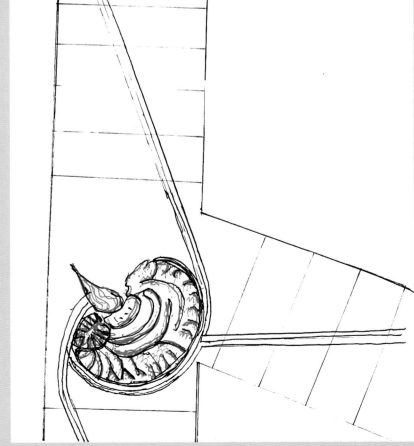

22

12.999948 BILLION YEARS
CONSCIOUSNESS

Music and counting, worship of fecundity, Paleolithic and Neolithic culture. It has taken about 13 billion years for the universe to create sentient life on this planet, and many scientists say it cannot be done much quicker. That is because all the main jumps have had to occur before this one, *Homo sapiens*, can come on to the scene.

It is hard to say when consciousness jumped out of life—is an amoeba conscious? Information processing may go all the way down to the electron, but the great leap in organization is into culture, and it is with such sentient creatures as the birds, bees, and the chimpanzees that this occurs. Traditions, learning, and symbolic languages are now passed on. However, as far as we know, no other living creature except us has a highly developed language and manipulates concepts at the level of written abstractions.

The Paleolithic and Neolithic cultures invent symbolic forms such as music and cave painting which celebrate the cosmic cycles, the rhythms of the moon and sun, and the struggles of life and death, the hunt. The feminine principle and surprising fecundity of nature are honored. Art emerges, the tragedy of life is perceived.

Goddess in greywacke stone holds up culture with her hair. Signs of fecundity, counting, flute playing, and burial are to the left.

23

12.999995 BILLION YEARS
CIVILIZATION—COSMOS

The great civilizations and religions emerged between 3000 BC and AD 700, from the Egyptian, Sumerian, Roman, and Christian West, to the Hindu and Buddhist East, and also with the Muslim and Taoist world-views. More than 6,000 other nations developed within the interstices of these major formations. Peaceful evolution, stasis, and drift are punctuated by competition, war, and suppression. Empires, such as the Chinese and Roman, keep a broad peace amid warring tribes and nations. Civilizations turned mystical thinking into systematic religion, scripture, and poetic dogma. The great stone circles at Avebury and Stonehenge, and 500 lesser ones in the UK, focused on the cosmic regularities of the seasons, the rhythms of the sun and moon. Triangular geometries gave structural stability to the pyramids, and the regular geometries of Euclid, Pythagoras, and Plato were assumed to underlie all nature. Architects crystalized the dome in India and Rome. Under the gaze of civilization, what started as wild speculation froze as perfect form and doctrine.

The smallest stone circle is oriented to the north, and the smallest onyx pyramids from Egypt mark the water steps.

Dynamism of Modernity
Death of Wilderness
Loss of belief systems

24

12.9999996 BILLION YEARS
MODERN ECONOMY THREATENS ECOLOGY

Modernity creates the nation state and modern economy by 1600. Nations, where they could, evolved through economic transformations into secular nation-states. These became relatively stable units of the global economy. Then, over the last three hundred years, an international scientific community emerged as the indirect engine of development. The success of global capitalism, however, has created systemic problems: global warming, the impoverishment of a billion people, and, at any one time, about forty low-intensity wars. Supermodernism, which has emerged since 1960, is the latest stage of late capitalism. Under this regime, 400 multinational corporations (controlling one third of the world's production) create environmental imbalances. The global economy strains the global ecology. Another mass extinction starts, this one caused, ironically, by success. As the economy grows by 2 percent every year, 27,000 species are lost: a hundred a day, three an hour. And yet by 1960 more people lived better and longer lives than ever before—at least the lucky and rich ones. Two billion people have a life expectancy of seventy-five and each dispose of more domestic energy than the Roman Emperor Hadrian did. Spectacular inventions are enjoyed by many—birth control and the automobile—and the spectacle of moon explorations and the Olympics are enjoyed by a television audience of 4 billion. Yet a billion people or more cannot get adequate drinking water. Lack of political will or the institutions to change this situation lead to the contradictions of the age.

Rust belt, screws, blades wedge out pockets of growth; corridors remain, floods fight back.

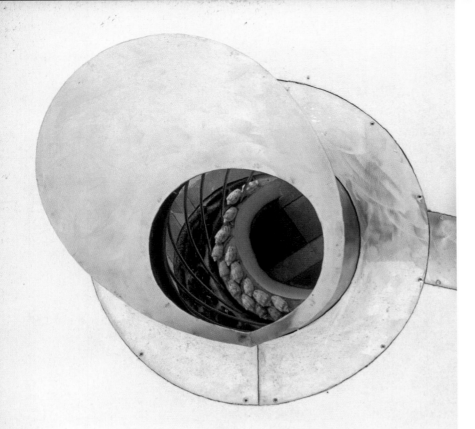

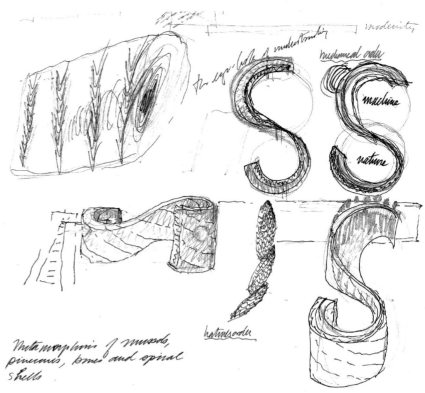

Metamorphosis of mussels, pinecones, bones and spinal shells

25

13 BILLION YEARS . . . PRESENT/FUTURE
EYE—REFLECTION—I—WORLD CULTURE—
SCIENCE—CRISIS

Religions, trapped in doctrine, have lost their imaginative stimulus; science has yet to produce a creative high culture. But the potential for understanding exists. Ours is the first generation to begin to see the story of the emergent universe and to be able to track it back to the first microseconds. The narrative can now be traced from the origin to the present, the story of a single, creative, unfolding event that is ongoing, which we can literally see, feel, and hear around us. It is a tale of increasing complexity, one that leads to greater sentience, understanding, and reflection—that leads ultimately to culture. In that sense, and contrary to what many have held since the time of the Greeks, we are not alienated from, but rather built into, the laws of nature; we are quintessential cosmic beings tuned to its laws and qualities. The wish to relate to this grounding, both through understanding and sensual apprehension, is an unconscious drive, even an instinct. Hence the hold of science and art on our sensibilities. The mind's eye can grasp the universe, the imagination can see its narrative as a whole—up and down. And what strange visions are on the distant horizon.

In 3 billion years the Andromeda galaxy, coming toward us at 3 million miles per hour, will hit the Milky Way, a galactic collision of spirals producing extraordinary events. As these curves go through each other their gravity fields will entangle, producing an elliptical supergalaxy. Streamers will be torn off, as John Dubinski has shown with a simulation at the San Diego Supercomputing Center. The wisping spirals of his model consist of stars and nebulae tens of thousands of light years long. Supernovae will explode into being, more seeds of universal organization.

Andromeda's black hole, thirty times as big as ours, may combine with it. If the earth is on the outside of a spiral arm at the epoch of collision we will get a nice whiplash into outer space; if it is on the inside, there is no escape.

And there are other cosmic events that have become predictable. As we have seen, Gaia, through life and its feedback systems, has coped with a sun that has become 25 percent hotter over 4 billion years. In another billion years from now life will begin to feel the sun's threat even more, and in another 3.5 billion it is predicted to be 40 percent larger, destroying all life. To try to deal with this, scientists at NASA have thought up a new version of an old "planetary slingshot" method, now used for speeding up spacecraft. In this optimistic scenario a 100-kilometer-wide asteroid could be passed in just the right orbit near earth to move it out every 6,000 years. Thus, as the sun expanded and gulped up planets, earth could move further and further away, possibly surviving another 6 billion years. This would be a more efficient method of survival than terra-forming another planet to make it habitable for humanity. Perhaps in this distant future a few earthlings will be intergalactic beings—but reflect, the collision of galaxies and the explosion of the sun are predictable.

A moment's reflection in a garden pulls the mind outward before it settles back on the weeds, everyday problems, and the way a weed might be seen in a different way.

Andromeda and Milky Way entangle their spirals in 3 billion years. (After John Dubinski, San Diego.)

FESTINA LENTE

Fortuna and Virtù

I have been extremely fortunate to be able to work on the gardens at Portrack, to collaborate with friends and scientists, and to be surrounded by amiable skilled craftsmen and women. After more than ten years of designing gardens and speculating on nature and enjoying the fruits of the earth, in all senses, I know just how lucky I am. Except for Maggie's death, which remains an intermittent pain and sadness, I have been blessed by the stars. I have children and I have Louisa, whom I love. I have been able to write on subjects that interest me and, through the garden, speculate on the basic truths and patterns behind the universe. What more could one want? As Voltaire ends his *Candide* by saying, in a world that may not be the best of all possible ones, it is necessary to cultivate one's garden. Most other pursuits are fruitless and fleeting and, like politics, unsure.

Through the gardens at Portrack I have received further commissions, and been allowed to extend similar ideas elsewhere. Two small gardens for a Maggie's Centre in Inverness, several DNA sculptures that are variations on a theme, a new kind of black hole (designed with Roger Penrose) for the IUCAA in Pune, India, a landform in Edinburgh, and a public park in Milan. Each of these continues experiments begun at Portrack, and each one is a part of what I see as the "Universe Project," the overriding idea being that the universe is the fundamental referent and measure to life and our life, at least in part because there are other referents and measures, too. Cosmogenesis has sublated notions that are religious. It has become, for me at least, the focus for iconography, art, and spirituality. Perhaps in a global culture it will become a unifying focus for others.

In any case, the local gods have been good to me for a while, for the reasons mentioned and for others that I will consider shortly. They make me reflect on the whole question of luck, and whether it really exists. When she got cancer, Maggie saw it partly as a repayment of dues for having lived such a charmed life for forty-eight years. Was it, as scientists ask, "bad luck or bad genes" or, as she half thought according to linguistic convention, a payback exacted for having had too much of the good life? I have been "blessed by the stars" and the "gods," even though I do not believe in the efficacious power of either—but I too follow language where it leads, and wonder about the accident of my life and its ups and downs.

During the Renaissance there was a popular distinction between Fortuna and Virtù and the fluctuating balance between them was a common topic. The words did not mean exactly what one might think, referring respectively to "fate" and to "directed control," and an individual's life would be subject to a mixture that would be hard to change. Only in the 20th century have scientists and forecasters repeatedly asserted, with a certain hubris, that we can shift the balance and successfully control human evolution. But a moment's reflection on the vagaries of the economy (not to mention the weather or war) should have long ago exposed such claims for what they are: advertisements for the particular control system on offer. Much of one's life depends on an accident of birth, the local economy, the stability of a nation, and global forces over which one has little control. Perhaps our ancestors were right, the chaotically shifting mixture of fate and self-determination cannot itself be controlled, and the proportion of one to another jumps around randomly.

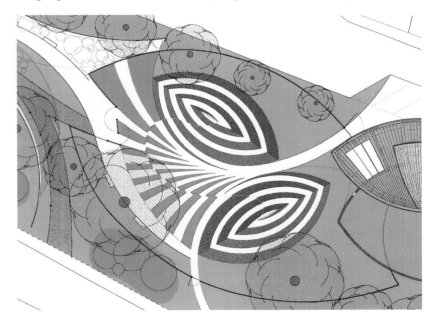

LEFT: "Festina lente": make haste to go slow. ABOVE: Gardens for Maggie's Centre, Inverness, with Page & Park Architects, 2001. The mounds represent cells sending messages back and forth to harmonize imbalances in the organism; a black and white garden leads to the hospital entrance.

The Romans were particularly obsessed by sudden swings in Fortuna, hence their association of it with fate. From their woeful experience comes our warning "don't tempt fate" or, if you do, it is better to neutralize the arrogance and to "touch wood." Latin wordplay, with emphatic alliterations, bangs home the message: "Fortuna favet fatuis," ("Fortune favors fools") and its counterpart, the answer, "Fortuna favet fortibus," ("Fortune favors the brave.") Even if fickle, there is hope, because "Fortuna meliores sequitor," ("Fortune accompanies better men.") Yet the balance between fate and directed control cannot be shifted, as a nice double entendre puts it: "Fortuna non mutat genus," ("Fortune does not change nature.") Cicero creates a clever inversion by combining the two themes: "Fortune favors the brave, as the old proverb says, but forethought much more." This became an adage of the late-19th-century scientist Louis Pasteur. "Fortune," he said, referring to inventions such as pasteurization, named after him, "favors the prepared mind," which shows there is a slight degree of control and self-determination, even within the constraints of luck.

This is hopeful. Even if you cannot beat Lady Luck, as gamblers call her, you can sometimes find a common cause. This is the attitude with which I approached the culmination of the garden, its center and the last area to be constructed. As work was progressing on this area, several technical and formal problems arose that needed a new kind of answer and, as luck would have it, scientists were just discovering, and partly inventing, an amazing new theory of the universe. Could my problems and their theories be, somehow, reconciled? Would Fortuna favor this marriage?

There were several problems that largely concerned bringing water up the cascade, having it enter the small pond at the bottom, and keeping it relatively level. In western Scotland there is often excessive rainfall compared to the rest of the British Isles and, with global warming, there is often a surplus of excess. Thus when we first looked at water sitting at the bottom of the hill, where the cascade would climb, and saw that it was a puddle most of the year, we assumed the water table could not be far underneath. We dug and dug and did not reach that level until after we had uncovered parts of the ancient River Nith that must have meandered here, a 500-year-old oak stump, and several distinct layers of sand, clay and stone. Then, at about ten feet below the level we had first assumed, we finally struck water and from there started the cascade, as I have described. The problem, as we were to discover over the next year, was that the level of this water table kept moving up and down, and most curiously, not in synch with anything obvious—the lakes, the River Nith, or even the rainfall. Imagine a pond rising and lowering five feet, with a will of its own. The only reason we could fathom was that there may be some artesian effect created by the hill because, five days after a downpour, the pond would rise up suddenly.

At any rate, these sudden variations in level meant it would probably be best to pump water into the pond, to keep it relatively level. So Alistair set about devising a way to pump water from our lakes and that provoked the idea of an underground conduit and the necessity of a water pipe. Following this chain of ideas and necessities we thought of a hose, then a sprinkler, then a nozzle with sprays, then several spouts, then a linear spewing object culminating in wonderful patterns of mist and jets. Finally was the idea of a metallic fountain ending in a long tapering barrel from which liquid could shoot. This meant something silver-colored and mechanical would inevitably be imposed on something green and living, and if this were to be the case, then it might as well be a continuation of the natural curves. Before too long, as the pond was

TOP: Alistair Clark fine-tuning the end nozzle and three downspouts on the nose of the white hole. ABOVE: Working with Doug McCormick and Neil Brown to hammer in the mock-up to the revolving planter, with flowers growing in the middle of multiple universes.

excavated and the earth piled up, it was clear new landforms would emerge inevitably, so they had to be put to some use. From here it was a short step to the idea that these curved landforms related to the Universe Cascade and were therefore, according to the iconography, other universes (as I will explain). Moreover, in this scenario the metal fountain was a "white hole" bringing energy from the black hole of the universe to which it was attached. All this seemed inevitable, a parallel between the symbolic program and the emergent forms and functions. Fortuna seemed to be calling the tune. John Gibson made the metallic barrel of the fountain head, and Alistair tuned its several sprays.

At this stage I did not have a clear idea of where the design might go, and was worried that metal elements imposed on a landform would be, however necessary, crude and overbearing. Cover them with Astroturf, hide them, or at least make them part of the background? I vacillated between the alternatives. But as John Gibson got to work on a sliding bridge to connect the Universe Cascade with the land opposite, a final part of the puzzle started to fall into place. What if the spoil from the pond became three landforms, three different kinds of universe—could the metallic necessities be accentuated as parts of these types and play some positive role in a narrative of the universe? Here, Fortuna came to the rescue from outside the garden, in the form of contemporary science, and this development necessitates a little diversion back into the complexities of fast-breaking cosmology, and some of the most extraordinary notions ever thought.

Marvelous and Magical Enough?

Since the 1930s, the standard science of the very small has been very strange, so unusual as to lead to that famous introspective question posed by Niels Bohr that I have mentioned more than once: if you are not shocked by quantum physics, you do not understand it. Quantum weirdness has been a phrase bandied about ever since, and possible solutions to such perplexities as quantum gravity were sometimes rejected for not being bizarre enough. Why? Because they had to tie together the very biggest and smallest things in the universe and that takes intuitive leaps of a spectacularly risky kind. This perplexity is still very much with us today, especially with the big cosmological questions, those that tend to be oversold as the Theory of Everything (or TOE).

Ponder how much has changed since the quantum and relativity theories were formulated around 1900. In one century, quantum weirdness has been accepted as basic science, just as much as the astonishing curvature of spacetime and the radical characteristics of black holes. In other words, completely exotic theories of the very small and very big are now known to be as true as any science is, and tested to a much greater degree of accuracy than other laws. The macrocosm and microcosm are, from human perspective, crazy. It is only our little bit of mesocosm between the two that is normal, in tune with our size and intuitions and in which we feel at home. But as a whole the universe really is uncanny, as poets have always insisted, and it is time we stopped considering it to be routine, banal, predictable. If today's cosmology has one message it is this: it is simply impossible to take the universe for granted. This is not an argument to remain wrapped in wonder, for scientists a kind of original sin, but rather a plea to return to an appropriate sense of awe with which all great mystics and scientists, such as Einstein, have looked at the universe.

The question becomes one of how to approach the mystery at the heart of things, a question I asked myself when designing the center of the garden, the place toward which all paths lead, or around which they wander. As I was working on this center in 1999, and the Universe Cascade, incredible evidence was coming in. It appeared that the cosmos was actually accelerating in its expansion, and this supposition was being confirmed by further tests. This led to the new design of the cascade: a vase shape with slightly out-tilted edges near the top that represent the increasing speed.

The idea is that, after 11 billion years or so, the very weak force of "anti-gravity" (or something like it) kicks in and starts speeding up the rate at which the universe is expanding. This force is sometimes called quintessence, the fifth force. Alternatively, this may be the plenum vacuum. It is also conceived as Einstein's "cosmological constant," a fudge factor that he put into his equations to balance the universe, in 1919. He later referred to this as his greatest blunder, but it may turn out to have held a truth that not even he could have suspected. The evidence in 1998, from those standard units of measurement, distant exploding supernovae, is unambiguous. They were fainter than they should have been, and one plausible explanation is that in the last one-sixth of its existence the universe has been flying apart faster than before. This could be due to one of the greatest mysteries necessitated by quantum physics. The idea is that virtual particles come into and out of existence in a short instant and exert a pressure on spacetime. The quantum foam hidden inside the perfect vacuum is a kind of paradox: nothingness, full not empty, plays an active role in the cosmos. Virtual pairs of particles and anti-particles come into existence and annihilate each other, the thinking goes, and do so in nearly the shortest instant, known as Planck time. They last for about 10^{-43} (that is, a fraction of a second equal to one divided by 10 followed by 42 zeroes).

In 1948, a Dutch physicist Hendrick B. G. Casimir predicted that if parallel metal plates were held very very close together in a vacuum, this quantum force would push them together. Why? Because the longer wavelengths of the squeezed virtual particles would be excluded by the metal plates and therefore the wavelengths to either side of these plates would exert more pressure

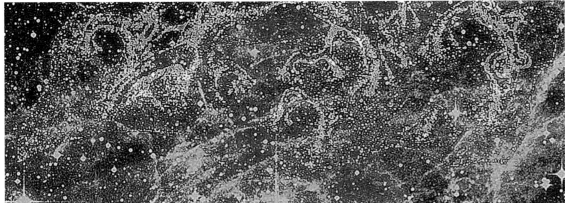

than those curtailed ones in the center. By the late 1990s this Casimir Effect had been confirmed several times: the quantum foam, the plenum vacuum, was not only real, but it exerted a measurable pressure. Nothingness was full of a seething quantum foam of fluctuations, of erupting and collapsing virtual particles that make up the fabric of spacetime.

And with this bit of news I realized how very lucky I was with the heart of the garden. By happy coincidence there were a series of parallels I could exploit. The first was between the bottom of the Universe Cascade and this quantum foam. Since, in order to pump water up to the top of the cascade, I had to dig down to the water table to get it, that meant the place where I had located the origin of the universe became located in the dark liquid, the brown water. The stairs, representing the early inflationary era, grew out of this mysterious foggy spume, just as the universe itself must have expanded very quickly from an unfathomable depth. A fluctuation in the quantum foam may have started it all, the whole process of the universe unfolding. Inadvertently, my model may have stumbled on the truth, or rather mimicked an emergence from the cosmic equivalent of the primeval ooze. And there was another fortuitous parallel. Maybe we will never be able to see back under this foam, this Planck time, back to the beginning. Like the opaque liquid at the bottom, will the way be forever blocked? Mysticism may start in mist and, as the church says, end in schism, but the origin and end of the universe are also shrouded in mist.

In 2001, further parallels between the garden and scientific discovery came to light, again fortuitously, just as the cascade was being finished. The breakthrough came from three different experiments on the initial expansion of the universe given the curious titles Boomerang, Maxima, and Dasi, and fortunately they

ABOVE: The quantum foam or the shape of spacetime as virtual particles come into and out of existence in the shortest possible time The quantum foam, the foreground, was the seed for the galaxies, the background, in the collage. (after Kip Thorne). RIGHT: The inflationary universe, the cascade steps expanding faster than the speed of light, emerge from the brown quantum foam.

came to similar conclusions. They looked at the background microwave radiation left over from the origin of the universe, similar to the fuzz that can be discerned on a television set dialed between stations, and found that it came in three distinct frequencies. Quickly naming these jiggling hot spots "acoustic waves" and, for the benefit of the press gathered in Washington, the "music of creation," they showed how the pressure waves reverberated through the dense plasma of the early universe. Contrary to some announcements, it was not the big bang they had heard or seen, but the noise generated when the inflationary period suddenly stopped.

The evidence showed the fine structure imprinted on the early microwaves, three harmonic peaks corresponding to three instruments or notes, as it were. These sounds, that no one heard billions of years ago, not only confirmed the inflationary theory, but also suggested that early quantum fluctuations were expanded to the scale of the whole universe, thus seeding the galaxies we now see. In other words, the universe as a tiny quantum vibration, a primeval musical score, has been blown up to a full symphony, and the first view of this is visible as three harmonic peaks of radiation. All this evidence added weight to notions already twenty years old, ideas of inflation, superstrings and a singular cosmic origin about 13 billion years ago, the hot stretch of spacetime.

Furthermore, it gave more credence to the reigning hypothesis that the universe is "flat" in the mathematical sense. Though curved locally around black holes, light can travel in straight lines across the observable universe on a flat membrane, as it were. Our universe has just the right balance of energy and matter. Not too hot and not too cold: such fine-tuning over 13 billion years got us here, so the Goldilocks outcome of the Anthropic Principle is again confirmed. No big crunches or fly-aparts lie ahead, or so it would seem. However, this conclusion seems at odds with the other evidence I have just mentioned: that the universe's expansion is speeding up! Such contradictions between emergent theories are not surprising and they remind us that new mysteries appear at the edges of ones just solved.

Mystery upon mystery—but the really strange result of these three harmonic peaks was a completely uncanny idea. They seemed to show that dark matter, which has perplexed physicists for twenty years, is not radically weird enough; something more bizarre must be added to the equations. But before considering this strange stuff, we might well ask, how do we know it's really there?

Some forty years ago astronomers had noticed, and then doggedly insisted, that galaxies did not behave the way they should, according to the laws of Newtonian forces and gravity. As they rotated, the stars at the edge of the galactic circumference should have been moving much slower than they actually were, and they should have been thrown out of the galaxy. Indeed, clusters of galaxies should also be spinning apart. But they are not. So some bigger force must be holding these structures together. These, and other observable paradoxes, led to the notion that there must be a lot of dark matter at work, maybe very small things like neutrinoes or very big objects like dark planets. Given puerile sobriquets to distinguish their size—WIMPS and MACHOS—as if the universe were some kind of multinational corporation made up of weaklings and alpha males, this dark stranger continued to elude direct perception. We know it is there because of many inferences, but we cannot see it and maybe never will (perhaps a better metaphor for it is the Cosmic Unconscious).

In any case, the three harmonic peaks observed in spring 2001 strongly suggested that this invisible matter made up 30 percent of the stuff in the universe. And then in spring 2003, as this book is going to press, even more delicate measurements (made by the Microwave Anisotropy Probe, or MAP) have given the amount of dark matter in the universe a more precise figure of 23 percent. The emerging consensus is that the ordinary matter that we see (galaxies, stars, interstellar dust and gas) constitutes a mere 4 percent of universe stuff. The remaining majority, apparently 73 percent, is not matter at all, but "dark energy." These recent measurements are extraordinary, and they also fix other important dimensions. For instance, in 1990 the age of the universe was reckoned to be between 10 and 15 billion years. By the turn of the millennium it was narrowed down to between 12 and 14.2 billion. Now it has been given a more precise age of 13.7 billion years and the rate of expansion has been determined at 71 kilometers per second per megaparsec. These latest, long-awaited figures show how fast universal space is stretching apart, an expansion caused by the original kinetic energy, and then only comparatively recently, by dark energy, quintessence, the fifth force.

It is this weak but omnipresent force of anti-gravity that finally gets the upper hand after 11 billion years, and starts to drive the universe apart faster and faster. The pressure of all those zillions of virtual particle pairs coming into and out of existence faster than you can think about them may be, in the end, the strongest engine of inflation. Such discoveries were said to have cultural implications. Some philosophers claimed they dealt another blow, the third after Copernicus and Darwin, to the human ego. We are not at the center of the universe, we are not made in God's image (but rather that of the primates), and now we find we are not even constructed from the majority substance. Such is Modernist logic, according to which the universe is considered a kind of Cosmic Bingo, in which only one super force should be the winner.

For me, however, the idea of a possible fifth force was fascinating and suggestive. In terms of the garden it was something of a godsend because, as I surveyed the tiny pond being dug at the bottom of the cascade, it suddenly, and accidentally, made sense of previous decisions. In functional and symbolic terms it clarified several ideas. Immediately apparent was that the water, already conceived as the quantum foam, was in rough terms 70 percent bigger than the approach path planned as a bridge to the cascade. And the Universe Cascade itself, the observable universe—made of relatively thin steps—was about 4 percent of the total area. So the three basic percentages fell into place, and made sense of the plan.

The question then became how to approach this center. In Chinese and French gardens it is important to withhold both the grand vista and the protected, intimate heart. They occur behind the courtyard house or château wall. Since at Portrack the Universe Cascade is at the center of the garden and is the culmination of approach, views of it were to be suggested yet resisted. The idea is to feel pulled to a center by axes, glimpses and paths, yet to be kept from it. Thus a series of walls, screens, and zigzags interrupt direct access. Trees veil it and only vignettes may be seen through small holes created in the top wall. In effect, it should be a struggle to figure out how things work, how to get to the heart of things, and how to understand them. Mysteries veiled are the more intently pursued, an idea suggested by Einstein's remark that although the universe is a very complex place it will, after hard and ingenious sleuthing, give up some secrets. God may be extremely subtle, he averred, but not malicious. The Renaissance garden captured some of this idea with the advice, festina lente, "make haste slowly." That is, perceive acutely, contemplate, and do not run. Hence, to reach the cascade one has to descend over a curved path and push out a bridge hidden under the metal frame. This limits traffic to one or two people and makes them proceed slowly.

Functionally it was necessary to have metal elements not only to guide movement, but also to pump water in and out. Thus the terraces, the spoil from the pond, end in silver-colored membranes and this innocent fact just happened to parallel one of the most extraordinary cosmological theories of our time, the idea of membranes, and the concomitant notion that we inhabit a multiverse. Again I was lucky to stumble on some fascinating coincidences between design and contemporary research. The strongest contender for the Theory of Everything (TOE) is called Membrane Theory or M-Theory and, in its originator's words, it plays quite openly on the overtones behind "M." Mystical, magical, and marvelous, the notion goes, as unthinkable as the idea that comes with it: that folded "branes" of universes might be stacked right next to each other like folded metal shelving devised by some ingenious architect. Versions of this TOE are made to sound even madder with such appellations as D-brane and p-brane. Stephen Hawking believes all these brane models are just different versions of one overall M-Theory, an idea that, since 1998, has been spun out of Superstring Theory. This is the speculation that six or seven extra space dimensions of tiny strings curl up on themselves and vibrate

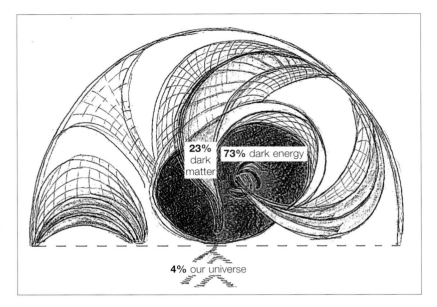

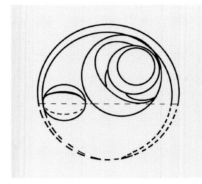

in circles only 10^{-35} meters around. These can be stretched out and become "open" strings, but still the six curled-up dimensions are so small they cannot be seen or felt or measured. Only gravity might be able to work on these folded-up lines. It is the various vibrations of the string that create all the different particles, and thus they quiver our universe into existence as a grand symphony. Apart from the way M-Theory ties together so many well-tested ideas, it necessitates gravity and falls out of the math.

Furthermore, it suggests the idea that there are many universes sprouting from each other like soap bubbles, each undergoing a different degree of inflation, each having slightly different laws, or the idea that there are a series of universes lying on different

TOP: Dark energy, dark matter, and the observable universe—the three kinds of substance. The hypothesis, based on observations announced in 2003, is that the observable universe is only 4 percent of the overall matter and energy, 96 percent of which is "dark."

Digging down to the water table to create a small pond resulted in a lot of excess earth, 23 percent of which became the dark matter (center), while the resultant water became the remaining dark energy. Overlapping arcs of circles, ovals and ellipses generated a series of curves that determined the terraces and paths. Resisted axes with switchbacks culminate the curved pathways to the center. Porous walls and trees reveal and veil the goal, an onion to be peeled, a kernel to be unearthed.

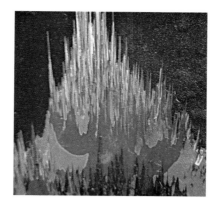

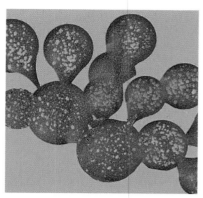

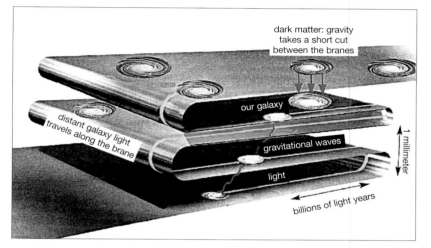

dark matter: gravity takes a short cut between the branes

our galaxy

distant galaxy light travels along the brane

gravitational waves

light

1 millimeter

billions of light years

membranes, where the usual four dimensions are apparent and seven of the remaining ones are so small that they are completely folded out of sight, like superstrings. The membranes in M-Theory are also like multidimensional soap bubbles, and since they are like surfaces they require one more spatial dimension than strings, which are like lines. Thus the fundamental objects are two-dimensional membranes making up an eleven-dimensional spacetime. Edward Witten, often said to be the most intelligent theorist working on this model, also claims that it resolves the five competing theories of superstrings. The math is elegant and compelling, although so overpoweringly complex that no one, not even Witten himself, has mastered it.

So whether one agrees with Lee Smolin's ideas, or Linde's model, or one of the M-Theories, a new strange idea is taking root.

Three versions of the multiverse. TOP LEFT: Branching bubble universes, with different laws, inflate from each other. TOP RIGHT: A similar model, conceived by Andrei Linde, shows the runaway fractal growth of many bubbles. BELOW: M-Theory has the usual observable universe stretched out on membranes. Light, electromagnetism etc. have to travel along the membrane, but gravity and anti-gravity can go across them (using up its force). This would explain many paradoxes including why the electric force is 10^{43} times stronger than gravity. Parallel universes may exist invisibly alongside ours, on their own membranes less than a millimeter away. (Diagrams after *Science Times*, October 29, 2002; *Scientific American*, August 2000; *New Scientist*, September 29, 2001.) OVER PAGE: Four universes from above.

We could inhabit one of many universes. This is an odd notion, only a few years old, and it is now commonly held by a number of eminent physicists I have mentioned, and others I have not, such as the Astronomer Royal, Sir Martin Rees. It is not yet a broad consensus with a firm body of evidence so much as a good hunch about what ideas might be propitiously developed.

The question becomes again: is the unlikely idea of a multiverse unlikely enough to be true, to resolve the great conundrum of quantum gravity? At this stage of creative suspense, who is to say? Let the physicists and speculators on the cosmos have their exploding, fractal bubbles and their p-branes and D-branes. They will no doubt have many more types of brane before I finish gardening.

In the meantime I had to make sense of these mysteries and so, in order to move the excavated earth into coherently similar piles, I settled on a different solution to the puzzle of the multiverse: it is made up of several, parallel "banana universes." Bananas? Arbitrary, you may think, just some kind of ad hoc expedient thrown into the bouillabaisse of competing theories, and I cannot deny a culinary component to the metaphor. But note their consistency, explanatory power, and functional cogency.

First of all, they have a consistent, self-similar geometry of warped space. They are generated by laws that bear a fractal relationship to each other—arcs of intersecting circles, ellipses, and ovals. The multiverse is a bunch of related bananas, not a mixed fruit salad. All these universes are necessarily curved back on themselves because of gravity, like black holes, and are also sheet-like membranes at the same time. That is, banana skins fall out of equations, just as Newton's apple fell out of the tree. Relativity Theory plus M-Theory = Bananaverse.

Secondly, it stands to reason that the three universes I have constructed (the three curved landforms) would have different fates according to their different laws. The one to the right of the cascade is obviously a failed universe where nothing has had time to evolve because gravity was relatively too strong. This can be seen by all the lines of gravitational collapse which curve into the hill and lead nowhere (see pages 244–5). The landform on the left, pumping water through its nose and pulling it up to the cascade through the mouth, has laws that are better balanced, something that is evident by the balance in water energy (i.e. our quantum foam again) (inset photo page 244). Water that shoots out moves a series of baby bananas that circle around a growth of superstrings. The landform in the center, the one that leads to the cascade, shows its force fields continuously being pulled into the metal membrane. These forces are attracted to the metal sheet, as are most things, including light and electricity, in our own four-dimensional universe. Remember M-Theory insists that sound waves, atoms, magnetism, and people all travel along the membranes while only gravity and anti-gravity can go across them (making these forces so relatively weak).

The failed universe, in the center background, suffered gravitational collapse before interesting things could evolve. The banana universe, to the left and inset, recycles dark energy down its membranes into the quantum foam, putting a rotational energy into nine baby universes. These have the three main axes and seven more folded in superstring dimensions. The center universe, to the right, with its large metal membrane, pulls in all the other forces and leads people to the cascade, our universe.

Thirdly, although obvious, it may be worth pointing out that all these bananas work functionally—as landform, fountain, path, and bridge—and skeptics will say that this is the real reason for their form.

Be that as it may, Banana Theory has one great advantage over competing models of the multiverse: no graduate student or astrophysicist will ever lose sleep trying to fathom its mathematics. Bananas are for eating. They also warn us to take all cosmological theories half-seriously (with a pinch of cinnamon), to be delighted by the promise of the extraordinary ideas now dominating the field, the grand visions opening before us, but also to suggest that they all have some fundamental problems, and maybe always will. "Bananas" say that the era of cosmic certainty, the BIG TOE, has yet to arrive, and they make comfortable landforms on which to sit and contemplate the mystery at the heart of things.

Cosmogenic Art

What can all these metaphors and sometimes fanciful theories possibly mean? At the very least they suggest the unfathomable nature of ultimate reality—and its enticing allure: the fact that we are impelled to seek answers to the basic questions, that curiosity about the universe is a basic drive, and that mystery is its engine. Secondly, they imply that the universe does not look like membranes any more than it looks like superstrings, vases, trumpets, bubbles, inflationary fractals, or bananas. To reiterate, it looks just like itself (not something familiar like string) and, in any case, one cannot get outside it to look back.

But it is also a question of scale: many of these metaphors and images are appropriate at one level of detail and wrong at another. For instance, according to many visual investigations, through telescopes and computer simulations, the biggest structures of the universe are gigantic superclusters of galaxies called Great Walls and Great Attractors—tangled webs of clumping stars and gas brought together by gravity and dark matter. So then, is the universe really made up of interconnected filaments—like a great brain? Yes, at these particular scales there really are some parallels between nerve cells and galactic webs, the microcosm and macrocosm. Yet webs are just one more image of the ultimate reality, another in a continuous, unending succession of visual concepts. Metaphor replaces metaphor in an emerging process of discovery and invention. It is as if the development of the universe were directly reflected by the unfolding of theories—an expanding, creative cosmos mirrored by an unfolding cosmogenic art. Maybe that process is itself the deepest truth?

Whatever the case, we continue to search, and that investigation is a spiritual, cognitive, and inevitable journey. Call it what you will, the cosmic passion to wonder and question is built into us, as it is into any sentient creature that wanders about the earth. What I hope to have shown through the Garden of Cosmic

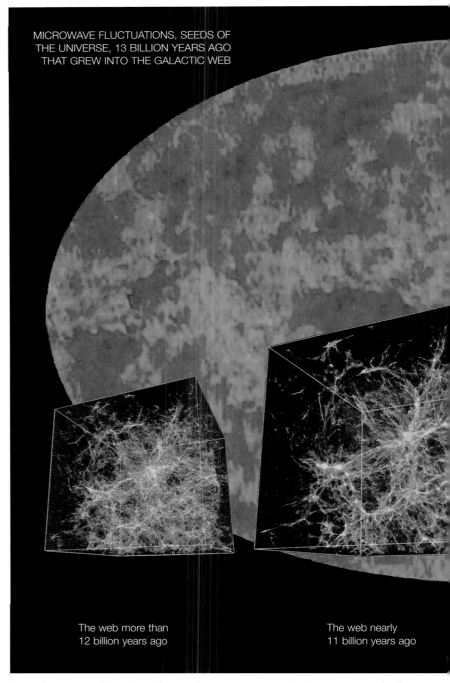

MICROWAVE FLUCTUATIONS, SEEDS OF THE UNIVERSE, 13 BILLION YEARS AGO THAT GREW INTO THE GALACTIC WEB

The web more than 12 billion years ago

The web nearly 11 billion years ago

Speculation is that the ideas of our time reveal the universe to be unbelievable, fantastic, provocative, surprising—it is beautiful and horrific by turns. Gaia and mass extinctions show nature to be Janus-faced, at once cruel and benevolent, chaotic and bountiful, self-organizing and entropic. And the universe as a whole is, as Inflation and M-Theory show, more uncanny than the creations of science fiction, or the traditional depictions of religious myth. The new metaphors should shake us out of our dogmatic ennui. They should show us we cannot take an underlying reality for granted, that a preparedness for the counter-intuitive must guide our action, that nature has many more fascinating layers to be unearthed, exposed to light, and grown into new forms. Perhaps an infinitude of delightful patterns.

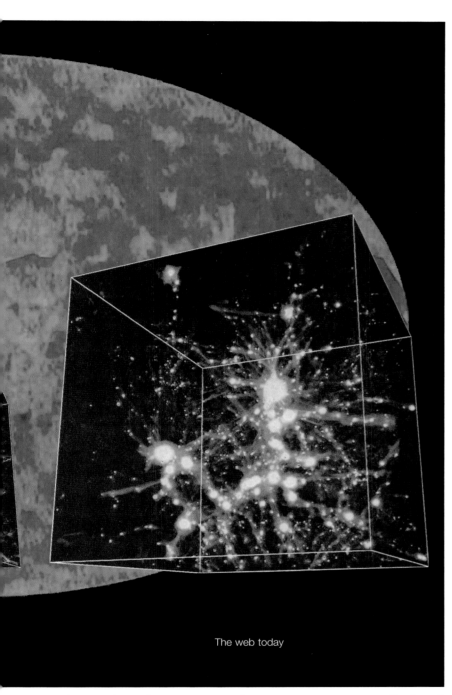

The web today

The Garden of Cosmic Speculation is an attempt to find and celebrate the fundamental aspects of the universe—its laws and its basic organizational types—and to create a new language of landscape from them. The aim is to create new metaphors, such as "Invisibilia," that can illuminate old ones such as "Black Hole," and to substitute new ones, such as "Hot Stretch" for

The universe as giant brain, simulations of the cosmic web over time. From energy fluctuations, 13 billion years ago, that formed into clumps of gas, galactic clusters emerged. These giant walls of structure are also called great attractors because, like strange attractors, they pull all matter toward a basin, thereby leaving voids that look like bubbles—and the whole web like a brain. (After simulations by Dr. Jeremiah P. Ostriker and Dr. Renyue Cen, Princeton University, 2001.)

questionable ones, such as "Big Bang." The goal is to forge a relationship with the universe that is more immediate and real than that given by modern science and religion, which may cut us off from those dual realities—of beauty and horror—that make life so poignant and precious. Consider the banal way nature is conceived in the classroom and in the press. To take just one instance, look at the way the most amazing molecule of life, DNA, is framed by teachers, scientists and, as I have mentioned, the artist Damien Hirst. This extraordinary unit of the universe is presented as a clunky, multi-colored stick and ball plaything that is neither expressive nor even ugly, neither graceful nor exciting. It is depicted as just another dead, neutral object, a chore to be studied rather than the unit of life to be celebrated. Artless art, depressing science.

Now consider how the philosophers and scientists of modernism frame DNA poetically and rationally, for instance the Oxford don, Richard Dawkins. This "Professor for the Public Understanding of Science" highlights the nasty aspects, which do indeed exist. The "Selfish Gene" is his summation in a best-selling title of 1976. It's a cliché that has selfishly devoured the minds of a generation and, unfortunately for Dawkins, allied his message with Thatcherism and rapacious capitalism (neither of which he particularly admires). Like the "Big Bang" and other modernist metaphors, this one is bound to be popular within a macho culture of Bond films and Pentagon rhetoric. A reason for its popularity is that it confirms the suspicion that our selfishness has genetic causes, that nature is really "red in tooth and claw."

The problem with this as a poetic response to nature is that it is a fully alienating metaphor; the problem with it as science is that it is only half true. It turns out, even according to the research on which Dawkins' summation depends, that selfish genes most often produce altruistic genes—those that sacrifice themselves for their descendants—because in the long run altruism pays off in the struggle for existence; ironically, it out-competes selfishness.

The conclusion, once again, is that nature shows an underlying duality: terror is there, but it is no more basic than beauty. To privilege the selfish gene rather than the altruistic gene, the choice of a nasty image over a benevolent one, is really another form of corniness, the sentimentality of the tough. On the other hand, religious leaders who say Darwinian competition can be reconciled with God, as several now do, imply that God is either not very omnipotent, or not very nice. A good God cannot, as nature does, sacrifice nine in ten so that the tenth may prosper.

This brief discussion of complex issues hardly does them justice, but it does highlight the necessity of a view of nature, and the universe, more basic than the reigning ones. Call it the cosmogenic view. Like the cosmic orientation of ancient religions, it acknowledges the wonder and mystery of the most powerful and grand thing there is, the ground of being and the basis for existence. Like the scientific orientation of the present it seeks the truth of an unfolding creative event, cosmogenesis, as a self-organizing process that includes us in the plot. As the Anthropic Principle shows, we are fundamentally built into the laws of the universe, its fundamental constants being balanced "just so" to allow us to emerge. Like the artists' orientation, exploiting our desire to discover new patterns, this view assumes curiosity and aesthetic experience are deeply connected so as to support each other.

All of these are speculations about nature and our nature and they have led me to a cosmogenic art that is critical while being celebratory. This art, the subject of another book, proposes the layering of ideas and patterns into a complex whole. The layers should make one slow down, think, and wonder about received notions. It should celebrate the beauty and organization of the universe, but above all resupply that sense of awe which modern life has done so much to deny. If it works with nature it does so as an equal, making choices, selecting critically, and taking nothing for granted. Perhaps in the end neither man nor the universe is the measure of all things, but rather the convivial dialogue that comes from their interaction.

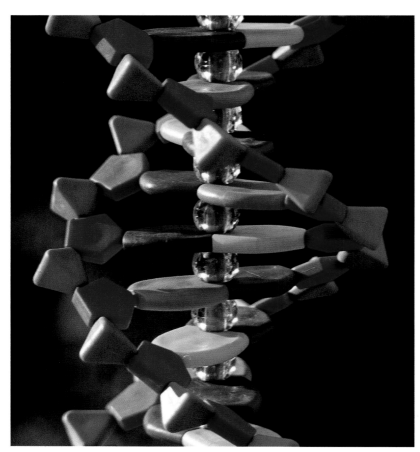

ABOVE: A teaching model of DNA. ABOVE RIGHT: Pharmacy DNA, Damien Hirst, London, 1998. RIGHT AND OPPOSITE: DNA for Kew Gardens, Charles Jencks, London, 2003.

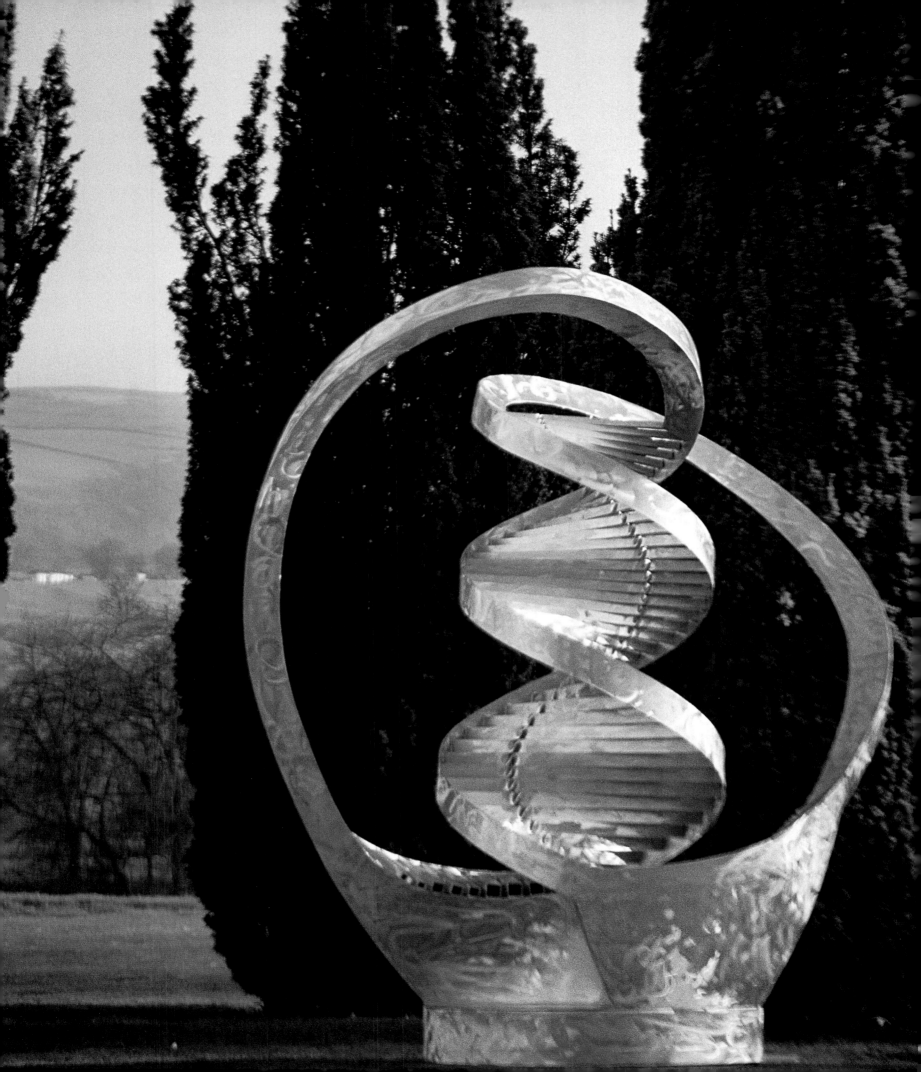

INDEX

INSTEAD OF A BIBLIOGRAPHY

My son Justin asked me for a good book explaining the universe, a reasonable request, and I was stumped. It's easier to mention fifty or so recent attempts, a result of the explosive flowering of cosmology (to use a suitably mixed metaphor), many of which have wonderful insights and none of which is definitive. All I can give here are some research tactics, my own favorites—hardly a scholarly selection—and the strategy for reading between fields: the sciences, the arts, books on spirituality, the Internet, and the weekly media.

To start with the last, I have found Britain's *New Scientist* to be the most refreshing, up to date, and informative and, for those Americans who look to the daily newspaper, the Tuesday science section of *The New York Times* is most helpful. But frankly, since science and cosmology are developing, in their Golden Age, at a mad pace, one has to read very widely. This speed of change is itself a good reason to be happy to be alive today: cosmological watching is now very dramatic, and the universe is telling us every day (through imperfect translators) how really amazing it is.

Often the best way to understand complex evolving structures is to see them change and there used to be a few good videos made by the BBC's *Horizon* and Channel Four's *Equinox* programs, both in association with American PBS outlets or companies like the Discovery Channel. Unfortunately, in the age of "the race to the bottom," such films are now a rarity, but one should keep alert because a few gems are occasionally pulled off the basement floor, among them Ian Stewart's Royal Institute Christmas Lectures of 1997, *The Magical Maze*, also published by Weidenfeld & Nicolson (London, 1997). A mathematician, he has also written many important, popular books explaining patterns in nature, among them *Nature's Numbers: Discovering Order and Pattern in the Universe* (Weidenfeld & Nicolson, London, 1995). For those who want to be immersed in this endlessly fascinating subject, there are the more detailed works of Brian Goodwin and Philip Ball.

For a beginner's overview of the cosmos, there are two authors whom I can recommend for combining just the right mix of intelligent analysis and excited research. Heinz Pagel's *The Cosmic Code: Quantum Physics as the Language of Nature* (Bantam Books, New York, 1983) is still a relevant and classic introduction to the basic ideas. So too are Paul Davies' two brilliant summaries: *The Cosmic Blueprint: New Discoveries in Nature's Creative Ability to Order the Universe* (Simon & Schuster, New York, 1988) and *The Mind of God: The Scientific Basis for a Rational World* (Simon & Schuster, New York, 1992). These books are much more illuminating and profound than Stephen Hawking's *A Brief History of Time* (Bantam Books, New York, 1988), the most over-hyped, over-bought, and under-read book in the history of the universe (and on the subject, too). However, his later work, *The Universe in a Nutshell* (Bantam Press, New York, 2001), makes up for the shallowness of the first and supplies some wonderfully informative diagrams. From them one can begin to understand superstrings and M-Theory, especially when read alongside Brian Greene's *The Elegant Universe: Superstrings, Hidden Dimensions and the Quest for the Ultimate Theory* (Random House, London, 1999). Roger Penrose's *The Emperor's New Mind: Concerning Computers, Minds, and the Laws of Physics* (Oxford University Press, New York, 1989) and Martin Rees's *Our Cosmic Habitat* (Weidenfeld & Nicolson, London, 2001) broach some fascinating ideas that stem from this cosmic search.

The study of living nature, the genome, and Gaia, are equally important for understanding our place in the universe and equally significant for the garden, but I will not even attempt to summarize my favorites. Furthermore, there are many adequate textbooks: Philip Whitfield's *The Natural History of Evolution* (Marshall Editions, London, 1993) and *The Book of Life*, edited by Stephen Jay Gould (Ebury Hutchinson, London, 1993) are just two worth noting. Suffice it to say that virtually all the many books and articles of Stephen Jay Gould are interesting and relevant, and James Lovelock's and Lynn Margulis' work on Gaia theory is absolutely essential. His *Gaia: The Practical Science of Planetary Medicine* (Gaia Books, London, 1991) has a concise analysis combined with informative diagrams.

For a more spiritually oriented version of similar ideas, connected with Complexity and Chaos Theory, see Fritjof Capra's *The Web of Life: A New Synthesis of Mind and Matter* (HarperCollins, London, 1996). Although science and religion are often opposed in assumption and sensibility—and I don't believe in a facile reconciliation—I do believe one can learn things from the spiritual traditions that the culture of science has blotted out. Here, the writings of Alfred North Whitehead or, more recently, David Ray Griffin, David Bohm, Charlene Spretnak, Matthew Fox, and Thomas Berry have been very helpful.

Since the majority of my life has been involved with the arts, more particularly architecture, it would be even more invidious, and interminable, to list influences I find important. Still, I can mention authors or creators without having to enumerate their works. First and foremost is Le Corbusier, an architect and painter always involved with translating nature's patterns into a building art. The painters at the early Bauhaus—Kandinsky, Itten, Klee—explored the artistic dimensions of the cosmos, as did the Constructivists and Expressionists. An exhibition of 1986, originating in Los Angeles at the Los Angeles County Museum of Art, *The Spiritual in Art: Abstract Painting 1890–1985*, with an informative catalogue of the same name, explored many of these artists, as did a later exhibit and book, *Cosmos: From Romanticism to the Avant-garde*, put together by the Montreal Museum of Fine Arts in 1999. Another fascinating juxtaposition of old and new texts and images is *Celestial Treasury: From the Music of the Spheres to the Conquest of Space* by Marc Lachieze-Rey and Jean-Pierre Luminet (Cambridge University Press, 2001).

There are many good books that explore a territory in common between the most primitive cosmic speculation and contemporary art, for instance Colin Renfrew's *Figuring it Out: The Parallel Visions of Artists and Archaelogists* (Thames & Hudson, London, 2003). Land or earth artists and some gardeners and landscape designers often mine common ground, as is discussed in Lucy Lippard's *Overlay: Contemporary Art and the Art of Prehistory* (Pantheon Books, New York, 1983) and John Beardsley's *Earthworks and Beyond* (Abbeville Press, New York, 1989). Very suggestive inquiries into the relation between past and present landscape ideas are also explored by Allen Weiss in *Unnatural Horizons: Paradox and Contradiction in Landscape Architecture* (Princeton Architectural Press, New York, 2001) and in the collection of essays by James Corner, *Recovering Landscape: Essays in Contemporary Landscape Architecture* (Princeton Architectural Press, 1999). In addition, some garden histories explore some cosmic dimensions of landscape, for instance Geoffrey and Susan Jellicoe's *The Landscape of Man* (Viking Press, New York, 1975) and Christopher Thacker's *The History of Gardens* (Croom Helm, London, 1979). Surveys by Sutherland Lyle and Jane Amidon note some contemporary examples of the same type.

A sculptor/rock collector, Richard Rosenblum, provides rare insights into Chinese practices in *Art of the Natural World: Resonances of Wild Nature in Chinese Sculptural Art* (Museum of Fine Arts, Boston, 2001). I find all of these art and landscape examples sympathetic, yet my own work, which is influenced by Erwin Panofsky, Ernst Gombrich, and the traditions of iconography, is also focused on content, symbolism, and the multivalence of meaning. See, for instance, *Towards a Symbolic Architecture* (Academy, London, 1985) and *The Architecture of the Jumping Universe* (John Wiley, London, second edition 1997), especially the sections on cosmic iconography.

BOOKS BY CHARLES JENCKS

Meaning in Architecture (contributor and editor with George Baird), Braziller, New York, 1969; Barrie & Jenkins, London, 1969.

Architecture 2000, Predictions and Methods, Praeger, New York, 1971; Studio Vista, London, 1971.

Adhocism (with Nathan Silver), Doubleday, New York, 1972; Secker and Warburg, London, 1972.

Modern Movements in Architecture, Doubleday, New York, 1972; Penguin Books, London, 1973, second edition 1985.

Le Corbusier and the Tragic View of Architecture, Harvard University Press, Cambridge, Mass., 1974; Allen Lane, London, 1974, second edition 1987.

The Language of Post-Modern Architecture, Rizzoli, New York, 1977, revised 1978, third edition 1980, fourth edition 1984, fifth edition 1988, sixth edition 1991; Academy, London, 1977, 1978, 1980, 1984, 1991.

The Daydream Houses of Los Angeles, Rizzoli, New York, 1978; Academy, London, 1978.

Bizarre Architecture, Rizzoli, New York, 1979; Academy, London, 1979.

Late-Modern Architecture, Rizzoli, New York, 1980; Academy, London, 1980.

Signs, Symbols and Architecture (editor with Richard Bunt and Geoffrey Broadbent), John Wiley, New York & London, 1980.

Skyscrapers—Skycities, Rizzoli, New York, 1980; Academy, London, 1980.

Post-Modern Classicism, Rizzoli, New York, 1980; Architectural Design monograph, London, 1980.

Free-Style Classicism, Rizzoli, New York, 1980; Architectural Design monograph, London, 1982.

Architecture Today, Abrams, New York, 1982; Current Architecture, Academy, London, 1982, second edition 1988.

Abstract Representation, St. Martin's Press, New York, 1983; Architectural Design monograph, London, 1983.

Kings of Infinite Space, St. Martin's Press, New York, 1983; Academy, London, 1983.

Towards A Symbolic Architecture, Rizzoli, New York, 1985; Academy, London, 1985.

Charles Jencks (extra edition of A & U), No. 1, Tokyo, 1986.

The Architecture of Democracy, Architectural Design monograph, London, 1987.

What is Post-Modernism?, St. Martin's Press, New York, 1986; Academy, London, 1986, second edition 1988, third edition 1989, fourth edition 1995.

Post-Modernism, The New Classicism in Art and Architecture, Rizzoli, New York, 1987; Academy, London, 1987.

The Prince, The Architects and New Wave Monarchy, Academy, London, 1988; Rizzoli, New York, 1988.

The New Moderns, Academy, London, 1990; Rizzoli, New York, 1990.

The Post-Modern Reader (editor), Academy, London, 1992; St. Martin's Press, New York, 1992.

Heteropolis—Los Angeles, The Riots & Hetero-Architecture, Academy, London & New York, 1993.

The Architecture of the Jumping Universe, Academy, London & New York, 1995; second edition John Wiley, London & New York, 1997.

Theories and Manifestos of Contemporary Architecture (editor with Karl Kropf), John Wiley, London & New York, 1997.

New Science—New Architecture?, Architectural Design special issue 129, December 1997.

Ecstatic Architecture, Academy, John Wiley, London & New York, 1999.

Millennium Architecture, Academy, Wiley, Architectural Design (guest editor with Maggie Toy), 2000.

Architecture 2000 and Beyond (critique and new predictions for 1971 book), Academy, John Wiley, London & New York, 2000.

Le Corbusier and the Continual Revolution in Architecture, The Monacelli Press, New York, 2000.

The New Paradigm in Architecture, revised edition of The Language of Post-Modern Architecture, Yale University Press, London & New Haven, 2002.

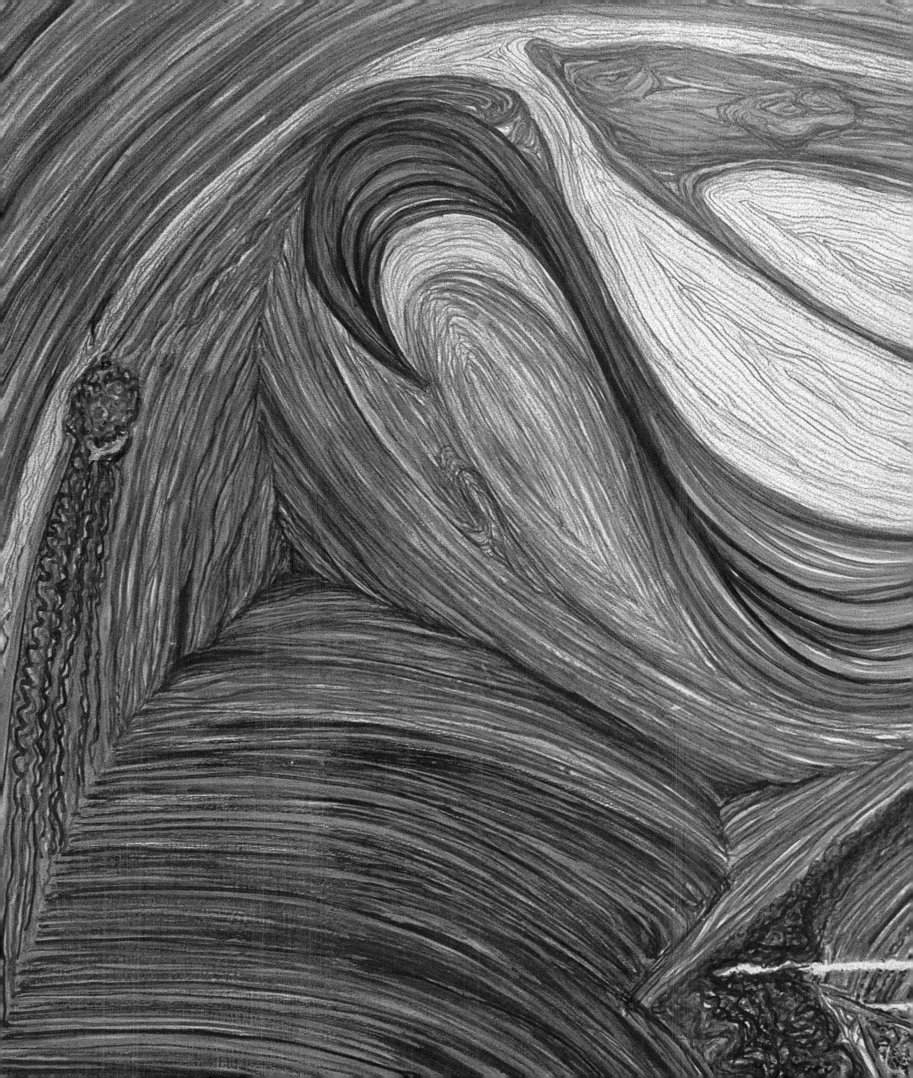